and University of Tampere.

Democratization in Eastern Europe

Domestic and international perspectives

Edited by Geoffrey Pridham and
Tatu Vanhanen

London and New York

First published 1994
by Routledge
11 New Fetter Lane, London EC4P 4EE

Simultaneously published in the USA and Canada
by Routledge
29 West 35th Street, New York, NY 10001

© 1994 Geoffrey Pridham and Tatu Vanhanen

Typeset in Times by
Ponting–Green Publishing Services, Chesham, Bucks

Printed and bound in Great Britain by
Clays Ltd, St Ives PLC

Printed on acid free paper

British Library Cataloguing in Publication Data
A catalogue record for this book is available from the
British Library.

Library of Congress Cataloging in Publication Data
A catalogue record for this book has been requested

ISBN 0–415–11063–7 (hbk)
ISBN 0–415–11064–5 (pbk)

Contents

vi   *Contents*

Part III The external dimension

Part IV Conclusion

Figures and tables

FIGURES

TABLES

Czechoslovakia, most recently in the 1990 and 1992 parliamentary elections in that country. He is a member of a research team investigating party formation in East-Central Europe since the end of communist rule, funded by the UK Economic and Social Research Council under its East–West programme.

Preface

This book originated from a workshop on 'Democratization in Eastern Europe' chaired by Hans-Dieter Klingemann and Tatu Vanhanen at the ECPR Joint Sessions of Workshops, University of Essex, in March 1991. Fifteen papers were presented in that workshop, which sought to discuss the problems and causes of democratization in Eastern Europe from different theoretical and empirical perspectives. The workshop brought together colleagues with different area and country specialisms; and it proved to be a stimulating and enlightening occasion. There were those with expertise in East European and Soviet politics, some with previous experience of theoretical or comparative work on democratic transitions (in Southern Europe) and others from the field of international relations and psephology. By and large, the workshop discussions cohered well, allowing us to gain comparative and particular insights into a process that was still in its early stages. Geoffrey Pridham was then invited to become co-editor; and eventually Hans-Dieter Klingemann was unable to continue in this capacity.

There followed some delay in preparing this work for publication. However, in the end, this delay had its benefits. There were two major stages of revising chapters and a final updating before submission of the manuscript to the publishers. We were, therefore, able to take advantage of the further course of democratic transition in Eastern Europe, with completion of the book two-and-half years after the workshop.

An initial selection was made from the workshop papers to restrict our geographical focus and tighten up our thematic approach. Seven of the chapters included in this book are based on presentations to the 1991 workshop. One additional chapter (that by Lewis, Lomax and Wightman) was commissioned later. Altogether, the book draws on much ongoing research on different aspects of transition to democracy in Eastern Europe. In particular, it has benefited from the team project

on 'Regime Change in East-Central Europe: Political Parties and the
Transition to Democratic Politics', funded for three years (1992–94) by
the East–West Programme of the (British) Economic and Social
Research Council (ESRC). All the members of this team, coordinated
by Michael Waller, are included in this volume – the others being Paul
Lewis, Bill Lomax, Geoffrey Pridham and Gordon Wightman.

Comparative approaches and perspectives have been adopted by
these various contributions and were encouraged by the editors in the
revision process. We decided to concentrate in this book on the
countries of East-Central Europe and certain ones in the Balkans
(Poland, Czechoslovakia, Hungary, Romania, and Bulgaria) rather than
attempt complete coverage of the former Eastern bloc states. This does
not mean that other countries in the region are excluded, for they appear
briefly where further comparisons are necessary.

Geoffrey Pridham, Bristol
Tatu Vanhanen, Helsinki
September 1993

Introduction

Geoffrey Pridham and Tatu Vanhanen

The sudden wave of democratization which erupted in Eastern Europe in 1989–90 provides a formidable challenge to political scientists trying to explore the causes and patterns of democratization. They were not able to predict or even anticipate the collapse of socialist systems in Eastern Europe and the consequent democratization. Samuel Huntington had concluded in 1984, in an article on whether more countries would become democratic, that there was less likelihood of this occurring in Eastern Europe than elsewhere in the world (Huntington 1984). However, political scientists were by no means alone in their failure to foresee the momentous events in Eastern Europe; and, it must be remembered, even the best of comparative research is more in the business of analysing and interpreting rather than predicting developments in different countries. The problem of predicting democratization is explored in detail in the third of our chapters, by Vanhanen and Kimber.

Now, however, the problem is whether one can find reasonable theoretical explanations for the democratization processes still in train in Eastern Europe. Broaching and perhaps solving this problem might increase our ability to explain democratization in general and also in other areas of the world. This edited book represents an early attempt to confront this historical occurrence of democratization in Eastern Europe. The problem is explored from different theoretical perspectives and by using different methods. It is hoped this concerted effort will facilitate a collective explanation, or at least one which is more balanced than any single perspective could provide.

A number of basic questions are immediately raised by the developments of the past few years. How far does the corpus of regime transition theory and of comparative work on democratization over the last two decades assist us with our task? Or, do we need in any way to start anew with theoretical perspectives? How much mileage is there in drawing on the empirical study of previous transitions to democracy in Southern Europe and Latin America for insights and directions in focusing on the dynamics of systemic change in Eastern Europe? And, last but not least, are we in fact being too assumptive about there being 'democratization', at least in the whole of the former communist bloc?

'Democratization' is a conveniently loose term to describe what is happening, although it is acknowledged the outcome is the establishment of a liberal or constitutional democracy familiar to students of Western Europe. For our purposes, 'democratization' is seen as the overall process of regime change from beginning to end, including both stages of what are generally called in the comparative literature 'transition' to a liberal democracy and its subsequent 'consolidation'. Clearly, this is a process far from complete in the countries of Eastern Europe. In fact, any generalization about the region as a whole would see them as still in the course of transition and as far from consolidating their new systems. If the earlier (and somewhat easier) democratic transitions in Southern Europe are any guide – they took on crude average about half a decade – then those occurring in Eastern Europe are probably several years short of completing that process. This does, of course, ignore the likelihood that some countries will achieve transition and move to consolidation earlier than others in the region.

By 'democratic transition' we refer to a stage of regime change commencing at the point when the previous totalitarian/authoritarian system begins to collapse, leading to the situation when, with a new constitution in place, the democratic structures become routinized and the political elites adjust their behaviour to liberal democratic norms. Transition tasks involve, above all, negotiating the constitutional settlement and settling the rules of procedure for political competition, but also dismantling authoritarian agencies and abolishing laws unsuitable for democratic life. In comparison, 'democratic consolidation' is usually a lengthier process, but also one with wider and possibly deeper effects. It involves in the first instance the gradual removal of the uncertainties that invariably surround transition and then the full institutionalization of the new democracy, the internalization of its rules and procedures and the dissemination of democratic values.

Theoretical approaches to democratic transition have not represented any coherent or even elaborate body of work. In fact, they have tended to diverge between two schools of thinking, the functionalist concerned with long-term developments of a socio-economic structural kind and the genetic which gives priority to short-term, usually political, determinants of the actual transition process. But, as Pridham argues in this volume, there is some compatibility between these two approaches that may help in our analysis of the change in Eastern Europe. Therefore, it does not readily follow that transition theory should be abandoned or reworked from first principles in the light of this experience. It still provides viable directions for assessing what has been happening in that region. But there is certainly a compelling need for adapting, developing and broadening its scope and, not least, for questioning some of its assumptions.

For instance, theories on transition have tended to emphasize the paramount role of elites – especially political ones, but not exclusively so – in the course of transition and with respect to key moments of decision. It is this aspect of transition theory that has probably received the sharpest criticism from those working on the current transitions. As David Ost argued in an early response to the change: 'Until we place the concept of civil society in the forefront, we will not be able to theoretically address developments in Eastern Europe' (Ost 1990). And, as so many of the publications on the events of 1989 underline, the role of the masses proved decisive in the collapse of the communist regimes, with it invariably being described as a 'revolution' (McSweeney and Tempest 1993: 414–15). It is important, nevertheless, to consider the transition process as a series of different and sometimes fluctuating stages that allow varying opportunities for elite action and mass influence. And, in particular, we need to give more attention than in the past to interactions between the two, especially at decisive moments of regime change. This point is examined by Pridham in his chapter in this volume, introducing his state/society model of democratic transition.

Another dimension of democratic transition, underplayed in previous work and early dramatized by the shift to democratization in Eastern Europe, is the international. It has been assumed in the standing literature on the subject that domestic forces were crucial and that external influences were at best secondary, although there was already some rethinking of this assumption with respect to Southern Europe before the events of 1989–90 (Pridham 1991). The latter have undoubtedly forced comparativists working on democratic transition to broaden their perspectives and to confront more seriously the relative weight of external and domestic determinants of regime change. This may well produce differential answers such as the conclusion that international forces were rather less crucial in the transitions of the South than the East (Pridham 1994).

A third and final way in which transition theory has been deficient has been its neglect of historical explanations. No transition, however radical, can break completely with the past because of inheritances (including negative ones) from the previous regime and the impact of historical memory and national culture. Historical perspectives have not been totally lacking in some work and have been vaguely implicit in the functionalist approach looking at the impact of structural factors over time. A sense of historical sequence is apparent in Rustow's series of transition phases, albeit within a very short time-span; and it is evident in other work linking the possibilities for democratic consolidation with the nature of the previous transition (Schmitter 1987; Pridham 1990, ch. 1). But the historical approach needs enlarging and applying backwards in time to assess the roots of democratization and the chances for its success. This lesson has been espoused by Michael Waller in his study of groups and political change and by Cotta in looking at political continuities and authoritarian legacies. Such an approach has an obvious relevance to a region like Eastern Europe where the 'unfreezing' of East/West relations has led to the emergence of some old historical conflicts during transition, as featured in the 'rebirth of history' interpretation of this development.

Empirical studies of earlier transitions have as a rule illustrated the various directions set out in theoretical work. That has strengthened interest in the causes if not preconditions of democratization and shifted attention to the dynamics of the transition process, given that cross-national and national case-studies have been usually inspired by genetic thinking about political choice and strategy. But, in effect, research on transitions in Southern Europe and Latin America has moved thematic concerns somewhat beyond the rather narrow concerns of the theory. First, it has painted a richer and more complex picture of transition processes, while – not surprisingly – identifying significant differences between simultaneous cases. This has served to pinpoint the need to look at different, sometimes conflicting, elite groups in transition as well as at the context or environment of the process.

Second, comparative or 'middle-range theory' studies have begun to draw inter-regional conclusions. Thus, Schmitter attributed the greater likelihood of new democracies remaining in Southern Europe than in Latin America to a more supportive international framework in Europe and to the greater presence of civil society (Schmitter, introduction to O'Donnell, Schmitter and Whitehead 1986). Applying inter-regional comparisons to Eastern Europe quickly highlights one rather basic difference from earlier examples of regime change, for we are here looking at a dual transition with economic transformation (marketization) paralleling democratization. This has presented a further challenge to the established literature on transition which has not previously coped with such a dual process in quite this way. Functionalist theory emphasized economic preconditions for democratization, and there has been some discussion about the relationship between economic and political liberalization as well as the effects of capitalist development on the potential for democracy. But earlier work had of course focused on systems which were already located in the capitalist world. This volume is in part attracted by the value of inter-regional comparisons, involving Southern Europe, although our essential concern is with the political rather than the economic process as the contributions by Pridham and Cotta show.

The difficult transitions in Eastern Europe remind us that the eventual outcome may not, in some cases, be one comparable to the established democracies of Western Europe. Indeed, there has been a certain 'culture-bound' attitude to expectations about the change in the East, certainly on the part of Western governments but also in academic research. This is perhaps because many who had previously worked on democratic transitions in the West have been turning their hand to the most recent and in many respects appealing examples of this phenomenon. As Paul Lewis, one of the authors in this volume, points out elsewhere, the situation in Eastern Europe is not 'particularly clear-cut in terms of the idea of democracy and conceptions of the basis for its development in the area' (Lewis 1993: 293). For many in the region, democracy remains an ill-defined objective with diverse associations and there still remain some alternative conceptions of it (Lewis 1993: 294–6). Furthermore, some basic differences about the nature of democracy have surfaced between West and East – with preferences veering respectively towards standard or procedural liberal democracy as against expansive or participatory democracy – this being partly influenced by different historical experiences of state/society relations (Rengger 1994). But, conceptual differences aside, the magnitude of transition problems cautions against optimism about these alternative versions of liberal democracy, for an authoritarian relapse in one form or another cannot at this stage be excluded in some cases.

The general approach and focus of this volume is influenced by these foregoing considerations about the literature on democratic transition. At the same time, it does not claim to be comprehensive and is concerned with democratization *sensu stricto*, namely with the process of political (regime) change. Within that frame of reference, the approach has been threefold and responds to the lesson that democratic transition should be viewed at different if not interconnecting levels. Thus, some comparative and historical chapters attempt to add breadth and depth to the study of the Eastern European democratizations. The chapters in Part I explore democratization essentially with respect to domestic factors. But they differ in their approaches in that Vanhanen and Kimber focus on long-term structural factors while Pridham and Waller consider historical and conjunctural factors in the same process. In Part II, we view the process systematically with special regard to the emergence of new party systems. The functioning of parties is seen as a decisive test of the emergence of political pluralism and also of their effectiveness as gatekeepers between the new systems and (civil) society. We turn, in Part III, to the international dimension already recognized as a principal component of the change in Eastern Europe. Niklasson and Hyde-Price look in turn at how far external factors were important and what form they took.

We should add that the different schools of transition theory are represented in this volume, as in the approach of the two editors. However, despite our harmonious cooperation, our intentions have remained ultimately modest in that recasting transition theory is not within our remit; and, it is in any case perhaps too soon to attempt that. However, some of our conclusions may possibly influence any further debate about transition theory in the light of experience in Eastern Europe.

The eight chapters of this book thus embrace different theoretical or specialist approaches. To make it easier for readers to gain an overview of our joint work, we introduce each chapter briefly and try to indicate how they are related. The Conclusion (Chapter 9) to the book draws together the results of this study in more detail.

POLITICAL CHANGE IN HISTORICAL AND STRUCTURAL PERSPECTIVE

For Geoffrey Pridham, comparing democratic transitions in Eastern Europe to earlier democratizations in Southern Europe is helpful in forming new perspectives on the former. Pridham regards the two schools of theoretical approaches to regime transition, known as the functionalist and the genetic or as respectively macro- and micro-oriented, as contradictory to some extent. But he emphasizes that they are possibly more compatible than might be supposed when applied to empirical research such as on Eastern Europe. Pridham himself focuses on historical and conjunctural factors in transitions. He differentiates three separate but interconnected levels of the transition process – the state, inter-group relations, and society – and hypothesizes that the more interaction among the three levels, the more likely the transition is to be unstable, uncontrolled and subject to upheaval. Pridham indicates that several lessons can be drawn from Southern European experience for the transitions in Eastern Europe. The main one is that there is no such phenomenon as a straightforward or easy transition to liberal democracy. More specifically, he differentiates between environmental, political-institutional and dynamic lessons. Altogether, there are similarities but also crucial differences between the two regions in their respective experiences of democratic transition.

Michael Waller sees the revolutionary events of 1989 as the culmination of a long series of political developments. His argument is that in order to understand democratization in Eastern Europe we have to take into account a group process of politics. The effect of the gradual formation of political groups from 1977 was to undermine the hegemony of communist parties and prepare the ground for political change. He differentiates three sets of factors: historical, systematic, and conjunctural. While historical factors comprise long-term cultural and economic developments, for instance, systemic ones refer to the overall effects of communist rule in these countries. Conjunctural factors include the shift in the Soviet Union's policy toward Eastern Europe, the attraction of the European Community, and the desperate economic plight in which all countries of the region found themselves. These three sets of factors set the parameters within which change took place in Eastern Europe. They also affected the formation of political parties and groups, which Waller analyses. His approach is significant as it highlights the basic need to underpin liberal democracy with associative life.

Tatu Vanhanen and Richard Kimber focus on domestic structural preconditions of democracy. Their intention is to find out to what extent the collapse of hegemonic regimes and the breakthrough of democracy in Eastern Europe could be explained by some systematic and structural factors. The study is based on Vanhanen's earlier comparative studies of democratization and on his evolutionary theory of democratization, using empirical data on 147 states, including all East European countries. This failure to make correct predictions for East European countries challenged Vanhanen to experiment with different combinations of his explanatory factors. The results show that if these alternative combinations of explanatory variables had been used, in addition to the original combination, it would have been possible to anticipate democratization in Eastern Europe on the basis of 1980 empirical data. Richard Kimber has analysed Vanhanen's data by a different statistical method using neural networks. In most points the results are approximately identical. The argument of their chapter is that democratization in Eastern Europe was not merely due to unique historical events and external factors but also to some particular structural factors, which have the same significance everywhere and which, therefore, make it possible to predict the possibility of democratization.

EMERGING PARTY SYSTEMS AND INSTITUTIONS

Maurizio Cotta explores the emergence of new party systems in Eastern Europe in diachronic and comparative perspective. He is not as such concerned with what type of democracy will be adopted in those countries, but a major aspect of that is the party system. Cotta concentrates on continuities and discontinuities with the past and how they help to shape party systems of new democracies, using re-democratizations in Western Europe (Austria, France, Germany, Italy, Greece, Portugal, Spain) as points of comparison. He finds that almost all the conditions limiting the possibility of continuity with past democratic experiences and with the old parties are stronger in Eastern European countries than in the group of 'discontinuous' Western European countries. Therefore, pre-Communist Party systems cannot provide the basic structure for the new party systems of the post-communist era. Their legacies are on the whole marginal. In such a situation idiosyncratic and situational factors – like institutional choices (concerning electoral systems or parliament–executive relations) made during the transition; leaders' personalities; specific issues appearing on the political agenda; success or failure in solving economic problems; or even external influences – can play a much stronger role in determining the nature of the new party systems. Consequently, we can expect further significant transformations of party systems in many of these countries. Cotta's analysis therefore helps us to understand better why new party systems are still unstable in Eastern Europe.

Turning to Kimmo Kuusela's chapter, it is worth recalling that the institutional choice of electoral system may significantly affect the nature of an incipient party system. Hence, it is important to look at the founding electoral systems as a formative influence on the emergence of multi-party systems after communist rule. One general feature of the changes made to electoral practices in Eastern Europe was a shift away from the majority allocation rule, which was universal with non-competitive elections, toward more proportional procedures. Kuusela relates this trend to proportional procedures in Eastern Europe before the Second World War. To some extent, new electoral systems differed from country to country depending on local conditions that affected the choice of the system. Kuusela sees the founding electoral systems in Poland, Hungary, Romania, Czechoslovakia and Bulgaria (and East Germany's 1990 electoral law) as having guaranteed a reasonable connection between the parties' support among the voters and their representation in the parliaments. On the other hand, he criticizes the excessive complexity of the East European electoral systems and argues the need for their reform. The problems Kuusela identifies are not merely technical, for they can have significant political consequences. The familiar trade-off between fair representation and political stability has to be established.

This very consideration influences the discussion by Paul Lewis, Bill Lomax, and Gordon Wightman of the emergence of multi-party systems in East-Central Europe. They emphasize that a major requirement of the emerging liberal democracy is the achievement of balance between a party system that reflects the divisions and conflicts in post-communist society and the formation of governments with effective powers derived from and sustained by a reasonably representative parliament. They start from the assumption that the emergence of effectively operating multi-party systems should be understood as a major feature of the potential consolidation of new democracies. While communist regimes came to a rapid end in Eastern Europe, democratization is likely to be protracted – not least because of the cultural and historical backgrounds of the countries in question, combined with the magnitude of economic as well as political change facing them. Political parties have begun to aggregate and articulate political views and interests, sustain leaders and organize their support, and generally to structure the political landscape. However, recognition of the important role played by parties during democratic transition came rather late in several cases. In Poland and Czechoslovakia, it was first thought that social movements like Solidarity and Civic Forum could substitute for parties and transcend the divisions familiar in Western democracies. But it soon became obvious that these broad movements were not able to cope with the need for differentiation and the complexity of demands evident in a post-communist, pluralist society.

THE EXTERNAL DIMENSION

Tomas Niklasson argues that we cannot find a satisfactory explanation for democratization in Eastern Europe without reference to the role of external actors. He focuses on the relationship between changes in the Soviet Union under Gorbachev and the development in Eastern and Central Europe during 1988 and 1989, indicating how the transition processes in Eastern Europe differ from earlier cases of democratization. His main hypothesis is that international actors have played and can play a more important role in the development of this region than has been the case in other regions. Niklasson brings into play the argument that the world is more interdependent today than ever before. The most important external role in Eastern European democratization was played by 'the Soviet connection', i.e. it was at the same time a domestic liberation and national liberation from Soviet influence. Niklasson, however, regards the changes in the Soviet Union as neither necessary nor sufficient conditions for what happened in Eastern Europe. He emphasizes that without the pressure within the East European states themselves changes would not have followed automatically from changes in the Soviet Union. His general conclusion is that regardless of the actions of the Soviet Union or Mikhail Gorbachev, there was an internal dynamic in all the six Eastern and Central European states that led to a situation ripe for radical change. The changes in the Soviet Union made the explosion come earlier, but an explosion would have come even without Gorbachev. At the same time, the linkage was not just one way, for developments in Eastern Europe started a dynamic of 'Eastern Europeanization' in the Soviet Union itself.

Adrian G.V. Hyde-Price takes into consideration other types of external factors and how the process of democratization in Eastern Europe can be supported and encouraged by them. His argument is that key international organizations – the European Community (EC), the Conference on Security and Cooperation in Europe (CSCE), and the Council of Europe – could be used to mitigate the serious problems threatening transition in Eastern Europe. These include (a) economic dislocation with growing unemployment, widening social and economic inequalities, falling living standards and a deepening mood of insecurity, (b) national and ethnic tensions, (c) the possible emergence of forms of 'authoritarian populism', and (d) the fear of inter-state conflicts in Eastern Europe and especially the Balkans. Western Europe has already exerted a powerful and pervasive influence on Eastern Europe by virtue of its political, economic, and cultural characteristics. Western countries and multilateral organizations can buttress democratic reforms in Eastern Europe by offering political support and advice and by providing economic aid and cooperation. Hyde-Price assumes that given its magnetic attraction as a focus of European integration, the Community can in particular exercise a considerable influence on the democratization process in the East. In this respect, the chances of the CSCE and the Council of Europe are more limited. In conclusion, Hyde-Price suggests that the strategic aim of Western policies towards Eastern Europe should be to enmesh these countries in an ever-deepening network of political, economic and social interdependencies; but he stresses that democracy cannot be imposed on the peoples of Eastern Europe. External agents can only provide a favourable international environment to democratic reform. In the end, the main burdens of democratic transition will have to be carried by the East Europeans themselves.

By and large, these different contributions to our volume provide a multi-dimensional approach to the process of democratization in Eastern Europe. Structural, historical, conjunctural, political-systemic and finally international determinants of regime change are all crucial in our understanding of that process. There may well be some disagreement on the relative significance of these determinants, hardly surprising when confronting what is a contemporary and still incomplete development. But we return to this basic problem in the Conclusion.

BIBLIOGRAPHY

Huntington, S. (1984) 'Will more countries become democratic?', *Political Science Quarterly* 99: 193–218.

Lewis, P. (1993) 'Democracy and its future in Eastern Europe', in D. Held (ed.) *Prospects for Democracy: North, South, East, West*, Cambridge: Polity Press.

McSweeney, D., and Tempest, C. (1993) 'The political science of democratic transition in Eastern Europe', *Political Studies*, September: 408–19.

O'Donnell, G., Schmitter, P., and Whitehead, L. (eds) (1986) *Transitions from Authoritarian Rule: Prospects for Democracy*, Baltimore: Johns Hopkins University Press.

Ost, D. (1990) 'Transition theory and Eastern Europe', Paper for Conference on Democratization in Latin America and Eastern Europe, Pultusk, Poland, May.

Pridham, G. (1990) *Securing Democracy: Political Parties and Democratic Consolidation in Southern Europe*, London: Routledge.

—— (ed.) (1991) *Encouraging Democracy: The International Context of Regime Transition in Southern Europe*, Leicester: Leicester University Press.

—— (1994) 'The international dimension of democratisation: theory, practice and inter-regional comparisons', in G. Pridham, E. Herring and G. Sanford (eds) *Building Democracy? The International Dimension of Democratisation in Eastern Europe*, London: Pinter.

Rengger, N. (1994) 'Towards a culture of democracy?: democratic theory and democratisation in Eastern and Central Europe', in G. Pridham, E. Herring and G. Sanford (eds) *Building Democracy? The International Dimension of Democratisation in Eastern Europe*, London: Pinter.

Rustow, D. (1970) 'Transitions to democracy: toward a dynamic model', *Comparative Politics*, April: 365–87.

Schmitter, P. (1987) 'The consolidation of political democracy in Southern Europe', Paper for Stanford University, July.

Part I

Political change in historical and structural perspective

Part 1

1 Democratic transitions in theory and practice

Southern European lessons for Eastern Europe?

Geoffrey Pridham

INTER-REGIONAL COMPARISONS AND DEMOCRATIC TRANSITION

The simultaneous transitions to liberal democracy that commenced as a whole in Eastern Europe at the end of the 1980s, in some cases earlier, are certainly a development of major historical significance, but they are still in a relatively early phase and their outcomes are as yet unknown. Democratic transitions are intrinsically hedged with uncertainty; and there is no firm guarantee of success. For this reason, there is a need for putting these recent developments into comparative perspective.

Comparative approaches have featured prominently in the study of democratic transitions, particularly as these have tended to involve largely contemporaneous processes within certain regions, specifically Southern Europe and Latin America. Engaging in inter-regional comparisons obviously magnifies the problems of cross-national analysis in accommodating national patterns and cultures and, if applicable, differences of area culture – such as 'Central Europe' and 'Mediterranean Europe'. Variations in international environment may also have a bearing on this process of change, as O'Donnell, Schmitter and Whitehead found when comparing Latin America with Southern Europe and their transition outcomes (O'Donnell, Schmitter and Whitehead 1986). Eastern and Southern Europe do however have a similar orientation in their transitions towards links with the European Community. This does not of course deny the importance of the domestic dynamics of system change and national-specific factors which help to determine that process.

This chapter is therefore exploratory and seeks to compare and draw insights and lessons from the earlier transitions to democracy in Southern Europe and to apply these to the Eastern European transitions currently in progress.

THEORETICAL APPROACHES TO DEMOCRATIC TRANSITION: A STATE/SOCIETY MODEL

There are generally two schools of thinking on democratic transition theory, known as the functionalist and the genetic or as, 'respectively' macro- and micro-oriented. The former gives paramount attention to structural or environmental – notably, economic and social – determinants of political system change; and it views regime changes as preconditioned by particular conditions like economic development or cultural patterns or simply modernization. On the other hand, the genetic school has usually given a priority to conjunctural and volitional variables and especially political determinants of regime change, and has therefore emphasized the importance of political choice and strategy by actors during the transition process. The assumption here is that this process is inherently fluid and is not automatic, and that a successful outcome is not preordained.

While these two approaches are philosophically different and have often been seen as in conflict, they are possibly less contradictory than might be supposed when applied to empirical research. The functionalist school focuses on longer-term processes especially prior to transition occurring, but also conceivably following its achievement: socioeconomic change of the kind highlighted by these theories cannot of course be telescoped into the relatively short time-span of democratic transition – which, averaging the Southern European cases, took around half a decade. Genetic theorists precisely concentrate on this very period once the authoritarian/totalitarian regime collapses and early democratization begins. This weighs in favour of genetic interpretations so far as the actual transition is concerned, but it does not have to deny some value in functionalist explanations.

Conceivably, structural determinants may well play a vital role in undermining authoritarian regimes over time, this being a variation on the theme of such regimes failing to adapt to social and economic changes or pressures for modernization. But they cannot exclude a significant element of strategic choice or, for that matter, political mistakes by authoritarian leaders. At the other end of the time-scale, it is very arguable that the functionalist and genetic schools are most compatible when looking at subsequent democratic consolidation – a process which is both longer-lasting and involves institutional and societal levels in conjunction. In between, the shorter transition process is likely to be dominated by political and institutional concerns, although there is usually room for structural factors to impinge. Experience so far in Eastern Europe highlights this, given the process of economic transformation parallel to that of regime change. That may also depend on how far a particular transition is more 'top down' or 'bottom up' in its dynamics, or on some combination of both directions. But, as O'Donnell and Schmitter note about such macro-structural factors, 'at some stages in the transition, in relation to certain issues and actors, these broad structures filter down to affect the behaviour of groups and individuals; but even these mediations are looser, and their impacts more indeterminate, than in normal circumstances' (O'Donnell, Schmitter and Whitehead 1986, Pt IV: 5).

In general terms, the transition process runs from the point at which the previous authoritarian system begins to be dismantled, through the constituent phase of the new democracy to its inauguration and early operation. A variety of transition pathways may be identified cross-nationally, for ultimately each national case has its peculiarities, although comparative approaches seek to relate the national-specific to the general. What follows here is an attempt to group different themes under distinct headings as a way of identifying different types of democratic transitions. It develops points from the above discussion.

Firstly, *the historical dimension* is important in so far as it brings into play functionalist concerns while providing a necessary context to the transition itself. Historical perspectives are too often neglected in the theory on regime transition, although there is clearly a case for considering the previous type of regime as an important determinant, helping to shape the transition pathway. Our focus here is on the intermediate patterns and dynamics of system change from the authoritarian decline onwards, as distinct from the broad historical sweep of developments favoured by the functionalist school.

This may be called conveniently *the 'pre-transition' phase* in which the dictatorship's weaknesses become malignant, and it begins to disintegrate and the course is set for eventual regime change. In particular, we are concerned here with the causes of authoritarian regimes 'opening up' and subsequently breaking down. Such change may arise from developments like military defeat, basic economic failure, socio-economic transformation and the disintegration of the dominant coalition between elite groups supporting the regime (Morlino 1987: 74). These causes are not exclusive of each other and may interact to produce a negative dynamic: for instance, policy failure, such as economic, may provoke strategic divisions between hardliners and softliners in the ruling coalition.

Invariably, this 'pre-transition' phase is marked by some form of liberalization of the authoritarian regime, which makes limited concessions to domestic or international pressure. As Morlino puts it,

Liberalisation is the process of concession from above of greater and larger civil and political rights, never too large and complete, but of such a nature that allows authoritarian elites to control the civil society, both at elite and mass levels. Basically, liberalisation brings about partial institutional change in an attempt to overcome the authoritarian crisis. Such a goal is attained by enlarging the regime's base of social support without giving up military rule completely.

(Morlino 1987: 55)

A qualitative distinction has however to be drawn between liberalization and democratization. The former is essentially defensive, being an attempt by an authoritarian regime to control change. According to Morlino, democratization, on the other hand, involves

the real recognition of civil and political rights and, where necessary, . . . a complete transformation in the service of a reconstruction of civil society. Political parties and a party system emerge. The organization of interest groups, such as labour unions, takes place. The elaboration, or adoption, of the principal democratic institutions and procedures that will characterize the regime, such as electoral laws and a specified relationship between executive and legislative powers, occurs.

(Morlino 1987: 55)

The principal concern with the historical dimension is to emphasize the link between the form of 'pre-transition', the shift to democratization and the mode of transition. For instance, liberalization may itself stimulate democratization as a result of which authoritarian leaders lose control; alternatively, a failure to liberalize or liberalize enough could lead to an accumulation of problems, producing an explosive type of transition.

There are other ways in which 'history' affects transition to liberal democracy. One thinks of the legacy of an authoritarian period for a subsequent democracy, implying its effects on national political culture – these are likely to be fairly profound, particularly in the event of long-lasting authoritarian regimes. Or, there may even be pre-authoritarian legacies, involving some survival or remnant of representative institutions such as parties and associations from earlier democratic systems. Morlino contends that previous democratic experience 'affects deeply the new democratic arrangements; it is part of the historical memory of the people preserved, in turn, by the mechanisms of political socialisation' (Morlino 1987: 66). Such factors come into play during the ensuing democratic transition all the more if some form of continuity has maintained them during the authoritarian period. Cultural patterns may persist autonomously, even for long authoritarian periods, as Maravall showed in the case of Spain (Maravall 1982). These have consequences for the inauguration of new democracies, for the resumption of pluralistic politics and maybe also for the course and length of the transition period.

The longevity of authoritarian regimes is therefore a principal but by no means an absolute determinant of democratic transition. Variation in type of previous regime is important too, for this is very likely to condition the nature of subsequent democratic transition. For example, limited pluralism under authoritarian rule is likely to provide a basis for early democratic activity. The degree of 'penetration' of the state, not to mention of society, notably by totalitarian-type systems, is likely to affect both the inauguration of democracy as well as its mode of transition. Fishman has underlined this distinction between state and regime as 'important not only for identifying the source of the democratising initiative, but also for understanding the subsequent trajectory of political change: the location of the impetus for political change within the circles of power has implications for the ability of the transitional political formation to carry out functions associated with state and regime' (Fishman 1990: 432). He concludes:

> This line of analysis suggests that democratic transition is more likely to be successful where state and regime can be distinguished from one another. Where the distinction is not easily drawn – because of 'fusion' between the two in a military dictatorship, or totalitarian penetration of the state by the regime, or confusion between the two under personal rulership – special problems are likely to emerge in the process of democratisation.
>
> (Fishman 1990: 434)

Also, not to be forgotten, the type of previous regime will certainly determine the kind of political reaction – at both elite and mass levels – to this very experience. That tends to encourage a negative (anti-authoritarian/totalitarian) value system that can be important for a time in promoting legitimacy for a new democracy, such as in discrediting alternative systems. We think of anti-fascism in post-war Italy and of course anti-communist feeling in contemporary Eastern Europe, not to mention the emergence of anti-military attitudes, following dictatorship, as likely to reinforce the armed forces' withdrawal from politics.

Furthermore, there are different *modalities of the transition process*. These are sometimes typed very broadly as evolutionary or revolutionary, although such a distinction may distract from the complexities of this process. In part, differences derive from the exact causes of authoritarian breakdown, but they are also due to various combinations of environmental as well as top–down and bottom–up determinants of regime change. For instance, Stepan identifies eight different paths to democratization: internal restoration after external reconquest; internal reformulation; externally monitored installation; redemocratization initiated from within the authoritarian regime, either by civilian leadership or by the military as government or as institution; society-led termination; party pact; organized violent revolt; and, Marxist-led revolutionary war (Stepan 1986, Pt III, ch. 3). Not all of these apply to our two regional sets of transitions, but they highlight the wide range of possibilities for the mode of system change.

The purpose of the following comparative framework is to accommodate these complexities and to encourage a dynamic rather than static approach to transition. It is based on the hypothesis that there are broadly three separate but interconnected levels of the transition process: the state, inter-group relations and society.

The state and society levels are self-evident, the former consisting of institutional structures and power agencies as well as the role of those political elites exercising power (or such as the military as government in the case of military dictatorship); while the latter simply refers to civil society, associational life, social movements and participation in general. The inter-group level comprises different sets of relationships, especially between political elites (notably, different parties) and between political and non-political elites (such as economic and military).

Surrounding these levels is the environment, which may comprise the international framework, the state of the economy (which can in turn have international and domestic aspects) and simply events which may have an impact at different levels or on one level more than another during transition. One may include also – somewhat schematically – the aforementioned historical dimension, as being transmitted to the politics of democratic transition, for it may affect elite and inter-elite attitudes depending on previous political experience (e.g. degrees of involvement in the previous regime); and, 'history' can influence the society level depending on how far this has been controlled by the outgoing regime.

Such a framework disaggregates the different levels according to the type of transition examined, but also allows one to measure the extent of interaction between them. Thus, a working hypothesis emerges: the more interaction between the three levels together, the more likely the transition is unstable, uncontrolled and subject to upheaval. As a whole, since any regime obviously encompasses links between all levels in one form or another, then a change of regime is bound to involve significant if not substantial alteration in these links. A totalitarian-type, and to a lesser extent an authoritarian, regime creates a much closer relationship between the state and society levels through the predominance of the first over the second. The advent of liberal democracy loosens that relationship and provides for autonomous political activity at the society level.

Thus, conclusions can be drawn about *the style and scope of transitions to liberal democracy.* Styles may conventionally range from the evolutionary to the revolutionary; they may be incremental or protracted, alternatively consensual (transaction) or not (rupture); and they can even be restorative, particularly when authoritarian interludes have been brief. In all these cases, we are in effect talking about different forms and degrees of links between the three levels. For example, an evolutionary transition involves a much less abrupt and probably less substantial departure in institutional arrangements (state level) – accepting the common need for creating a constitutionally responsible government and the rule of law – than a revolutionary transition, which in turn is likely to include some element of society impacting on the state. A simple restoration of democracy after an authoritarian interlude will probably entail minimal state-level change, and it may or may not be accompanied by the direct influence of society. It is also highly conceivable it will show a marked continuity of political elites with the pre-authoritarian period. Clearly, the distinction between consensual and non-consensual transitions revolves around inter-group relations, especially among political elites. This may also affect their relations with non-political elites.

As to scope of transition, this primarily means whether the process is essentially elitist or rather participatory. Does it, as in the first case, concentrate on the state level (changes in institutional arrangements, implementation of the constitution) and the inter-group level (con-stituent stage)? Or, as in the second instance, does the transition embrace the society level to the extent of allowing or producing persistent pressures which force elites to modify their strategy and behaviour?

Finally, we are concerned with *the outcomes of transition* in the sense of different versions of liberal democracy. There are certain basic conditions for liberal democracy, e.g. responsible government, political pluralism, subordination of the military to civilian authority; but at the same time there must be room for institutional and structural variation. The most obvious versions are parliamentary and (semi-)presidential systems and liberal democracies which are centralized or federal. But, the key to a successful transition is a qualitative change occurring in political dynamics that sets the course for the end of transition and encourages the prospects for democratic consolidation.

When uncertainty persists, however, the transition remains out of control or there is no clear sense of direction or outcome; then the dangers or risks that are likely to be present become more threatening. They may assume various forms: direct threats from anti-system forces opposed to liberal democracy (reactionary military, political extremes); severe and persistent policy problems (e.g. economic, social dislocation or violence), creating government overload at a time of system fragility; and, widespread disillusionment with the democratic experiment and an unfavourable domestic or international environment.

As to the end-point of transition, a minimalist definition would be that this is reached when a new constitution has been proclaimed and inaugurated. Linz admits that the choice of end-point is rather arbitrary, 'but there is little doubt that the successful realisation of a free election, the convening of a new parliament on whose confidence the government depends, or the installation of a new president in office, would be such a moment' (Linz 1990: 157). Clearly, the new constitution is integral to a transition period, for the degree of consensus behind it offers an element of stability in the future politics of the democratic system. For this reason, there is a preference here for including in the transition period the start-up of constitutionally elected government – in effect, the first couple of years following the proclamation of the constitution.

SOUTHERN EUROPEAN EXAMPLES OF DEMOCRATIC TRANSITION

The transitions to democracy that occurred in Spain, Greece and Portugal in the latter half of the 1970s emphasized certain dimensions to democratic transition. In particular, common environmental factors and similarities of background condition received strong recognition (in terms of the Mediterranean region) and not merely internal causes of national system change; while more systematic attention was given dynamic in place of descriptive approaches to the theme. Comparisons with, say, post-war transitions in Western Europe (specifically, Italy and West Germany) also, on the environmental level of discussion, pointed to the importance of different time contexts. This only encouraged new or revised attempts at comparative or theoretical work (e.g. O'Donnell, Schmitter and Whitehead 1986; Herz 1982; Pridham 1984, 1991a).

While some debate centred on the existence or not of a 'Mediterranean model' of democratic transition (Pridham 1984; Lijphart *et al.* 1988) –

prompted by similarities of historical and political background as well as the contemporaneous processes in these countries – differences in style of transition were apparent, such as between the Spanish and Portuguese cases: a fairly controlled and rather elitist and consensual process in the first, a military coup followed by political and economic upheaval in the second. Stepan includes both Portugal and Greece as cases of transition initiated from within the regime, but through the military as institution rather than as government – in Greece, it was the generals, concerned about the army's position following Turkish aggression in Cyprus, who gave the push to the colonels (Stepan 1986, Pt III: 77). Post-war Italy he classified as a mixed case of both internal reformulation (Mussolini's overthrow by the Fascist Grand Council) and externally monitored installation (Stepan 1986, Pt III: 69). Spain was a fairly straightforward case of initiation from within the authoritarian regime by civilian leadership, combined with pactism.

Literature on the Southern European transitions has largely favoured genetic explanations over functionalist ones. The levels of economic development – sometimes termed 'semi-peripheral' with respect to the rest of Western Europe – did not make them sure cases for democratization (Vanhanen 1990: 131). This was all the more true a decade and a half ago when their transitions began, for their modernization has proceeded particularly since then. Spain offered, admittedly, a partial exception, as a fairly convincing case of socio-economic transformation commencing before political system change and creating some pressures for the latter from the 1960s. One might add that developments like Franco's impending death and Portugal's colonial wars which acerbated systemic crisis gave a visibility to political causes of regime collapse; and this is all the more evident if we include Italy's defeat in war as the primary cause of her transition to democracy. We proceed now to apply the state/society model to these cases of transition.

The historical dimension

The historical dimension immediately identifies some differences if not contrasts between the Southern European cases, especially over the longevity of authoritarian regimes and, therefore, distance from previous democratic experience. Greece, for instance, experienced the shortest previous authoritarian regime (it may be described simply as a military dictatorship) with the colonels holding power from 1967 to 1974. Again, there is some basic difference between Italy's fascist regime, claiming self-consciously to be totalitarian – or, as neither wholly totalitarian nor simply authoritarian (Di Palma 1982: 107) – and the other three cases

24   *Political change in perspective*

which were straightforwardly authoritarian. These differences had some influence on the course of transition politics in the various countries. For instance, while Greece's transition was the shortest in time, that in Portugal encountered difficulties in igniting democratic political life after such a long authoritarian period (Gladdish 1990).

Furthermore, one can observe liberalization occurring, notably at the economic level in both Iberian states; but in each case this was not accompanied by any substantial political liberalization. In Portugal, the Estado Novo was 'too archaic, too disconnected and inflexible to be able to respond to changes in the environment' to conduct any 'parallel reorientation of politics' (Bruneau 1984: 25–6). In Spain, the 'economic miracle' that took place under the Franco regime created such a transformation that political ramifications were eventually inevitable. Despite attempts by the ruling elite to respond to change (e.g. some liberalization of press censorship), they could not prevent different non-political groups – especially economic elites – distancing themselves from the regime and paving the way for its eventual disintegration (Malefakis 1982: 217ff.). If there is a lesson here it is that any strict separation between economic and political forms of liberalization is rather artificial and ultimately impossible. The answer of the technocrats in authoritarian clothes that an 'opening up' could be confined to one level proved to be myopic. Indeed, one could go so far as to say that liberalization is probably doomed to failure or is at best only a transitory solution, although that may need to be qualified by the timing – for a belated or reluctant liberalization is especially likely to have this result.

What significance did these differences have for the Southern European transitions? Firstly, the matter of pre-authoritarian democratic experience was pertinent in helping to determine the resumption of democratic life and in providing a historical reference for political actors and organizations. The longest authoritarian period was Portugal's, so that memories of the 1910–26 parliamentary republic were extremely distant; while Spain's previous democratic experience was a decade closer in time and made more powerful by the painful memories of the civil war. This contributed over time, with social modernization, to some 'remaking' of the Spanish political culture broadly favouring moderate politics (Maravall 1982: 20). Italy's two decades of fascism still allowed political actors from the 1920s to play a major role in the transition after the Second World War.

Secondly, continuity with earlier democratic life cannot of course be dissociated from authoritarian interludes. The type of previous regime mattered such as in the extent to which it suppressed opposition activity, as a primary source for subsequent democratic elites. It was severe in fascist Italy and also in the first decade of Franco's system, although systemic evolution in the latter made it possible for groups and movements in opposition to emerge eventually. This political activism that surfaced in the 1960s in Spain was somewhat in contrast to the relative apathy that characterized political tendencies in Salazar's Portugal. In the latter, the long authoritarian period produced a distinctly 'subject' political culture within a framework of centralistic bureaucratic tutelage (Opello 1985: ch. 9). It was also due to the international isolation and absence of modernization that characterized Portugal under the Estado Novo.

Political legacies are essentially about how to handle the past in terms of the present or ongoing political experience. Inevitably, the past acquires a different set of perspectives once the old regime has been rejected or removed and once the new politics is set on course, both in terms of mass political attitudes and also elite behaviour. As Di Palma noted in the case of post-war Italy, 'the definition of what Fascism was, its disposition, and the reactions to that disposition became entangled with and cannot be understood outside the contentious issues associated with the transition' (Di Palma 1982: 116). This was partly as de-fascistization achieved limited results, but also because the Italian transition itself – with its inter-party compromises and defeat of the Left in the late 1940s – persisted in fuelling controversy long afterwards (Pasquino 1986, Pt I: 65–6).

The past also presents its own problems, notably when transition pacts or consensus-building involves some kind of deal with former regime figures or groups. Spain's largely evolutionary transition illustrated these problems of the Francoist legacy, all the more given sharp historical memories. The compromise between Franco's legacy and the new democracy that marked the Spanish transition in turn presented problems for transition management since it 'left intact . . . the corpus of military and paramilitary institutions that had functioned for so long to prevent change' (Maxwell 1982: 242).

The basic distinction between the Spanish and Portuguese transitions – the latter seen as 'revolutionary' in some of the literature (cf. Bruneau 1984; Opello 1985) – is one of style of transition and to some extent its scope; but this tells us little about their transition dynamics. Here, the focus on the three levels can help.

The state level

In Southern Europe, we are really looking at changes of regime rather than transformation of the state, if we mean by the latter its political, institutional and bureaucratic structures. Accepting the alteration in the functions of political institutions – to allow for responsible constitutional government – there was nevertheless a remarkable continuity in those structures.

This was particularly noticeable in post-Franco Spain, where not only was the Cortes transmuted from a barely consultative to a parliamentary role, but also the police apparatus and the bureaucracy remained almost untouched (Abel and Torrents 1984: 13–14). The same was surprisingly true to a large degree also in post-fascist Italy with the restoration of the old state in a new guise (Di Palma 1982: 116). The most visible change, on the other hand, was the abolition by referendum of the monarchy in Italy and Greece for essentially the same reason: its association with the former regime.

Since the change in the functions of political institutions is of course crucial as the *sine qua non* of democratic transition, it follows the constituent process (the formulation of and agreement on a constitution) is a central component of democratic transition. This leads directly to the question of inter-group relations, since it is invariably political parties (specifically their parliamentary arms) which negotiate that process, although other groups may sometimes have a direct or indirect influence on it.

Inter-group relations

The level of inter-group relations is certainly quite variable between the Southern European transitions if we take political groups. In general terms, there is a consensual process of a cross-party kind in both Spain and post-war Italy (until 1947), with the less consensual procedure in Portugal and Greece. In Greece, Karamanlis supervised the 1975 Constitution – a revision of the 1952 one, with new elements – without calling a constituent assembly. It was formulated in the Parliament without the explicit agreement of the opposition (Featherstone and Katsoudas 1987: 21). These different patterns had various consequences for transition politics and beyond, such as in stabilizing regime change in Spain at this crucial moment and helping to neutralize moments of tension; while in Portugal and Greece problems of party-political polarization tended to be reflected in subsequent disputes over the constitutional settlement.

In Portugal, the years 1974–5 had been dominated by a series of major crises and coup attempts, but the period from the 1976 Constitution was less traumatic in that the option for liberal democracy had at last been made. All the same, the Constitution was based on a somewhat uneasy agreement between the parties and the military, which continued to enjoy a policy influence through the newly created Revolutionary Council, a body not abolished until the constitutional revision of 1982. In fact, broad consensus on the Constitution was not fully achieved until a further revision in 1988, on its socio-economic objectives. Clearly, therefore, this problem was indicative of the long and fairly complicated transition in that country.

In Spain, there has been no general disquiet over the Constitution and no revision – as was noted on its tenth anniversary celebrated in 1988 – except for the major issue unresolved by it, concerning the regions and their powers. Significantly, this emerged as one of the overriding problems of the Spanish transition, given its link with military discontent (based on the army's traditional attachment to the 'unity' of Spain) and, in the Basque case, with terrorism. Post-war Italy also witnessed difficulties in implementing its Constitution, if one recalls delays in creating the constitutional court and in introducing regional government for reasons of conflicting party interests. There is a probable connection here with the fact that republican Italy's democratic system took a long time to consolidate.

But this focus on political elites, specifically political leaders and parliamentary groups – albeit central to the transition process – is only one aspect of this dimension. Equally telling is the relationship between them and non-political elites, as revealing about the width of support behind transition and its interim chances of success. To some extent, non-political elites may take their cue from political leaders and parties. This was by and large true of economic elites in these countries, thus confirming the dominant role of parties in these new democracies (Pridham 1990: 114–15, 136–7). Even in post-1974 Portugal, when radical economic experiments took place, the industrial and agrarian elites tended to accept change while it lasted. In some cases there were preferential links, although these were not usually one-directional, as the relationship between the Italian DC and the Catholic Church illustrated only too well in the decades after the war. The Church hierarchy under Pius XII emerged as a considerable force pressing for an anti-communist solution to the transition. In the other three cases, however, Church leaders chose to play a more discreet role and surfaced in transition politics only when special ecclesiastical interests were apparently challenged.

The most difficult relationship was predictably with the military following right-wing authoritarian rule. That was itself suggestive of the wider condition of democratization in that a transition from authoritarian to democratic rule requires a basic change in civil/military relations.

Apart from the special case of Portugal, where the military played the key role in overthrowing the Estado Novo and then a co-role in constitutional government until the early 1980s, the main problem arose in Spain. Unreconstructed elements in the military presented the most direct threat to the transition here, as witnessed by several coup attempts. It was only in the course of the 1980s that government leaders managed to extract the military from the political game by a policy of institutional reform (Boyd and Boyden 1985: 117ff.). In both Greece and post-war Italy, the military was largely discredited by national defeat in war; although in Italy's case the involvement of some military circles or figures in plots against the state occasionally proved unsettling.

The society level

The society level once again played a variable role in the Southern European transitions. It was most in evidence in post-1974 Portugal because of the mushrooming of popular movements advocating radical change. Portugal thus showed elements of both 'top–down' and 'bottom–up' pressures during transition. In Spain, however, the transition was a rather elitist process; in fact, some called it a 'revolution from above' for this reason – a term which nevertheless misleads somewhat. It was not literally true all the time, as in early 1976 when there was some danger of popular pressure threatening to disrupt matters before the bold option for system reform became adopted by Suarez and the King in the summer of that year. Thereafter, the Spanish transition remained a largely controlled process, but at a price – the down-side of '*consenso*' was the increasing risk of public disaffection over the new democratic life, since the extent of elite-level compromise caused confusion. This disappeared, however, with the shock impact of the 1981 coup and the political excitement over the alternation in power in 1982. In Italy, the parties not only collectively dominated the constituent process but also operated as channels of mobilization, hence as integrative agents at the societal level. As a whole, therefore, the transitions in these countries were essentially elite-level processes, subject on occasions to mass-level intervention.

Transition outcomes

As to transition outcomes, there was an overall tendency to prefer parliamentary over presidential models of liberal democracy. That was clear from the start in Italy and Spain; while in Portugal, and to some extent Greece, semi-presidential elements existed temporarily until constitutional revisions in 1982 and 1985 respectively. Centre–periphery models varied between the centralism of Italy, Greece and Portugal and the quasi-federalism of Spain – Italy later adapted to regional devolution, but not until the 1970s. In this institutional sense, as Lijphart and others concluded, the new Mediterranean democracies were as varied as other systems in Western Europe (Lijphart *et al.* 1988).

TRANSITIONS IN EASTERN EUROPE: LESSONS FROM THE MEDITERRANEAN?

The greatest appeal of the Southern European models of democratic transition for Eastern Europeans is simply their successful outcome, for despite the uncertainties and upheavals of their transitions the four cases examined above have subsequently consolidated their new democracies.

It was the Spanish model of evolutionary system change that has received the greatest attention in some countries of Eastern Europe, because of the effective way in which it was managed and because it seemed to offer lessons about problems of continuity with the previous regime. During a visit to Madrid in April 1990, Dubcek – later a president of the Czechoslovak parliament – flattered his hosts by saying that Spain could, despite national differences, serve as a model 'because of the spirit of consensus in which the process of transition from totalitarianism to democracy took place' (*Espana 90*, June 1990: 2). Madrid became virtually the Mecca for transition actors from Eastern Europe, with a whole run of visits there from such other figures as Havel, Roman, Mazowiecki and Yeltsin to talk with Spanish political leaders. As one Spanish government adviser commented wryly: 'One of Spain's main exports these days is the know-how of its transition period' (*The Times*, 23.1.90). During the changes in the autumn of 1989, the Hungarian press gave much coverage to the earlier Spanish transition experience. To some extent, leaders from other Balkan countries similarly looked to Greece specifically with the link between democratization and EC entry in mind; but the Portuguese transition model found no real takers, although there were several parallels with Romania's experience after 1989 over the revolutionary start to the process and the persistent instability and problems of consensus-building that followed.

One may be rightly sceptical about this exercise in cross-national comparisons among political elites. Techniques and procedures, perhaps pitfalls and insights are rather more applicable than any idea of grafting national models on to embryonic democracies elsewhere, for ultimately national-specific features have to be accommodated. So, what general and particular lessons can be drawn from Southern European experience for the latest transitions in Eastern Europe?

The main, indeed simple, lesson from the Mediterranean warns that there is no such thing as a straightforward or easy transition to liberal democracy. In an essay on the change in Eastern Europe, Di Palma recalls that the Southern European transitions also occasioned pessimism in their early stages, and for similar reasons to do with the trauma and rapidity of change (Di Palma 1990: 231–2). All the four countries there faced some serious difficulties: the fragile state of the economy as well as problems of finding consensus in Portugal; the military and regional problems in Spain; and, in Greece, there was the question of redefining the country's international priorities and also problems of delayed modernization and national identity. Italy too faced severe problems because of economic instability at first and as the high degree of political polarization of the transition persisted well into consolidation. The last case was really the most difficult of the transitions because of extreme political divisions then and the tense international context with the advent of the Cold War. It is important to recall that even the Spanish transition, much lauded and somewhat idealized in Eastern Europe, had severe moments of crisis and uncertainty and occasioned periods of pessimism about its outcome.

This might serve to put regime change into some perspective for transition actors in Eastern Europe and quieten some of their fears. To a significant degree, it is a matter of riding, managing and simply coping with uncertainty (O'Donnell, Schmitter and Whitehead 1986, Pt IV). There is usually substantial scope for the skills of political leadership, notwithstanding the different constraints which operate. But we need to apply Southern European experience more specifically.

These lessons may be grouped as (1) environmental, (2) political-institutional and (3) dynamic:

1 Similarities deriving from a common regional environment have some bearing on transition. Countries which share the same broad regional context are going to face similar geopolitical concerns and possibly also comparable historical experience, where similarities of culture and social structure might come into play. As a general rule, historical legacies from both pre-authoritarian democracy and the authoritarian period – the former depending on the longevity of the latter – were a powerful influence on the politics of transition in the South. Furthermore, one clear lesson from looking at 'pre-transition' there is that any distinction between economic and political forms of

liberalization by authoritarian leaders proves untenable. The overall momentum of change does not ultimately allow that distinction to be maintained.

These points of comparison are of course enhanced when we are talking about transitions occurring not merely in the same region but also simultaneously. Some cross-fertilization between simultaneous transitions may occur, although this has happened much more in Eastern than in Southern Europe (where the start of the three transitions was more spaced out). At the same time, significant variation in the types of transition is evident, not merely between Italy and the other three because of the different time context, but also between the concurrent Iberian and Greek cases. It is also evident in the simultaneous cases of transition in Eastern Europe. Taking Stepan's paths to democratization, there are examples of or attempts at initiation from within the authoritarian regime (Bulgaria, Romania, perhaps Albania; and a failed attempt in Hungary) and examples of society-led regime termination, as in Poland, Czechoslovakia and also East Germany.

2 On political–institutional lessons, Lijphart has already drawn several lessons from Southern European experience, for democratization in Latin America (Lijphart 1990). He includes the following: that it is important to accommodate societal divisions through consensus-oriented democratic arrangements; that proportionality in elections and parliamentary rather than presidential government are therefore to be recommended; and, similarly, federalism is appropriate where necessary; and, in general, constitutional protection and rigidity are preferable for new democracies. His objections to presidentialism, for instance, are that it runs risks in a new and fragile democracy through the concentration of executive power in one person, that it is inimical to collective decision-taking and that the principle of separation and balance of presidential and legislative powers is difficult to achieve in practice (Lijphart 1990: 76).

While Lijphart's lessons are also broadly valid for Eastern Europe, they suffer somewhat from institutional preconceptions and, to state the obvious, they ignore national differences within Southern Europe. For instance, semi-presidential as distinct from presidential structures might be recommendable at least as a transitional option. In Greece, this allowed Karamanlis to act for a while as a stabilizing influence which bridged political polarization and cushioned the first change of power in the new democracy. In Portugal, Eanes, albeit far from charismatic, acted similarly as an institutional reference point at a time of troubled transition and unstable coalitions. He also expressed and perhaps satisfied the military's uncontroversial co-role in government at this time. Again, consensus procedures, while perhaps preferable, are not to be treated as gospel for transition actors. Some degree of party battle is ultimately conducive to healthy democratic politics; and at some stage of a transition inevitable tensions arise between systemically induced consensual pressures and the normal resumption of party life. At a deeper level, it might also be a safety valve for purging historically conditioned resentments which may need to be resolved before new democracies are securely on track.

3 Lijphart thus failed to identify lessons other than institutional ones; and here we turn to what may be called dynamic factors in transition. For instance, the international context is usually the source of significant impacts and influences during domestic system change, whether in the form of external transition events or the policies of foreign governments or the activities of international organizations. Reaction to the recent dictatorial past might well impact on transition politics, but that also depends on what type of system has preceded (whether more totalitarian or simply authoritarian) and what kind of excesses have occurred. Finally, the style and scope of transition is relevant here in that this determines the degree of uncertainty in the process and probably influences the chances of success and certainly the pace and speed of transition.

These three groups of lessons all highlight familiar problems when looking at the more recent transitions in Eastern Europe. At the same time, some important differences emerge, in particular with respect to dynamic factors under (3). Clearly, environmental influences were at work in Eastern Europe where there was much more cross-fertilization between the simultaneous cases, for there were many more transitions occurring at shorter intervals than in Southern Europe. Also, the international context has been more salient by virtue of the crucial role played by Gorbachev's Moscow in these events, against a background of Soviet control or influence over their political and economic systems. Moreover, in Eastern Europe we are talking about more extensive change with economic as well as political systems being transformed, and generally of a faster pace of socio-economic modernization and hence greater stresses and strains. There is a real danger of economic reform and its devastating consequences in Eastern Europe threatening the political process of democratization. We can spell out these similarities and differences more exactly by applying briefly the same framework of state and society to the Eastern European transitions.

The historical dimension has clearly so far played a salient part in their regime change. In fact, the historical past has come to weigh fairly heavily on the current transitions as reflected in a 'rebirth of history' school of interpretation (e.g. Glenny 1990; Roskin 1991; Rothschild 1990). This has been evident in the question of political traditions as a factor relating to the prospects for (re-)establishing liberal democracy (Batt 1991: 44ff.). Usually, this has taken the form of references to interwar legacies and the brevity of parliamentary government then. However, the 'return' of parliamentary and democratic institutions has contrasted somewhat with the general lack of success of 'historical' parties. There are other forms of tradition which may be negative or positive in their consequences for transition, such as the debate in Poland over the 'authoritarian temptation' with reference to the new constitution and Walesa's ambitions as president. Balancing this problem is the argument for a strong presidency as a transitional focus for decision-making in the case of fragmented party systems and unstable coalition governments. Then, we need only recall the re-emergence of traditional forms of ethnic and regional nationalism to identify a potent impact of history on transition politics.

Nevertheless, much also depends on how transition actors manage or exploit issues from the past. On the one hand, the momentum of transition and prospects for a new departure encourage hopes for a break with tradition. The rapidity of the successive collapses of communist regimes in Eastern Europe in the autumn of 1989 underlined more dramatically than in Southern Europe how contagious liberal democracy can be, reinforced as this was by the opening up of Eastern Europe to Western influences and especially by the role of the mass media. It showed only too well that liberalization did not ultimately work, although this took longer to realize in some countries than in others. In Hungary, the process of economic liberalization that occurred long before democratization – and was promoted if somewhat ambivalently by Kadarism – allowed eventually for some limited form of associational activity, which later on provided the basis for democratic opposition groups (Sword 1990: ch. 5; Batt 1990).

Soon, however, the problem of political legacies surfaced by way of 'overcoming the past', to borrow a phrase from post-war Germany – and one repeated in the Federal Republic after unification. The question of political revenge for communist rule and of the purge syndrome, which was handled generally with moderation in Southern Europe, has been much more virulent in Eastern Europe, e.g. the Stasi links of former East German elites; the division between the Walesa and Mazowiecki strategies over rooting out communist personnel; and, the 'lustration' law in the Czechoslovak Republic (White 1991). It also explains the failed hopes of 'reform communists' in these countries and the uncomfortable public perceptions of 'unfinished business' and calls for a 'second revolution' in Romania under Iliescu. The issue of the past and of solutions for solving it is a painful but necessary one to confront, and it has a particular significance for the formation of political attitudes in these new democracies.

The relationship between regime and state is a notably difficult one in Eastern Europe because of four decades of communist rule, or of longer periods of nondemocratic rule in some cases if we include the interwar autocracies and Nazi occupation. Whether communist systems can be characterized as totalitarian or authoritarian, they nevertheless achieved greater interpenetration between party and the state structures than the Mediterranean dictatorships save perhaps fascist Italy. This can produce difficulties for establishing the authority of the state in the new democracies, as the somewhat poignant matter of the past role of secret services has shown. A severe problem is obviously presented by regional and ethnic nationalism, as this represents a thorny centre-periphery cleavage which may or may not be reasonably solved through variations on the federal model. Clearly, this has failed in Yugoslavia, and serious strains have been evident in the Czechoslovak Republic leading to its replacement by two separate states. The milder experience of Spain and the Basque problem suggests how much this kind of problem can complicate the transition process. And it is unlikely that the new constitutions of Eastern Europe, several of them still being formulated, will completely resolve this matter.

As to inter-group relations, indications are still unclear since we do not yet know whether some constituent processes will eventually turn out to be consensual or not, i.e. between different political tendencies. The practice of operating 'round tables' in the first phase of some of these transitions was a sign of consensus (Batt 1991: 28–30; Sanford 1992); but it is no guarantee of the same being adopted in constitution-building. One related question is the evolution of party systems, for the principal umbrella movements have been transmuted into parties and in general there has been a profusion and instability of parties and political groups (Batt 1991: 54–5; Szajkowski 1991). That is, however, a normal feature of this early phase of democratic transition as Southern European experience also demonstrated (Pridham 1991b).

Relations between political and non-political elites are less easy to identify because of the lack of evidence, but there are some signs. Obviously, given Southern European experience, the role of the military is of particular concern. But so far developments in Eastern

Europe have been largely different. The twin dependence of armies on the national Communist Party and on the Soviet military link under communism appears to have undercut their role with regime change. It has only been in Romania that the army played a part in the early events of transition; while, clearly, in Yugoslavia the resort to force has obviously placed the military in the centre of developments. On the other hand, economic elites are likely to be more salient than in Southern Europe as a consequence of economic system change; and it does not follow they will automatically become subordinate to political parties.

The society level has indeed been very important, although it is difficult here to do justice to the complexities of each national case of transition. We are talking about the role of the Church in Poland and East Germany, for instance, as well as intellectual and cultural groups and varieties of dissidents, particularly in the first stage of transition. The degree to which they were overall important suggests a much greater element of 'bottom–up' momentum in the Eastern European transitions than in Southern Europe, although there is significant cross-national variation. For a time Hungary represented a more 'top–down' process, while Czechoslovakia featured a significant 'bottom–up' pressure and Poland demonstrated elements of both. Disputes about whether Romania experienced a revolution or a plot similarly reflect on this dichotomy. But one should not over-utilize such a dichotomy, given the importance of external developments and in particular the withdrawal of Soviet support for the communist regimes.

As to transition outcomes, this is much too soon to say. Some transitions will take longer than others, as happened in Southern Europe. Institution-building is still in progress, although there is a fairly distinct tendency towards (semi-)presidential models, excepting Hungary; and, centralism tends to predominate over federalism. But, in general, we are still observing new and hence fragile democracies which have a long way to go and many obstacles to surmount before transition and certainly consolidation is accomplished.

As a whole, therefore, there are some similarities between the transitions to liberal democracy in Eastern and Southern Europe; but there are also some crucial differences, both as to the scale of transition as well as to the time context in which it has occurred. In this sense, our comparative approach helps to counterbalance the short-term assessments that have often prevailed in interpreting recent change in Eastern Europe. At the same time, this historic shift to democratization tends to favour the genetic theories of regime transition as demonstrated by the dynamics of the process and the way in which the past interacts with the present. This is not to the exclusion of economic factors in such change, for clearly they are extremely important (significantly more so than in the Southern European transitions), but they cannot be treated in a deterministic manner as usually suggested by functionalist theories.

BIBLIOGRAPHY

Abel, C., and Torrents, N. (eds) (1984) *Spain: conditional democracy*, London: Croom Helm.

Batt, J. (1990) 'Political reform in Hungary', *Parliamentary Affairs* 43: 464–81.
—— (1991) *East-Central Europe from Reform to Transformation*, Royal Institute of International Affairs, Chatham House Paper, London: Pinter.

Boyd , C., and Boyden, J. (1985) 'The armed forces and the transition to democracy in Spain', in T. Lancaster and G. Prevost (eds) *Politics and Change in Spain*, New York: Praeger.

Bruneau, T. (1984) *Politics and Nationhood: post-revolutionary Portugal*, New York: Praeger.

Di Palma, G. (1982) 'Italy: is there a legacy and is it Fascist?', in J. Herz (ed.) *From Dictatorship to Democracy*, Westport: Greenwood Press.
—— (1990) 'Le transizioni democratiche in Europa orientale: una prospettiva comparata', *Rivista Italiana di Scienza Politica* 20: 203–42.

Espana 90 (1990) Bulletin of the information service of the Spanish Foreign Ministry.

Featherstone, K., and Katsoudas, D. (1987) *Political Change in Greece*, London: Croom Helm.

Fishman, R. (1990) 'Rethinking state and regime: Southern Europe's transition to democracy', *World Politics* April: 422–40.

Gladdish, K. (1990) 'Portugal: an open verdict', in G. Pridham (ed.) *Securing Democracy: political parties and regime consolidation in Southern Europe*, London: Routledge.

Glenny, G. (1990) *The Rebirth of History: Eastern Europe in the age of democracy*, London: Penguin Books.

Herz, J. (ed.) (1982) *From Dictatorship to Democracy*, Westport: Greenwood Press.

Lijphart, A. (1990) 'The Southern European examples of democratisation: six lessons for Latin America', *Government and Opposition* 25: 68–84.
—— Bruneau, T., Diamandouros, N., and Gunther, R. (1988) 'A Mediterranean model of democracy? The Southern European democracies in comparative perspective', *West European Politics* 11: 7–25.

Linz, J. J. (1990) 'Transitions to Democracy', *Washington Quarterly*, Summer.

Malefakis, E. (1982) 'Spain and its Francoist heritage', in J. Herz (ed.) *From Dictatorship to Democracy*, Westport: Greenwood Press.

Maravall, J. (1982) *The Transition to Democracy in Spain*, London: Croom Helm.

Maxwell, K. (1982) 'The emergence of Portuguese democracy', in J. Herz (ed.) *From Dictatorship to Democracy*, Westport: Greenwood Press.

Morlino, L. (1987) 'Democratic establishments: a dimensional analysis', in E. Baloyra (ed.) *Comparing New Democracies*, Boulder: Westview.

O'Donnell, G., Schmitter, P., and Whitehead, L. (eds) (1986) *Transitions from*

Authoritarian Rule: prospects for democracy, Baltimore: Johns Hopkins University Press.

Opello, W. (1985) *Portugal's Political Development*, Boulder: Westview.

Pasquino, G. (1986) 'The demise of the first Fascist regime and Italy's transition to democracy', in G. O'Donnell, P. Schmitter, and L. Whitehead (eds) *Transitions from Authoritarian Rule: prospects for democracy*, Baltimore: Johns Hopkins University Press.

Pridham, G. (ed.) (1984) *The New Mediterranean Democracies: regime transition in Spain, Greece and Portugal*, London: Frank Cass.

—— (ed.) (1990) *Securing Democracy: political parties and regime consolidation in Southern Europe*, London: Routledge.

—— (ed.) (1991a) *Encouraging Democracy: the international context of regime transition in Southern Europe*, Leicester: Leicester University Press.

—— (1991b) 'Political parties and elections in the new Eastern European democracies: comparisons with Southern European experience', in Hellenic Foundation for Defence and Foreign Policy, *Yearbook 1990*, Athens: Eliamep.

Roskin, M. (1991) *The Rebirth of East Europe*, Hemel Hempstead: Prentice Hall.

Rothschild , J. (1990) *Return to Diversity: political history of East-Central Europe since World War Two*, Oxford: Oxford University Press.

Sanford, G. (1992) *Democratisation in Poland, 1988–90*, Houndsmills: Macmillan

Stepan, A. (1986) 'Paths toward redemocratisation', in G. O'Donnell, P. Schmitter, and L. Whitehead (eds) *Transitions from Authoritarian Rule: prospects for democracy*, Baltimore: Johns Hopkins University Press.

Sword, K. (1990) *The Times Guide to Eastern Europe*, London: Times Books.

Szajkowski, B. (ed.) (1991) *New Political Parties of Eastern Europe and the Soviet Union*, Harlow: Longman.

Vanhanen, T. (1990) *The Process of Democratisation*, New York: Crane Russak.

White, S. (ed.) (1991) *Handbook of Reconstruction in Eastern Europe and the Soviet Union*, Harlow: Longman.

2 Groups, parties and political change in Eastern Europe from 1977

Michael Waller

Descriptive accounts of the fall of the communist power monopoly in the East European countries are now becoming legion. In this chapter the main lines of that story will be taken as given. Its aim is rather to suggest a framework for analysis that might enable the process of change in Eastern Europe to be put into perspective. It will be argued that, whilst the revolutionary events of 1989 did indeed represent a rupture of epochal significance, they were the culmination, in many cases, of a long series of political developments which were to influence both the process of system change, and the initial political forms that emerged from it.

This kind of process is particularly susceptible to a general analysis in terms of group formation because of its very fluidity. An understandable preoccupation with simply the formation of political parties alone robs the Eastern European experience in particular of much of its analytical interest. True, political parties are taking shape, and their development offers the comparativist a rich seam of exploration. But this is part of a broader process of political aggregation, which has been untidy, remarkably varied, and faces a future that remains opaque.

The countries covered in this essay are those that were part of the Soviet bloc in Europe: Poland, Czechoslovakia (now the Czech Republic and Slovakia), the GDR, Hungary, Bulgaria and Romania; whilst occasional references will be made to Yugoslavia and to the Soviet Union itself. Although it is often useful to distinguish between an East-Central Europe and the Balkans, the main arguments of this essay allow a collective reference to Eastern Europe.

Finally, and still in introduction, the emphasis in this chapter will be placed on the period immediately before the major turning-point of 1989. This was a time when a particularly interesting process of political aggregation was taking place, and it was a process that was to have a profound effect on the politics of the post-revolutionary period.

Some account of those later developments is offered here, but for a fuller treatment the reader must turn to other chapters in this volume.

A FRAMEWORK FOR ANALYSIS

Factors influencing change

Current change in Eastern Europe requires an analysis in terms of three sets of factors. The first set is *historical*. The various cultural, political and economic divides imposed by European history have left differing traces, and in each country of the region the past exercises a significant influence on the present. Any analysis of recent change must deal with layers of history, to some extent shared, and to some extent individually experienced. The factors that link Bulgaria with Romania and Serbia, and those linking Poland with Hungary have their roots in past centuries, as do the factors that differentiated Slovenia and Croatia from the other republics in the Yugoslav federation. The 'isobars' of culture, empire, levels of economic development that traverse the region are not of recent date.

The most recent and universally shared historical layer is the forty and more years of communist rule. Since the actors in today's drama are a product of that period, it must be seen as distinct in its workings from the previous history of these nations. Imposed on all of them except Albania and Yugoslavia in the aftermath of the Second World War, communist rule is often perceived as a 'glacier' that froze that history (for example, Rupnik 1990). Events since 1989 have made it clear that the simple fall of the communist power monopoly did not undo all the work of those forty and more years. Indeed, in the view of a substantial body of thought deriving from within those countries, the state socialism of the communist years had been consolidated into a distinctive societal form (Konrád and Szelenyi 1979). The period of communist rule in fact provides a second and distinct set of factors shaping the process of change in Eastern Europe, which can be termed *systemic*. They are systemic in that they stem from the very way in which the political system worked in those years.

The communist political system was not only authoritarian, but it characteristically atomized society, breaking up autonomous concentrations of power in the middle reaches of the political system, and making the organized articulation of interests impossible to sustain. Formed originally as a means whereby an authoritative party could mobilize undifferentiated masses, democratic centralism remained jealous of its prerogatives. The fount of all power, the party used its monopoly of the written and spoken word to brand the dissenter as both antisocial and irrational (Stojanovic 1981: 100–6; Waller 1981: 61–80). We shall shortly see that there was room in the system for a group process of politics, but it was one that was constrained, indeed shaped, by a system in which autonomous organization for political ends was not a part of daily political life.

It is important to be clear what to attribute to historical and what to systemic factors. All countries of the region experienced apparatus politics on much the same model (including Yugoslavia and Albania where the Communist Party came autonomously to power). All have found that the political and economic influence of the *nomenklatura* of the communist days has lasted long into the period since the fall of the communist parties themselves. Yet the way in which communism arrived in the various countries varied; once installed it created local dilemmas and pressures (in the crises of 1956, 1968 and 1980/81 the pre-communist history of each of the countries involved spoke quite clearly); and the ways in which communism fell from its monopoly of power differed quite markedly, also partly for historical reasons.

A third set of factors is *conjunctural*. If history and the effects of communist rule speak for continuity, it was conjunctural factors that provided the impulse for change, and have continued to influence the direction of change, in the direction of both stability and instability. To be included in such factors are the shift in the Soviet Union's diplomatic stance following from its need to integrate itself in the world economy, which led to its disengagement from Eastern Europe and the withdrawal of its support for the regimes of the region. Further conjunctural factors concern the west of Europe: the attraction of the European Community, which has had such an effect on the political evolution of Spain, Portugal and Greece; the prospect of loans and support – or, in the case of the southern tier, the lack of it. The rift that history created between the ex-Ottoman Balkan states and a Christian world to the north is being deepened by differential prospects in relation to the European Community. Further conjunctural factors concern the economic difficulties in which all countries of the region find themselves. The length of time during which the euphoria of freedom from Soviet influence and communist rule will offset the effects of this relative penury will be one of the most important conjunctural factors in the future evolution of Eastern Europe.

These three sets of factors – historical, systemic and conjunctural – set the parameters within which change has been taking place in Eastern Europe. It is their interaction that has given the process of change its at times surprising or paradoxical character. Conjunctural factors ushered in the prospect of change, but it is a change whose forward ideas are tinged with nostalgia. The past crowds physically onto the stage of the present in the form, for example, of the day-before-yesterday's political parties or, less nostalgically, of yesterday's *apparatchiks* turned businessmen.

Lest this sounds fanciful, consider an important example – the formation of political parties in the prelude to and after the first post-communist elections. Historical factors produced not only the return of a series of pre-communist parties but also a second series of parties deriving from the final years or months of communism. The systemic factors revealed themselves in various ways: first, in the fact that the latter parties were shaped by their experience as movements of dissent, mirror images of the unitary communist party that they had formed to contest; secondly, in the inability of leaderships to link up with clear constituencies, which must be read at least partly as an effect of the refusal of communism to allow interests to take organizational form or even to achieve a clear articulation.

The workings of the conjunctural factors are at times easy enough to discern, but less so at others. To what extent, for example, was the democratic choice, in the form of a competitive party system, historically determined, in the sense that it constituted a reversion to a pre-communist past, and to what extent has it been a conjunctural matter, a strategic contemporary decision, conscious or otherwise, in a Europe where a democracy dividend is clearly on offer?

The theoretical literature on transitions to democracy from authoritarian rule contains a distinction between genetic and functional factors which corresponds in part to the distinctions that are being made here (Pridham 1990); and it could be argued that to posit a set of systemic factors is simply to subdivide the historical factors into those pertaining to the communist and pre-communist periods. Quite so; it is a distinction between the living and the dead, between myth and experience. At the same time, it would not be surprising if transitions from communism exhibited certain characteristics that mark them off from other examples of transition from authoritarian rule.

Towards a group analysis of change in Eastern Europe

Textbooks on democracy, and on the individual political systems that exhibit it, view political parties and pressure groups as the essential channels of representation and of popular participation. Moreover, they are presented as more or less fixed constellations. The structure of democracy is to be understood through these abiding elements. The political parties of Western Europe have indeed in many cases had a remarkable longevity, and the party systems themselves have been portrayed in one celebrated analysis as having been 'frozen' over a considerable period (Lipset and Rokkan 1967).

Pressure groups tend also to be seen as abiding – and rightly so, since the more powerful of them have seen both continuity and organization entrenchment. It is a commonplace in the political science literature on pressure groups that the permanence and invisible operation of the more mighty powerholders of Finer's (1967) 'anonymous empire' are to be contrasted with the weakness of noisier and more ephemeral movements and 'cause' groups. At the centre of liberal democracy is abiding organization: less organized movements lie in the antechamber to liberal democracy, destined to anguish over the implications of consolidation and organizational integration, or frustrated by an inability to achieve it. The parties and the major pressure groups that we are presented with have thus been around for some time; and they constitute the universe that we must analyse, and we naturally analyse it in terms of them and their place within it.

The point of this disquisition is simply to point out that the analyst of liberal democracy is rarely faced with dynamic circumstances of flux, in which even the attribution of labels such as 'party' or 'pressure group' must, at least temporarily, occasion reflection and doubt. Yet such circumstances exist at the time of writing in Eastern Europe. True, each election brings a little more order, in the sense that, at the level of parliaments and governments, a process of differentiation is producing political parties that play the role that we are accustomed to see parties playing in established liberal democracies. Yet against such palpable facts of life a post-authoritarian resistance to the very notion of party is to be encountered in certain countries, which expresses itself, for example, in low turn-out at elections.

Perhaps most remarkable has been the almost total mismatch compared with Western Europe between the development (or lack of it) of a social-democratic presence in the parliaments on the one hand, and the evolution of the trade unions on the other. In this mismatch, the continuing strength of the reformed communist parties is a key factor. Understandably, there is a strong resistance, inside the countries of the region and outside, to consider these parties as comparable with other parties of the emerging party systems. Is this simply a matter of perceptions, which the process of institutionalization of the new order will cause to wither away? On the other side of the equation, the political role that the trade unions will play, and their relations with government and political parties, are still quite unclear.

For the moment we are presumably justified in believing that the familiar categories of Western political systems will be reproduced in the new Eastern Europe. But the point of analytical interest is the way in which this process is taking place, the nature of the influences that are shaping it, and the extent to which it will not in fact reproduce familiar patterns and will therefore force adjustments in the discussion of parties, groups and interests in the political process.

In any analysis of the evolution of group formation in Eastern Europe, the historical, systemic and conjunctural factors outlined above are of central importance, and must be used to illuminate the way in which the communist system, fundamentally inimical to group autonomy, is being slowly transformed so as to accommodate both competitive party politics and a conventionally accepted arena for the articulation of group interests.

First, it is important to dwell longer on one particular and crucial feature of the communist power monopoly. It was mentioned above that the autonomous articulation of interests was ruled out by that monopoly, but the way in which this was actually done calls for reflection. The central mechanism of the party's monopolistic control was its apparatus – the officials who staffed the various departments of the party's bureaucracy. These officials are often referred to collectively as the *nomenklatura*. But in order to understand the lingering effect that the communist past is having on the reshaping of Eastern European politics it is necessary to be a little more precise, firstly, about who exactly comprised the *nomenklatura* and, secondly, how the apparatus went about its business of control.

The term '*nomenklatura*' is commonly used in three senses. It has connoted, first, the list of strategic posts that the secretariat at a given level within the party's apparatus was competent to fill. But it came to connote also the people who held these posts. In a sense these office-holders constituted the elite of each communist political system, but in fact, since at the lowest level the list included collective farm chairmen and headmasters and headmistresses, it is a very diluted sense of elite that is involved (Macshane 1981: 163–9).

On the other hand, in a third (strictly speaking erroneous) connotation the term does indeed refer to the heart of the elite – those members of the party apparatus itself who were its inner core (Voslensky 1980). These were the leading members of the departments of the party's committees at national and regional level. By the very nature of their function they were skilled in the use of power and position, they were at the centre of networks of political and – so it was to transpire –

financial influence, and they were part of a web of patronage which they could either exercise or benefit from, or both.

As for the way in which the party exercised its monopolistic control, one feature in particular was to have a massive impact on the process of group formation, not only during the communist years but also during the transition period that was to follow. The party did not outlaw political organization as such; it actively encouraged it, but channelled it in a characteristic way through the 'mass organizations'. Thus trade unions, women's federations and youth leagues flourished, but under the party's direct control. The mechanisms involved here were, again, the power of appointment to (and dismissal from) responsible positions in these strategic organizations and control over the means of communication. The trade unions, for example, were in this way politically emasculated, but they were given a real social function – in fact, they became the prime channel for the distribution of welfare benefits and ran palaces and houses of culture, pioneer camps for children and rest holiday centres and sanatoria for all employed people.

In such circumstances, what room was there for a group process of politics? The literature on the politics of communism carries a number of answers to this question. Two of the most celebrated concern the Soviet Union itself. The first is the view associated with Jerry Hough's term 'institutional pluralism' (Hough 1983, which includes a modification of his original view). Whilst there were many who were sceptical about claiming that the Soviet Union was in any sense pluralist, the view that at the heart of the system 'whirlpools' of interest formed, bringing officials in various bureaucracies of party and state to make common cause in defence of a given policy, found considerable favour, and was built on by Archie Brown and others who were able to discern schools of thought and policy alliances forming within the party's administrative and research departments, the institutes of the Academy of Sciences, and the governmental bureaucracies (Brown 1983). But such group influences operated only within the heart of a centralized and secretive system; they were far from constituting signs of a general associative life at the level of society as a whole.

A rather different case is the view put forward in 1984 by Teresa Rakowska-Harmstone that the federal structure of the Soviet Union, simply by providing the 15 republics of the Union with constitutions and governmental institutions, was enabling those republics to resist, at least to some extent, the assimilating pressures of Moscow (whereas those entities with less than full republican status were to be seen as well on the way to full assimilation). This case is not, of course, the stuff of group politics that theorists of democracy present. It is worth noting here, however, partly because of the corroboration that events gave to Rakowska-Harmstone's view, but also since no account of the process of group formation during the transition from communist rule can ignore the national factor. We return to this problem below.

Finally, this time in Eastern Europe itself, and particularly in the Polish case, communist power was never able to destroy nor even eclipse the associative power of religion.

These various aspects of the political practices characteristic of communism have been selected and presented here because they were to have a particular relevance to the process of group formation in the recent transition period in Eastern Europe. They help to explain the fact that the unseating of the communist party from its governmental position did not necessarily spell the end of the power of the *nomenklatura*, in group or individual terms. Similarly, they explain why – until the shift in property relations has proceeded further than its present very limited extent, and has substantially reshaped the structure of interests in this area – the same *nomenklatura* can be expected to fulfil a function not all that distant from its function in the past. Thirdly, they also explain why political parties and trade unions have taken so long to come into a stable relationship. And, fourthly, they explain how it comes about that once an area is opened up for autonomous group activity the initial result is a broad clustering around interests that are so generally shared as not to count, in common parlance, as interests at all, such as nation and Church, rather than a narrow clustering around more restricted issues and interests.

A periodization

In order to make the process of change intelligible a periodization is proposed which is a simple division into three periods of unequal length, as follows:

1 From 1977 (notably the creation of Charter 77 in Czechoslovakia) to the concession of the communist power monopoly. This will be termed the 'heroic period'. It is on this period that the present study concentrates.
2 The often very short period between that concession and the holding of the first post-communist election.
3 The period since that first election.

The cut-off dates of this periodization vary between countries and are in some cases blurred. For example, the formal concession of the party's monopoly was not as clear-cut in Bulgaria as it was elsewhere, the heroic period was collapsed in that country into months rather than years, and it is difficult to know which Polish election to consider the first post-communist one. But this raggedness is important. It reflects two facts in particular. Firstly, the party's loss of its monopoly was a far more gradual process than the choice of a single formal moment might suggest. Secondly, this in turn conceals a process whereby the fatal weakening of the party's monopoly caused by the withdrawal of Soviet support was matched by growing pressures from within their own societies. Those pressures involved the mobilization of the party's enemies, often in somewhat inchoate form. But in the circumstances there was great political significance even in inchoate mobilization. Indeed, we are dealing with embryos here, and the task is to determine what were the genes determining the future shape of the organizational patterns that would grow from these embryos.

The factors that make each of these periods distinct are as follows. The first period, during which the party's monopoly was in principle still operative, and was so considered by the world outside Eastern Europe, saw a remarkable development of autonomous political activity in Poland, Czechoslovakia, the GDR, Hungary, and late in the day in Bulgaria. It was strictly illicit; however, it not only persisted but also provided the foundations for the political processes that the world was later to witness, just as it provided four of the first post-communist presidents (Zhelev, Havel, Walesa, Göncz). That is to say, the situation of flux that attended the change of regime got under way in most of the region some ten years before Gorbachev came to power in the USSR. The aggregation of political preferences that was taking place during those years varied in its forms, but it had one crucial characteristic: the universally shared aim of removing the communists from power. This is, of course, to simplify, and we shall return below to details that qualify this generalization.

The second period was in a sense a transition within the transition. It saw the fall of the ruling parties from their monopoly position and the transfer of their power to the forces confronting them. It involved a process of negotiation which had strikingly similar features in all the countries considered here, except Romania. It was also marked by the all-important passing of legislation to guarantee rights of association and of the press, without which no process of competitive politics could take place, by the putting in place of an electoral system, and by the holding of a free election.

The general character of the third period is of a hesitant process of party formation, and at times consolidation, in a parliamentary context. It brought differentiation within the broad aggregating bodies of the first phase, in a process that has reflected a rivalry, often confused, between elites far more than the articulation of any grass-roots demands.

GROUPS IN THE PROCESS OF CHANGE IN EASTERN EUROPE

The following analysis of the formation of groups in the revolutionary period in Eastern Europe from around 1977 seeks to identify the centres around which political action rallied during those years, both within the system of rule and outside it. It is not so much a classification of groups, as an attempt to illustrate the processes of aggregation and of mobilization that gave the period its character. It is important to make this clear, since the most prominent aggregators of political preferences during these years – the 'forum' movements – were heterogeneous in terms of their social base, the nature and origin of their leadership, and the issues that they espoused, even if they all had a single underlying aim of challenging the ruling party's monopoly of power. To present them as the centrepiece of a process of group formation thus cuts across treatments of dissent of an earlier day, which tended to classify dissenting groups according to social base and issues espoused (Tökés 1979; Connor 1980).

The account given here will first plot change within the system through an examination of group formation. It will then seek to identify the issues and agencies that were most effective in articulating political preferences and in attracting support and allegiance outside the formal system.

The heroic period

It has been a characteristic of communist politics that the inflexibility of the system prevented the need for change from becoming manifest. When change did finally occur, it tended to be cataclysmic. It was, in familiar terms, a politics of lurches (Rusinow 1977: 139; MacEwen 1976: 37). It was therefore not at all surprising that the monopoly's final demise in Eastern Europe should have presented itself as a rupture. In fact, however, a great deal had been going on behind the party's opaque shield, not only in the development of dissenting movements but within the formal structures of government themselves. No account of the exit from communism in the region is complete unless both are taken into account.

Prominent within the system itself was the development of rival policy strands within the apparatus of rule in relation to the process of reform. In its crudest form, this was a matter of factional divisions within the party leaderships, and as such quite unexceptional. But two of its features are worth noting. The first is the emergence of a 'reform communism' in the Polish and Hungarian parties, itself carrying a strong echo of divisions within the Czechoslovak party during the Prague Spring of 1968. The pressures of the Solidarity period gave this strand within the Polish United Workers' Party a particular impetus. It was, in fact, Wojciech Jaruzelski himself, the party's leader, who acted as the chief proponent of a qualified change which would allow the party to preserve a dominant role in society in one form or another whilst making a minimum of concessions to social pressures which could no longer be totally suppressed, except at a now unacceptable cost. In the Hungarian case, a reformist tendency had long been visible during the Kádár years. This was to assert itself strongly, with Imre Pozsgay as its leading spokesman, in the *perestroika* period, in a process which was to lead to the change of the party's name from Hungarian Socialist Workers' Party to simply the Hungarian Socialist Party in October 1989 (Lomax 1991: 165–70).

But a rather more subtle and differentiated process of group formation was going on within the system, both in Eastern Europe and in the Soviet Union. It was a development of the bureaucratic politics referred to above as an example of the limited group autonomy that communist rule accommodated, and it concerned schools of thought involving, in a varying mix, members of research institutes, administrative personnel, and at times the departments of the party's central committee.

If the political conditions for the emergence of a public opinion had to wait until 1989 to appear in Eastern Europe, *expert* opinion was not subject to the same constraints, and had in fact been increasing its purchase in political life from the 1950s. As the pressures for change gathered steam, these collective voices from within the research and academic community became increasingly audible, and they gained in political significance precisely from the lack of an open system.

In the absence of public debate and of a political class extending beyond the party's *nomenklatura*, a collective expert voice, whether stemming from a single institution or not, carried a particular public responsibility. In a celebrated case, a group of engineers and adminis-trative officials in Slovakia opposed the project for a dam on the Danube at Gabcikovo on the grounds that it would lead to the contamination of the underground lake of pure water in the Bratislava area, whilst in Königswalde a group of scientists combined to contest the official view in the GDR at the time that economic growth should take precedence over protection of the environment (Slansky 1988;

Mallinkrodt 1984: 19). These are cases of group action amongst scientists and administrators, but many more cases could be cited where individual scientists have lent their support to more public group action.

A further and rather more surprising organizational base within the system turned out to be available for the autonomous expression of political preferences. This was the mass organizations. As long as the Stalinist political system held good, the mass organizations, that hallmark of the traditional system, could be relied on to transmit the party's policies to the grass-roots of society. But during and after the INF missile crisis of the early 1980s, the 'transmission belts' of the Stalinist system began, in two cases, to develop an independence. These two cases were the party's youth organizations, and the hitherto extremely official peace councils.

The fact that it was these two particular cases that were affected is significant. Firstly, youth was at the forefront of pressures for change in Eastern Europe; and secondly, the INF missile crisis, coupled with the CPSU's search for influence among left-wing parties and movements in Western Europe, placed the peace councils in a particularly strategic, if ambivalent, position. This is well illustrated by the case of the Hungarian Peace Council which, under its president Barabas, not only attended the conventions of European Nuclear Disarmament, but at one point had its representatives elected to the END council (Thompson 1987: 11). True, it was the fully autonomous organization FIDESZ that was to emerge in Hungary in the later phase as the party of youth, but the role of the official Hungarian party youth movement KISZ and of the Hungarian Peace Council in the earlier phase are a notable example of the extent to which dynamic political activity was being aggregated through organizations traditionally sponsored by the party. Further examples could be offered: the environmental action at Krivoklát by the Czechoslovak party's youth organization in 1988 (Waller 1989: 324) and the contestatory actions of the Slovenian League of communists' youth organization, whose paper *Mladina* became in the 1980s the mouthpiece of a sustained campaign against militarization of Yugoslav society and in favour of environmental protection (*END Newsletter* 1988: No. 9).

If these developments within two of the mass organizations are to be cited as cases of movement and change within the structures of the system, an important case of retrenchment has to be recorded – that of the trade unions. The official trade unions for the most part remained silent during the years of greatest change, and where they did not, as in the case of the Polish OPZZ, it was to support the traditional authority structures. With the single massive exception of Solidarity, only very late in the revolutionary process did trade unions play a significant mobilizing role.

In the non-systemic area emerging patterns of autonomous political aggregation are, as might be expected, much more difficult to categorize. One striking feature of the period, however, was shared by the GDR, Poland, Czechoslovakia; and it was to appear in Bulgaria also at the end of 1989: the emergence of a movement that acted as a spearhead, within the limits possible during those years, for all those movements that contested the Communist Party's monopoly of power. Certain central features of these 'forum' organizations, which were to go to form the basis for the political parties of the period from 1989, were noted above.

It is important to record the very wide diversity of these movements in terms of the circumstances of the birth and of the nature of their leaderships. The first to appear – Charter 77 in Czechoslovakia – began very soon to take on an aggregating role. In the words of one of its founders, Václav Havel, it 'broadened the scope for diverse other dependent activities and initiatives' (Skilling 1985: 38). That this role was acknowledged also by the ruling party was revealed in an internal report which, commenting on the rapid growth of 'illegal groups' during this period, said that 'a sort of free union has been set up between these illegal groups, bound to each other by the most active leaders, who are based on Charter 77' (*La Nouvelle Alternative*, June 1989).

In the case of the GDR, it was the Evangelical churches that featured in this aggregating role as the spearhead of dissident tendencies, and the trigger in this case was NATO's 'dual track' decision of 1979. Soon the Evangelical churches had placed themselves at the head of a pacifist and environmentalist movement, involving to a great extent young people, and acting through peace novenas, peace forums, 'church days' and 'blues masses'. The peace forums in Dresden, held on the anniversary days of the destruction of that town in the Second World War, were attended by as many as 5,000 people (Ramet 1984; Sandford 1983). All this happened with the ruling party's somewhat intermittent acquiescence, although the sequel was to show that, whatever reasons the SED had for its relatively tolerant attitude, that tolerance was not to be taken as a move towards reform of the communist system. As in Czechoslovakia, the leaders of this movement were to go on, after 1989, to occupy important positions in the new polity, although reunification was to make Germany a deviant case in the story of transitions from communism.

The Polish case is dominated, of course, by Solidarity which, having imposed itself in August 1980 in its original guise as an independent

trade union of workers, went on to rally behind it all forces hostile to
the ruling party and to the Soviet Union, Poland's traditional enemy,
which stood behind the ruling party. The Polish case is, however,
paradoxical. The immediate impact of Solidarity was far greater than
that of either Charter 77 or the GDR's Evangelical churches. At its
height it was claiming a membership of ten million, and it dwarfed all
other dissenting movements and organizations in Poland. And yet
Poland was exceptional among the countries of Eastern Europe in terms
of the number of autonomous political organizations, and even parties,
that managed to maintain themselves in being during the communist
period (Millard 1990).

Late in the day came a Bulgarian equivalent – so late, in fact, that
the Union of Democratic Forces, which represents a clear parallel with
Charter 77, Solidarity and the GDR's Evangelical churches, only came
into being once the communist regime of Todor Zhivkov had collapsed
in November 1989. Once in place, however, it played the same
aggregating role as those other movements and organizations.

No aggregating movement of this kind was able to develop in
Romania, in the exceptionally oppressive circumstances of Ceausescu's
rule. The case of Hungary, however, deserves particular note. Here, if
no single movement capable of aggregating all the voices of dissent
against communist party rule developed, this was partly because a
number of candidates for that role developed, no one of which acquired
the authority to speak with an overall collective voice. Thus the
Hungarian Democratic Forum (formed in September 1987), the Alliance
of Free Democrats (formed in February 1989 as the Network of Free
Initiatives) and the Alliance of Young Democrats (formed in March
1988) were to play a prominent role and were to emerge later on the
electoral scene (Lomax 1991: 165–70).

But there did develop in Hungary a process of aggregation around a
single issue, and one that was close to the national sensitivities of
Hungarians. The proposal to construct a system of dams on the Danube
in cooperation with Slovakia became an extremely important point of
focus in the struggle against the party's monopoly of power which was
as strong in Hungary as in the other countries of the region (Waller
1989: 318–19). The Danube Circle, which was formed to protest against
Hungarian participation in the project, and the movement of support
that it generated, repay thought. On the one hand this was an environmental issue, and its chief salience could be located in that fact were it
not that in the post-revolutionary period the Danube Circle has found
it very hard to maintain support for a strictly environmental movement.
On the other hand, precisely in the post-revolutionary period the

national aspects of the protest were to become stronger. The clustering of support for the Danube Circle against what was seen as an ill-considered extravagance on the part of an irresponsible ruling party had a lot in common with the mightier aggregating movements of dissent in neighbouring countries.

A second productive source of non-systemic political mobilization during the heroic period – organized religion – affected only two of the Eastern European countries during the period in question to any great extent – the GDR and Poland. In the first case, the Evangelical churches offered themselves overtly from 1978 as aggregating centres for collective action that were bound to be contestatory in the circumstances. But this abrupt rise in the churches' political profile took place at least to some extent as a result of a policy decision by the ruling party. The SED was at that time attempting to assert its German cultural credentials. It had, for example, reinstated Martin Luther as an important part of the GDR's heritage, and in 1978 it entered into a concordat with the Evangelical churches which would allow the latter some liberty of action in return for an acceptance of the party's political authority. Before that date the Evangelical churches had not been able to wield any great political influence, and such as they exercised through the pulpit did not constitute a major factor in the politics of the GDR, nor could they be considered until that time a significant focus for the aggregation of political activity.

The church's influence in Poland was both deeper and more discreet. Throughout the communist period it qualified the party's monopoly of power very considerably, without having a formal presence in government. Since some 85 per cent of Poles are practising Catholics, congregation on religious occasions could only be tantamount to political aggregation. The visits of the Polish pope to his homeland have been eloquent testimony to this. In addition, at a more formal level, the Church managed to maintain a small group of deputies in the *Sejm* whose allegiance was expressly to the Church. Significantly, at the round table talks at the beginning of 1989, the Church had only two representatives to Solidarity's 25. It could do the essentials of its business on that occasion through its hierarchy. In the longer term it could count on having a strong constituency within Solidarity itself. The way in which that constituency asserted itself during the transition period against secular opinion in Solidarity is part of that later story, but it attests the pervasiveness of the Catholic Church's influence throughout the period covered in this chapter (Davies 1984: 58–60).

Just as religious organizations in the form of the Evangelical churches were at the heart of the major oppositional movement in the

GDR during the heroic period, and thus gave that movement of dissent a religious colouring that was not necessarily subscribed to by all participants in the movement, so in Poland Solidarity enthroned the issue of freedom of association in trade unions within a more general movement. Outside Poland this period saw few attempts to set up independent trade unions. In Hungary, however, a Democratic Union of Scientific and Academic Workers was formed, but this was not until December 1989, and that interesting white-collar union must be considered more a result of the process of change than as an element of mobilization in bringing it about. Similarly in Romania, the fall of Ceausescu was followed almost immediately by the creation of an independent Federation of Free Trade Unions. Solidarity was in fact exceptional, in this as in many other ways. We shall see below that the development of the trade unions has been a complex story in the post-revolutionary phase.

During the heroic period, group formation was at its most dynamic in terms of its outcomes, and also most clearly discernible, within the structures of state and party power and in the broad aggregating movements described above. If the picture thus presented appears simple, it is because the circumstances during these years of tension were simple.

The second phase: the transfer of power

This presentation of the process of regime change in Eastern Europe in terms of group formation has concentrated on the period before the actual fall of the communist monopoly. The period of the transfer of power, and that which has followed the holding of the first free elections, will be treated more cursorily – partly for considerations of space, partly because other contributions to this volume provide further detail; but also partly because until a little more time has elapsed it will be impossible to see the clear contours of a more closely articulated group politics that can be expected to replace what might well be termed the surges of the immediate transition.

Any account of the transfer of power, however cursory, must draw out from a confused story four particular landmarks. These are:

1 The negotiation of the transfer.
2 The formal abolition of the party's power monopoly.
3 The passing of laws legalizing political associations.
4 The establishment of an electoral process and the holding of a free election.

The first of these landmarks revealed – except in the case of Romania, where the transfer of power took place without any negotiation – which were the major group forces in play. In those cases where the negotiations involved orderly round table discussions, it was possible to seat around the table a calculated and agreed balance of representatives. These meetings thus had a clear constitutional status. In Poland the balance of the delegations to the round table talks which opened on 6 February 1989 was carefully composed. Together with the communist party and Solidarity, the Catholic Church and also the official trade unions (the OPZZ) were represented. A similar attention to the representation of the major forces in play was to be found in Hungary when a comparable round table discussion took place in September of the same year.

In Bulgaria, the ten political organizations for which the Union of Democratic Forces spoke when the Communist Party's delegates met representatives of the opposition included political parties stemming from before the communist period, a Federation of Independent Students' Federations, the independent trade union organization *Podkrepa,* and a series of organizations that the revolutionary upsurge had produced, none of them dating from before 1989 but including three which had played crucial roles in that process: the 'Citizens' Initiative' Movement and the Discussion Club for Support of Glasnost and Perestroika, both of which were created in 1988, and Ekoglasnost, the aggregating role of which from early 1989 foreshadowed that of the later and larger Union of Democratic Forces.

Even in the GDR and Czechoslovakia, where in each case the party resisted as long as was politically feasible and thus fell in the heat of profound crisis, party and opposition finally came together to negotiate for the country's future. The pattern was the same. Civic Forum in Czechoslovakia and the newly created Neues Forum in the GDR acted as umbrella organizations for the forces opposing the party's monopoly; yet each of them contained individuals and groups which were to populate the political scene once the ruling party had vacated it, and were to undergo a process of differentiation in the ensuing period.

The formal rescinding of the provision in the constitution of each country for the privileged role of the communist party, had a particular symbolic significance in the circumstances. This occurred in Hungary on 18 October 1989; in Czechoslovakia on 29 November; in the GDR on 1 December; in Bulgaria in stages from 12 December to 15 January 1991; in Poland on 29 December. In Romania the Romanian Communist Party was so discredited that it was not seen necessary to revoke its leading role. Of equally symbolic importance were the decisions to abolish the workers' militias, and to put an end to another hallmark of communist party practice – the organization of the party in the workplace. To conclude the list of decisions charged with symbolism, the Warsaw Treaty Organization's intervention in Czechoslovakia in 1968 was repudiated in turn in each of the participating countries.

Abolishing the Communist Party's monopoly was a dramatic event, but it was essentially a negative one. On the whole less publicly celebrated was the series of laws that have been passed gradually over an extended period enacting a freedom of association. Yet this legislation has been the essential foundation for the creation of an associative political life and thereby of political pluralism. One of the first such enactments – the original registration of Solidarity in November 1980 – was indeed a moment of high drama, but Solidarity was to be outlawed at the end of the next year, and it was not until 17 April 1989 that the union was re-legalized. By that time, in fact on 11 January 1989, the Hungarian Law on Association had been passed. Not only freedom of association had to be embodied in law. The various press laws that were enacted have played an equally crucial role in preparing the ground for a politics that includes the free articulation of group pressures. It was a signal day when, on 8 March 1989, there appeared the first free newspaper to be published in these countries since the war – the Polish *Gazeta Wyborcza*.

Finally, and of all this constitutive series of events the one that most determined the shape of the future, electoral systems were adopted and elections were held. The simple facts of holding an election to an assembly to which the government would be accountable, and of establishing a constitutional right of association and of speech, had the effect that they must always have. Contending leaderships had to mark off their positions from those of their rivals; and they had to assemble sufficient support to appear as credible contenders for power at national level. Those who had small chance of succeeding in the latter task threw in their lot with others that had a greater chance.

In other words, whilst aggregation remained the name of the game, the manner of aggregation differed categorically from that of the first phase. This explains, if it needs any explanation, the compressed and at times anguished discussions of this brief period over modes of operation – movement or party? – and the abrupt contraction of viable political formations, or of those which entered the electoral lists (in the Hungarian case, from 65 registered parties, eight won 378 of the 382 seats in the assembly, with a 4-seat 'multi-party' residue) (Swain 1991). This is most certainly not to say that the prospect of an election produced coherent political parties: it did so but rarely, if at all. Nor is it to say that that prospect meant that the aggregation of preferences would be monopolized by political parties, for this also has not been the case, although the successful holding of free elections and such subsequent clarification of programmes and constituencies as has ensued have necessarily moved things in that direction.

Across the region the victors in these first elections were the 'forum' parties. The question of group representation and of sectional electoral constituencies was therefore not really posed, or was posed in crude terms. The appeal of the forum movements was a negative one – to oust the communists from power. Their function at this stage of the process of transition was akin to that of national liberation movements, whose appeal is to the nation as whole, and to support for a single, all-englobing issue. But it was not long before the elements from which the forum movements were composed began to separate out. When that process, together with the tally of parties outside the forum movements and the communist parties themselves, is examined, the truly transitional nature of the second period is revealed.

The third period: beyond the first elections

By the close of 1991, the end of the communist monopoly in Eastern Europe was a fact, free elections had been held in each country of the region at least once, and political organization for the furtherance of sectional interests had been legalised.The sequel of those first elections, however, has shown that these enabling factors are still only the foundations on which some new edifice had to be built. The expected developments on which a restructuring of interests would depend were slow to take place, notably the change in ownership relations that marketization is supposed to be ushering in.

The key features of this third period included, firstly, a process of differentiation within the forum parties, which yielded in most of the countries involved a clearer demarcation between the elements of the emerging party system. Secondly, there was a tendency for nation, region and Church to grow in political salience as focal points for group identities. Thirdly, the elites of the communist period demonstrated an ability to retain their power, partly in managerial structures which remained little affected by the transition, and partly through using their contacts and political skills to acquire new positions of power. This has had an effect on the structure of the employer lobby, with organizations representing a new entrepreneurial interest cohabiting with representatives of the large state-owned enterprises in tripartite discussions involving government, the trade unions and employers' organizations in each country.

Fourthly, the realm of politics conventionally identified as the 'left', and comprising on the one hand political parties with an ideology favouring 'red' or 'green' values, and on the other hand the trade unions and organized labour, is in a state of disarray. The remaining part of this study will therefore be devoted to discussing this part of the political scene, since it has an obvious relevance to the formation of group identities and the generation of group pressures in general, and to the relation between parties and trade unions in particular.

Those parties that stood under the social democratic label and which were not simply communist parties reformed and renamed, fared very badly in the first round of elections. The Bulgarian social democrats misjudged the second round of elections in October 1991 in their country and lost the representation that they had earlier had as a member organization of the UDF. In fact only in the Czech Republic has a social-democratic parliamentary presence been reasonably well established. Here the Czechoslovak Social-Democratic Party, unsuccessful in the first election, benefited from the break-up of the Civil Forum, and the six deputies that it gained in this manner increased to 21 in the federal parliament with the second election, held in 1992 (16 from the Czech Republic and five from Slovakia). The party had in the meantime been strengthened through the rallying to it of a number of particularly respected political figures, whilst a subsequent change of leadership was to lead to yet further strengthening.

The social-democratic parties had in many cases been dragooned during the communist period into joining, as junior partners, a 'front' dominated by the communists, and it was difficult for them to live this down. But also they suffered from a phenomenon of the transition the significance of which has still not been properly digested either within those countries or abroad. This is the simple fact that the communist parties, far from going away, achieved quite respectable scores in the first elections – a presence that they maintained in the second elections. With changed names (usually including the 'socialist', and only in the single case of the Czech Republic the 'communist' tag), with no chance of recovering the monopoly of power that they once held, freed from the association with a Soviet bogey, and still endowed with the organizational skills that have been so characteristic of communist parties, these parties bid fair, in at least two cases – the Hungarian and the Slovak – to grow into the social democratic space which others are having such difficulty in filling.

As for the green parties and green movements which had often enjoyed a high profile in the heroic period (and which before the Czechoslovak elections had been credited at one point with between 10 and 18 per cent support) (Jehlicka and Kostelecky 1992), they scored dismally in the elections, although they gained parliamentary representation in Romania, in the Slovak national chamber (but not the Czech or federal chambers) and in Bulgaria, where both Ekoglasnost and the Green Party were members of the Union of Democratic Forces.

But in many ways one of the most surprising developments has been in the trade union field. We saw that during the heroic period new and independent trade unions, with the exception of Solidarity, were slow to appear. With the fall of the communist regimes there was considerable change. Firstly, the ex-official trade union confederations – the mass organizations which in the past had functioned as 'transmission belts' linking the masses to the regime – now gradually but universally separated themselves from their earlier sponsors, and began to carve out for themselves a sphere of political activity independent of any political party. These were formidable organizations, both in terms of membership and of the funds that they disposed of. They were brought to part with the latter, but they have retained very high memberships. In 1991 the Hungarian MSZOSZ still enrolled 3 million of the 4.5 million members that it counted three years before. Despite Solidarity's claim in 1981 to have had a membership of 10 million, in 1991 it only counted 2.3 million members, against the 4.5 million of the ex-official OPZZ. In Bulgaria the independent trade union *Podkrepa* was a founder member of the UDF and played an important role in the unseating of the communist party but the ex-official trade union confederation not only remained in being, but emancipated itself from its earlier sponsors (now renamed the Bulgarian Socialist Party) and has been able to use its considerable muscle in the recent politics of Bulgaria. Only in Czechoslovakia was the Revolutionary Trade Union Movement of the communist days formally disbanded, on 2 March 1990. In its place was created a new Czech and Slovak Confederation of Trade Unions (Engelbrekt *et al.* 1991).

Secondly, the period from 1989 has seen the creation of a great number of new trade union organizations, yielding a complicated picture in which the ex-official unions, now independent, are engaged in political struggle with new-born rivals.

From somewhere within this complex set of heirs to the socialist heritage, in its syndicalist and party forms, will presumably arise eventually the forces that will contest the market-based policies of the new governments, once the social effects of those policies become manifest and the charm of liberation begins to wear thin. But at the time of writing the ultimate configuration of those forces remains quite opaque.

CONCLUSIONS

Andrei Sinyavsky has likened democracy to the cellular structure of a honeycomb – a graphic version of the pluralist view of democracy as a matrix of interests and organizations, the boundaries of which are mutually supporting in a stable and enduring structure. Sinyavsky was opposing this to the monolithic structure of communism, where an abhorrence of sub-system autonomy leaves an organizational vacuum between the leaders and the led. History has shown the latter to be unstable in that it starves the decision-making centre of information (hence, as the system reached the point of collapse in the Soviet Union, the call for *glasnost*) whilst offering no organizational buffers to disperse the incidence of demands on the centre and to protect it from the surges of discontent that have studded the history of communism, particularly in Eastern Europe, despite the image of planned harmony that communist party propagandists have presented.

The countries of Eastern Europe all claim to have put behind them the political system of communism, and to be seeking to establish a pluralist democracy. How, then, are they faring, and to what extent does the material presented in this study provide evidence for an answer?

In all the countries a framework has been won which would enable the political system to fill with the associative life, in terms both of political parties and of pressure groups, that has underpinned democracy in other places. The enabling legislation is in place, orderly and open elections have been held, autonomous associations with political or partly political aims have been registered in their thousands. Paradigms to shape a forward course are available and generally accepted, some drawn from a country's past, others from a Western model whose adoption offers material dividends.

At the same time, this essay has recorded a number of factors that have impeded the development of democratic politics in the region, and may be expected to have an influence also on future developments. To take a stance against the past does not do away with the influences, attitudes, indeed the people, of that past. Secondly, the single year 1989 was only the culmination of a revolutionary process, and such processes devalue norms and generate enthusiasms. There results a nervousness which cannot be expected to recede until, with time, new norms become habits of mind. Thirdly, time again can alone translate the juridical possibility for the formation of autonomous organizations to form into what established democracies know as the lobby – a mesh of interests and organization linked to government on a day-to-day basis.

There is a fourth, purely conjunctural, factor that will influence particularly the future of the transition in Eastern Europe. Whilst the link between affluence and democracy is difficult to demonstrate conclusively and in detail, few would doubt that a failure on the part of government to translate liberation from communism into tangible material benefits will make the consolidation of democratic politics difficult. Moreover, if to high unemployment and low wage levels is added a sense of disappointment that the dream of being a real part of Europe is not being realized, the likelihood will increase of populist appeals arising that will bypass and thus devalue the democratic process.

Many of the phenomena that a group analysis of politics in Eastern Europe reveals were shaped in the period before 1989, and are likely to have a continuing effect on the future of the transition. They include a tendency towards a broad clustering, first around the major opposi-tional forces of the revolutionary period at a time when communism ruled out the autonomous articulation of interests and demands, and later around large-scale objects of loyalty such as nation, region or Church, when in principle the way had been opened for the narrow clustering characteristic of democratic pressure group activity. They include also a tendency for the expression of political preferences to surge, either around these broad poles of attraction (and political leaders who choose to manipulate their appeal), or in the form of spontaneous action which bypasses the infant channels of political expression, as in the transport drivers' action in Hungary in late 1990.

Eastern Europe, of course, has no monopoly on surges of political passion and their manipulation, nor on strikes and demonstrations. Moreover, such occurrences attract the attention of commentators more than group pressures exercised away from the public eye. But it is the political salience of the former of these in relation to the latter that marks the present development of the transition in Eastern Europe. It remains to be seen whether the old adage that time alone will tell will redress the balance.

BIBLIOGRAPHY

Brown, A. (1983) 'Pluralism, power and the Soviet System: a comparative perspective', in S. G. Solomon (ed.) *Pluralism in the Soviet Union*, Basingstoke: Macmillan.

Connor, W. (1980) 'Dissent in Eastern Europe: a new coalition?', *Problems of Communism* 29, No. 1.

Davies, N. (1984) *Heart of Europe: a short history of Poland*, Oxford: Oxford University Press.

END Newsletter (1988).

Engelbrekt, K., Obrman, J., Pataki, J., Vinton, L., and Ionescu, D. (1991) 'Unions in the new Eastern Europe', *Report on Eastern Europe* 2, 13: 19–22.

Finer, S. E. (1967) *Anonymous Empire*, London: Pall Mall.

Hough, J. F. (1983) 'Pluralism, corporatism and the Soviet Union', in S. G. Solomon (ed.) *Pluralism in the Soviet Union: Essays in Honour of H. Gordon Skilling*, London: Macmillan

Jehlicka, P., and Kostelecky, T. (1992) 'The development of the Czechoslovak Green Party since the 1990 election', *Environmental Politics* 1, No.1.

Konrád, G., and Szelenyi, I. (1979) *The Intellectuals on the Road to Class Power*, Brighton: Harvester.

Lipset, S. M., and Rokkan, S. (eds) (1967) *Party Systems and Voter Alignments*, New York: Free Press.

Lomax, B. (1991) 'Hungary from Kadarism to democracy: the successful failure of reform communism', in D. W. Spring (ed.) *The Impact of Gorbachev: The First Phase, 1985–90*, London: Pinter.

MacEwen, M. (1976) 'The day the party had to stop', in *Socialist Register*, London: Merlin.

Macshane, D. (1981) *Solidarity: Poland's Independent Trade Union*, Nottingham: Spokesman.

Mallinkrodt, A. M. (1984) 'Wanted: theoretical framework for GDR studies', *GDR Monitor* No.10: 14–28.

Michel, P. (ed.) (1991) *Politics and Religion in Eastern Europe: Catholicism in Hungary, Poland and Czechoslovakia*, London: Polity Press.

Millard, F. (1990) 'Emergent pluralism in Poland: a short guide', *The Journal of Communist Studies* 6, No. 1: 99–109.

La Nouvelle Alternative, June 1989.

Pridham, G. (1990) 'Southern democracies on the road to consolidation', in G. Pridham (ed.) *Securing Democracy: Political Parties and Democratic Consolidation in Southern Europe*, London: Routledge.

Rakowska-Harmstone, T. (1984) 'Ethnic politics in the USSR', *Problems of Communism* 33, 3: 1–22.

Ramet, P. (1984) 'Church and peace in East Germany', *Problems of Communism* 33, No. 4.

Rupnik, J. (1990) *L'autre Europe: crise et fin du communisme*, Paris: Odile Jacob.

Rusinow, D. (1977) *The Yugoslav Experiment, 1945–74*, London: Hurst.

Sandford, J. (1983) *The Sword and the Ploughshare: Autonomous Peace Initiatives in East Germany*, London: Merlin/END.

Skilling, H. G. (1985) 'Independent currents in Czechoslovakia', *Problems of Communism* 34, 1: 32–49.

Slansky, P. (1988) 'Pollution: the tale of Bratislava', *The East European Reporter* 3, 3: 26–30.

Stojanovic, S. (1981) *In Search of Democracy in Socialism*, New York: Prometheus Books.

Swain, N. (1991) *Hungary's New Political Parties*, Manchester: Lorton Papers, No. 5.
Thompson, M. (1987) 'Movements meet in Coventry', *END Newsletter*, No. 30: 10–11.
Tökés, R. (1979) *Opposition in Eastern Europe*, London: Macmillan.
Voslensky, M. (1980) *Les priviligiés en URSS*, Paris: Belfond.
Waller, M. (1981) *Democratic Centralism: An Historical Commentary*, Manchester: Manchester University Press.
—— (1989) 'The ecology issue in Eastern Europe: protest and movements', *The Journal of Communist Studies* 5, 3: 302–28.
Wolchik, S. L. (1991) *Czechoslovakia in Transition: politics, economics, society*, London: Pinter.

3 Predicting and explaining democratization in Eastern Europe

Tatu Vanhanen and Richard Kimber

Political scientists were unable to predict the great movement of democratization in Eastern Europe from 1989–90. The problem we examine in this chapter concerns the question whether there are any systematic and structural explanations for the collapse of hegemonic regimes and the sudden breakthrough of democracy in Eastern Europe. Was it due to some unique local or historical factors, say, the personality of Gorbachev or to the reforms introduced by him, or was it due to some more universal factors that preceded Gorbachev's rise to power? And would it have been possible to predict the great wave of democratization in Eastern Europe on the basis of some explanatory variables? Our inquiry is based on Tatu Vanhanen's two comparative studies of democratization (1984 and 1990) and his later attempt to explain democratization in Eastern Europe by using different combinations of his explanatory variables (Vanhanen 1991a), and on Richard Kimber's parallel attempt to solve the problem by using a different method to analyse the same empirical data (Kimber 1991a). We have attempted to present the results of statistical analyses in a way that makes them comprehensible also for readers who are not familiar with the statistical methods used in these analyses.

VANHANEN'S THEORY OF DEMOCRATIZATION

According to Vanhanen's theory, democratization depends on the distribution of relevant power resources. Democratization takes place under conditions in which power resources have become so widely distributed that no group is any longer able to suppress its competitors or to maintain its hegemony. This theoretical assumption is based on a Darwinian interpretation of politics, according to which politics is a part of the general struggle for survival. Consequently, the central theme of politics concerns the struggle for scarce resources. This

crucial characteristic of politics is assumed to remain the same
across all cultural variations, because all human populations share
the same basic behavioural predispositions. As all available resources
are used in the political struggle for scarce resources, it is reasonable
to assume that the distribution of power follows from the distribution
of those resources. Power is concentrated in the hands of the few or
shared by the many, depending on whether important economic,
intellectual and other power resources are concentrated in the hands
of the few or distributed among the many. Therefore, the distribution
of power resources among competing groups can be regarded as the
most crucial social condition of democracy and democratization.
Democracy emerges when no group is any longer able to establish or
maintain hegemonic power. This, briefly stated, is Vanhanen's theory
of democratization.

The theory of democratization outlined above is simple, but it may
be difficult to understand for readers who are not used to applying the
principles of the Darwinian theory of evolution by natural selection to
the study of politics. In fact, this difficulty concerns most students and
researchers of political science and of social sciences and history in
general because the Darwinian revolution has not yet reached these
sciences. Therefore, it is advisable to attempt to explain in greater detail
why democratization is assumed to be causally related to the degree of
resource distribution. According to the Darwinian theory of evolution,
there must be a struggle for existence among the individuals of a
population because more individuals are produced than can be supported by available resources. This inference is based on the facts that
(1) all species have great potential fertility, (2) populations normally
display stability, and (3) natural resources are limited and, in a stable
environment, remain relatively constant. On the basis of these facts,
Darwin concluded that a struggle for existence is inevitable, this being
due to the permanent and universal scarcity of resources in nature. Only
some of the individuals of a population are able to reproduce and
survive. They become selected in the struggle for survival. Darwin
concluded that the survival in the struggle for existence is not completely random but depends in part on the hereditary constitution of the
surviving individuals. The individuals who in some respects adapted
even slightly better to their environment have better chances to survive
than those whose characteristics are less adaptive in the same environment. This leads to evolution by natural selection.

These principles of the Darwinian theory of evolution by natural
selection are well known and generally accepted when applied to other
species, but the point here is that they can be applied to our own species,

too, and that it is possible to deduce theoretical explanations for human politics from them. Politics can be interpreted as an expression of the universal struggle for existence in living nature. It is for us a species-specific way to compete for scarce resources and reproduction. The permanent scarcity of many important resources makes the competition and struggle for them inevitable among individuals, groups, and populations. Thus the evolutionary roots of politics lie in the necessity to solve conflicts over scarce resources by some means. Because everyone seems to have an equal right to those resources, and because they are scarce, we have to compete for them. We should understand that the scarcity of resources makes this competition and struggle inevitable for us, just as in other parts of nature, and that there is no way to avoid this struggle. It belongs to the nature of all living beings that they do their utmost to preserve their existence. Only those who are successful in this struggle are able to survive and reproduce.

Politics and political structures have evolved in the continual struggle for scarce resources to channel the competition for the distribution of scarce resources among individuals, groups and populations. It is reasonable to assume that everyone tries to further his/her interests and to get as much as possible in the political struggle for scarce resources. Power is used as a currency or as an intervening mechanism in this struggle. The more one has power, the more one can get scarce resources. Power can be understood as the ability to compel or persuade others to do something which they would not otherwise do. This ability to persuade or compel others rests on sanctions. Therefore, the distribution of power in any society depends on the distribution of sanctions used as sources of power. If the resources used as sources of power (economic, intellectual, coercive, or whatever they are) are concentrated in the hands of one group, the same group will be the most powerful group. If the resources used as sanctions are distributed widely among several groups, it is reasonable to expect that power becomes distributed among several groups, too. This relationship between the distribution of sanctions and the distribution of power is regular and constant because all individuals and groups have the same need to resort to all available resources in the continual political struggle for power. Those controlling most effective power resources have better chances to get power than those whose power resources are meagre or who are without any significant power resources. This argumentation leads to the hypothesis that the concentration or distribution of political power depends on the degree of resource distribution.

The variation of political systems from the rule of the few to the rule of the many follows from the reasoning discussed above. In societies where relevant power resources are concentrated in the hands of the few, political power is also concentrated in the hands of the few, and in societies where important power resources are distributed widely, political power also tends to become distributed widely. From this rule we can derive an evolutionary explanation for democracy and democratization. Democracy is the government by the many, and autocracy is the government by the few. The concentration of power resources leads to autocracy, and the distribution of power resources leads to democracy. So it can be hypothesized that *democratization takes place under conditions in which power resources have become so widely distributed that no group is any longer able to suppress its competitors or to maintain its hegemony.*

It is characteristic of this evolutionary theory of democratization that the same explanation is applied to all countries because human nature is assumed to be approximately the same among all populations. We do not need a different explanation for each country or for each cultural or regional group of countries. The assumption about the similarity of human nature across all cultural, racial, and ideological cleavages makes it possible to formulate universal research hypotheses on democratization and to test them by the same empirical variables in all countries. The problem is how to measure the variation in the distribution of power resources and the degree of democratization. Vanhanen has used six empirical variables to measure some aspects of the distribution of economic and intellectual power resources and two basic electoral variables to measure the degree of democratization. The variables and the indexes based on them are listed in Table 3.1 and further described in Appendix 3.1 (see pp. 85–6).

Vanhanen has investigated democratization in the world on the basis of this theory. A study of the period 1850–1979 (see Vanhanen 1984) indicated that the relationship between the Index of Power Resources (IPR), which combines the five explanatory variables used in his study, and the Index of Democratization (ID) remained relatively strong throughout the period of comparison (for variables, see Appendix 1). In the total group of 820 decennial comparison units, the correlation was 0.803, which means that IPR statistically explained 64 per cent of the variation in ID. Regression analysis was used to show how accurately the average relationship applied to individual countries. Historically, democratization started in the countries (Western Europe and North America) where power resources were the most widely distributed, whereas countries with low IPR values remained nondemocracies. Some deviations have always weakened this regular pattern: democracies which were expected to be nondemocracies because of

Table 3.1 Basic empirical variables and indexes

Political variables

Smaller parties' share of the votes cast in parliamentary and/or presidential elections (Competition)

The percentage of the total population which actually voted in the same elections (Participation)

Index of Democratization (ID)
 Competition
 Participation

Explanatory variables

Percentage of urban population
Percentage of non-agricultural population
Number of students per 100,000 inhabitants
Percentage literacy
Percentage share of family farms of the total area of holdings
Degree of decentralization of non-agricultural economic resources

Index of Occupational Diversification (IOD)
 Percentage of urban population
 Percentage of non-agricultural population

Index of Knowledge Distribution (IKD)
 Number of students per 100,000 inhabitants
 Percentage literacy

Index of Distribution of Economic Power Resources (DER)
 Percentage share of family farms of the total area of holdings
 Degree of decentralization of non-agricultural economic resources

Index of Power Resources (IPR)
 Index of Occupational Diversification (IOD)
 Index of Knowledge Distribution (IKD)
 Index of Distribution of Economic Power Resources (DER)

their low IPR values and nondemocracies which were expected to be democracies because of their relatively high IPR values. Usually, however, such deviations did not last long. In the case of Eastern European socialist countries, he came to the conclusion:

> Because their IPR values cannot be much increased as long as land ownership and other major means of production continue to be concentrated, I predict that these countries will probably remain below the threshold of democracy. On the other hand, the pressure for democratization will probably be enhanced, and the consequences of this pressure are incalculable.

(Vanhanen 1984: 132)

The social basis of hegemonic governmental structures is rather narrow in socialist countries because they are upheld only by the concentration of the means of coercion and of economic power resources. Other social conditions, particularly a high level of education, are conducive to the emergence of democracy. It was noted that it is difficult to estimate the relative importance of the different power resources. The gradual evolution of more democratic political institutions is always possible. So the possibility of democratization was left open, and was only predicted for Poland and Yugoslavia. In these two countries the IPR (Index of Power Resources) values in 1970 were so high that they should have been democracies, whereas Romania, the German Democratic Republic and Czechoslovakia were at the transition level of IPR, and the Soviet Union, Bulgaria, Hungary and Albania were below the transition level of IPR (Vanhanen 1984: 107–17, 132).

In a later study (Vanhanen 1990), in which IPR is based on six explanatory variables (see Appendix 3.1), the explained part of the variation rose to 70 per cent. The correlations ranged from 0.836 to 0.845 over the period 1980–8. The results of regression analysis indicated that Poland and Yugoslavia, because of their relatively high IPR values, were highly deviating nondemocracies, whereas the other East European countries were nondemocracies because of their low IPR values. So the results of regression analysis provided an explanation for the lack of democracy in Eastern Europe from 1980–8 but did not help to predict the collapse of authoritarian systems from 1989–90. Vanhanen concluded that the other East European countries were still nondemocracies 'because economic and some other crucial power resources are highly concentrated in the hands of the hegemonic party and state institutions'. They were not deviating cases in his study. However, he pointed out again that

> the social basis of power concentration in East European societies is not secure, because it is supported only by one structural factor, the concentration of economic power resources, and contradicted by several others, particularly by the fact that intellectual power resources are widely distributed and that the occupational diversification of the population has created inevitable interest cleavages that provide a natural basis for competing political parties.
>
> (Vanhanen 1990: 135)

The discrepancy between the first four and the last two explanatory variables is striking, but the analysis technique used in his study did not permit democratization to be predicted for countries whose IPR values were low (Vanhanen 1990: 93–9, 132–40). Therefore, democratization in Eastern Europe from 1989–90 contradicted predictions based on the IPR values of these countries in 1980.

The problem is: would it have been possible to predict democratization in Eastern Europe for countries whose IPR values were low if the same data had been analyzed differently? This is the problem we have to try to solve.

EXTERNAL FACTORS

First, however, it is necessary to refer to the role of external factors in Eastern Europe. The way socialist systems were established in the other East European countries after the Second World War differed crucially from the way socialism was established in the Soviet Union. In Russia domestic forces were crucial in the establishment of a socialist system, whereas such systems were imposed on the other East European countries (with the exception of Albania and Yugoslavia) by an external force (the Soviet Union) after the Second World War. Consequently, Vanhanen (1991a) has argued that the use of external power resources, which are not taken into account in his Index of Power Resources, provided an explanation for the breakdown of incipient democratic institutions and for the concentration of power in the hands of the communist parties in those countries after the Second World War. In the 1980s, when the threat of external intervention disappeared, domestic governments were no longer able to suppress the demands of democracy, and socialist systems collapsed. It can be argued that they survived 40 years with the support of external power resources. However, this explanation does not apply to the Soviet Union, Yugoslavia or Albania because their political systems were not dependent on external support. For these countries it is necessary to seek explanations in the distribution of domestic power resources or other domestic factors.

STRUCTURAL IMBALANCES

It might be possible to find a systematic explanation for the collapse of hegemonic political systems and the emergence of democracy in Eastern Europe in discrepancies in explanatory factors. The first four explanatory variables have predicted democratization in the Soviet Union for decades, whereas the concentration of economic power resources as indicated by the last two explanatory variables has been in harmony with the concentration of political power. The same structural imbalance existed in all East European socialist countries. Table 3.2

Table 3.2 The values of six explanatory variables and three sectional indexes in nine East European countries in 1980

Country	UP	NAP	Stud.	Lit.	FF	DDN	IOD	IKD	DER
1 Albania	37	40	11	70	0	0	38.5	40.5	0
2 Bulgaria	64	67	23	95	0	0	65.5	59.0	0
3 Czechoslovakia	63	90	26	99	5	0	76.5	62.5	0.5
4 GDR	77	90	48	99	5	2	83.5	73.5	2.3
5 Hungary	54	84	19	99	2	1	69.0	59.0	1.2
6 Poland	57	70	33	98	76	2	63.5	65.5	24.2
7 Romania	50	53	17	98	9	0	51.5	57.5	4.2
8 USSR	62	84	39	100	0	0	73.0	69.5	0
9 Yugoslavia	42	63	37	91	75	50	52.5	64.0	46.6
Arithmetic mean	56.2	71.2	28.1	94.3	19.1	3.9	63.7	61.2	8.8

Notes UP = urban population; NAP = nonagricultural population; Stud. = students; Lit. = literates. FF = family farms; DDN = degree of decentralization of nonagricultural economic resources; IOD = Index of Occupational Diversification; IKD = Index of Knowledge Distribution; DER = Index of the Distribution of Economic Power Resources. For identification of the variables, see Appendix 3.1.

illustrates the distribution of economic and intellectual power resources as indicated by the six social variables and the three sectional indexes in nine East European countries in 1980 (Vanhanen 1990).

Table 3.2 shows that in 1980 the values of the first four explanatory variables in Eastern Europe were as high or nearly as high as they were in Western Europe (see Vanhanen 1990: 127), whereas the values of the last two variables were zero or near zero for all countries (Poland and Yugoslavia excluded). The arithmetic means of IOD (the Index of Occupational Diversification) and IKD (the Index of Knowledge Distribution) are 63.7 and 61.2, respectively, for East European countries, and 77.5 and 66.1 for West European countries, whereas the arithmetic mean of DER (the Index of the Distribution of Economic Power Resources) is only 8.8 for East European countries but 66.5 for West European countries. This indicated a crucial difference in social structures between East European socialist countries and Western Europe in 1980. From the perspective of democratization, the problem in Eastern Europe was in the discrepancy between the first two and the third dimensions of resource distribution. The first two dimensions indicated that important intellectual and socio-economic resources were widely distributed within societies and that conditions for democratization were very favourable, whereas the concentration of the means of production was conducive to the concentration of political power. Because the three sectional indexes are combined into the Index of

Power Resources (IPR) by multiplying their values (see Appendix 3.1), the value of IPR remains at zero if the value of any sectional index is at zero. As a consequence, the IPR values of East European countries were significantly above zero only in the cases of Poland (10.1) and Yugoslavia (15.7). Therefore, on the basis of their IPR values in 1980, Vanhanen was able to predict democratization only for Poland and Yugoslavia. The other East European countries did not seem to be deviating cases, and he could not predict democratization because of their low IPR values.

PREDICTIONS BASED ON AN ALTERNATIVE IPR

The failure to predict democratization in Eastern Europe by his IPR led Vanhanen to consider alternative ways of combining the six explanatory variables. One way would be to combine the three sectional indexes by calculating their arithmetic mean. This way of combining the three explanatory factors is based on the assumption that a high level of resource distribution in one or two dimensions could partly compensate for the lack of resource distribution in other dimensions. To test the explanatory power of this kind of alternative IPR (IPR-2), he calculated the arithmetic means of the three sectional indexes for the 147 countries. Its explanatory power was tested by using it as the independent variable in a regression analysis in which ID-1988 was used as the dependent variable. The results show (see Vanhanen 1991a) that seven of the nine East European countries (Bulgaria, Czechoslovakia, the German Democratic Republic, Hungary, Poland, the USSR and Yugoslavia) were expected to be democracies on the basis of IPR-2 values, although they were nondemocracies. Romania was at the transition level of IPR-2, whereas Albania, because of its low IPR-2 value was expected to be a nondemocracy. In other words, it would have been possible to predict democratization for seven of the nine East European countries on the basis of the arithmetic mean of the three secitonal indexes (IPR-2), whereas on the basis of the original IPR democratization was expected only in Poland and Yugoslavia.

How should we interpret these clearly contradictory results and predictions? Would it have been better to use IPR-2 than IPR? It is true that IPR-2 would have produced correct predictions on democratization in the case of East European socialist countries, but, on the other hand, IPR explains more of the variation in ID (71 per cent) than IPR-2 (65 per cent) in the total group of 147 countries. Therefore, it may be theoretically better to combine the three sectional indexes into the Index of Power Resources by multiplying them than by calculating their arithmetic mean, even though this method prevented correct predictions being made for East European countries. However, it was a mistake to restrict attention to one particular combination of explanatory variables because we cannot be sure that the concentration of power resources in one dimension is always sufficient to nullify the distribution of power resources in other dimensions.

INDEX OF STRUCTURAL IMBALANCE

There is yet another way in which the discrepancy between various explanatory variables may be taken into account. The extent of the discrepancy can be measured by an Index of Structural Imbalance (ISI) which is based on the mean deviation of the three sectional indexes (IOD, IKD and DER) listed in Appendix 3.1. For example, in the case of Hungary (see Table 3.2) the values of the three sectional indexes are 69.0 (Index of Occupational Diversification), 59.0 (Index of Knowledge Distribution), and 1.2 (Index of the Distribution of Economic Power Resources). The arithmetic mean of these three sectional indexes is 43.1. The absolute differences of each score from the mean are 25.9 (IOD), 15.9 (IKD), and −41.9, and the arithmetic means of these differences (mean deviation) is 27.9. So Hungary's Index of Structural Imbalance (ISI) value is very high. The higher the ISI values are, the more single dimensions of resource distribution differ from each other. It is reasonable to assume that political systems are exceptionally insecure in countries with high Index of Structural Imbalance (ISI) values because some structural factors are conducive to democracy and others conducive to autocracy. In such countries, the destiny of the country's political system depends on the relative significance of these contradictory structural factors. Their relative significance may vary from country to country, and it may change over time within a country. Consequently, a political system may be in harmony with the most important aspect of resource distribution even though it is at variance with some other aspects of resource distribution. The high values of ISI indicate the existence of serious structural imbalance and imply that drastic changes in political structures are possible.

The values of Index of Structural Imbalance for the 147 countries of this comparison group, together with the values of sectional indexes (IOD, IKD and DER), are given in Appendix 3.2 (see pp.87–90). Figure 3.11 illustrates the distribution of ISI values in the group of 147 countries in 1980.

Appendix 3.2 and Figure 3.1 indicate that the Index of Structural Imbalance (ISI) values ranged from 0.3 (Honduras) to 33.9 (GDR) in

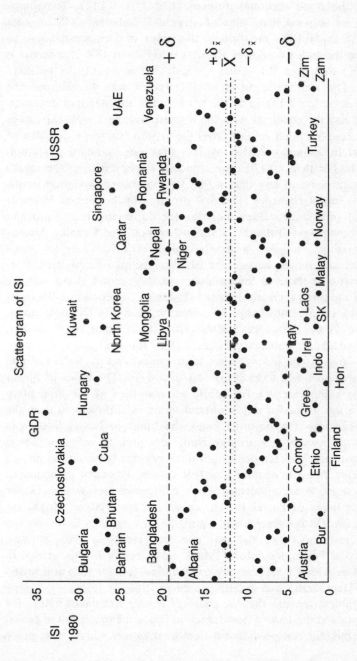

Figure 3.1 A scattergram of the Index of Structural Imbalance in the comparison group of 147 states in 1980

Abbreviations: Bur = Burma, Comor = Comoros, Ethio = Ethiopia, Gree = Greece, Hon = Honduras, Indo = Indonesia, Irel = Ireland, SK = South Korea, Malay = Malaysia, Zam = Zambia and Zim = Zimbabwe.

1980. ISI correlated negatively with the Index of Democratization in 1988 (−0.339), Index of Power Resources (−0.319) and the arithmetic mean of the three sectional indexes (IPR-2) (−0.112). These correlations are so weak that Index of Structural Imbalance (ISI) cannot be used to explain the variation in the Index of Democratization, or to replace the Index of Power Resources (IPR) or IPR-2, whereas it is possible that high ISI values indicate the insecurity of political systems. The arithmetic mean of ISI values was 12.039 and the standard deviation 7.131 in 1980. We can use one standard deviation to distinguish the countries with the highest and the lowest ISI values from the countries that deviate from the artithmetic mean of Index of Structural Imbalance (12.039) by less than one standard deviation. ISI was higher than 19.170 (one standard deviation from the mean) for 21 countries and less than 4.908 (one standard deviation below the mean) for 21 countries. The first group with the highest Index of Structural Imbalance values includes the following East European socialist countries: Bulgaria, Czechoslovakia, the German Democratic Republic, Hungary, Romania and the USSR. There are some significant differences between these two groups of countries. It is characteristic of those in the countries of the second group that the values of the three sectional indexes (Index of Occupational Diversification, Index of Knowledge Distribution, and the Distribution of Economic Power Resources) differ from each other only slightly, whereas structural imbalance characterizes those in the first group. One or two sectional indexes have high values, and the values of one or two other sectional indexes are low or at zero. The Index of Power Resources values are low for nearly all countries of the first group because a low value for any sectional index is sufficient to drop the IPR to near zero. On the other hand, the Index of Power Resources values in the second group range from very high to very low. There is a corresponding difference in political systems between the groups of countries. Because of their low IPR values, 19 of the 21 countries in the first group are nondemocracies. Singapore and Venezuela, for which the Index of Power Resources values are relatively high, are democracies. On the other hand, 12 of the 21 countries in the second group were democracies and nine nondemocracies in 1988, because the Index of Power Resources values vary greatly in this group. In fact, IPR provided a satisfactory explanation for the variation in the Index of Democratization in both groups in 1988.

The problem remains that the Index of Power Resources values for 1980 explained the lack of democracy in Eastern Europe in the period 1980–8, but did not predict the democratization which took place from 1989–90. How should this problem be solved? It was assumed above that, because of structural imbalance, political systems are more insecure in countries with high Index of Structural Imbalance (ISI) values than in countries with low ISI values. Let us restrict our attention to the group of 14 countries for which ISI values were higher than 22.0 in 1980 (Bahrain, Bhutan, Bulgaria, Cuba, Czechoslovakia, the German Democratic Republic, Hungary, North Korea, Kuwait, Qatar, Romania, Singapore, the USSR and the United Arab Emirates). Singapore was the only democracy among these countries. Its high Index of Structural Imbalance value was principally due to its extremely high Index of Occupational Diversification value (99.0). Because the other 13 countries were nondemocracies in the period 1980–8, it would have been reasonable to expect political convulsions due to structural imbalance to lead to democratization, at least in some cases, depending on which structural characteristics dominate in each country. Let us see what has actually happened in this group of 13 countries since 1988.

Democratization has taken place, or at least started, in all East European countries of this group (Bulgaria, Czechoslovakia, the GDR, Hungary, Romania and the former USSR), whereas the seven other countries have remained nondemocracies. Are there any structural differences between these two subgroups that might explain differences in political developments? The Index of the Distribution of Economic Power Resources (DER) values were low for all these countries, except Bhutan (67.9). They were extremely low (from 0 to 4.2) for the subgroup of socialist countries, including Cuba and North Korea, whereas they were slightly higher for the other four countries (from 10.1 to 15.5). More significant differences occurred in the Index of Knowledge Distribution (IKD) values. This value ranged from 57.5 (Romania) to 73.5 (GDR) in the subgroup of eight socialist countries, but from 31.0 to 45.0 in the subgroup of the four Middle East oil states; it was only 11.5 for Bhutan. It may be that the increase in intellectual resources through education and the distribution of such resources among wide sectors of the population was the most crucial structural change undermining the social basis of autocratic socialist systems, gradually replacing the concentration of economic power resources as the dominant structural factor. From this perspective, it is remarkable that intellectuals provided the leadership and the core of opposition in all East European countries. Education seems to be an extremely powerful causal factor in democratization. In fact, after democratization in Eastern Europe, practically every country in the world for which Index of Knowledge Distribution is 50.0 or higher is a democracy. Cuba and North Korea are the most conspicuous deviations from this rule, but because their social structures seem to be similar to those in Eastern Europe we can expect democratization in these two countries, too. The same prediction applies, although to a lesser degree, to Bahrain, Kuwait, Qatar and the United Arab Emirates, for which the ISI values are high. In these four oil states, the concentration of political power is principally based on the concentration of the most important economic power resources, as it was in Eastern Europe, but the rising standard of education challenges old power structures. Bhutan is a different case. In Bhutan the distribution of economic resources (DER) seems to be the only structural factor conducive to democratization. The Index of Occupational Diversification (IOD) and Index of Knowledge Distribution (IKD) values are still very low. Because it is much more difficult to improve the standard of education than to change the structure of the economic system, prospects of democratization are still poor in Bhutan. However, we should note that in Bhutan the pattern of explanatory variables is the same as in India and that when democratic institutions were established in India its IOD and IKD values were not much higher than they are now in Bhutan.

We can conclude that low Index of Power Resources values do not always indicate the concentration of power resources and a low potentiality for democratization equally reliably, because they may conceal structural factors conducive to democracy. The Index of Structural Imbalance (ISI) discloses the existence of potentiality for democratization, and, therefore, high ISI values can be interpreted as indicating that some structural factors are highly favourable for democratization whereas some others are highly unfavourable. Consequently, we should take high ISI values into account in predicting the prospects of democratization on the basis of Index of Power Resources (IPR). If the Index of Structural Imbalance values had been used in addition to IPR in the predictions of democratization (see Vanhanen 1984 and 1990), those for Eastern Europe might have been more accurate. It would have been possible to argue that although the concentration of power resources (low IPR values) of those countries predicted that hegemonic systems would continue, their extremely high structural imbalance values (ISI) indicated a potentiality for democratic change. It would, of course, have been necessary to make the same predictions for the other nondemocracies with the highest ISI values, too.

PREDICTIONS BASED ON IPR–ISI

The values for ISI can be used separately from IPR values, but IPR and ISI can also be combined to form a new Index of Power Resources and

Structural Imbalances (IPR–ISI). There are several ways of combining them, depending on how the significance of ISI values is weighted. They were combined by adding a quarter of the value of the Index of Structural Imbalance to the value of the Index of Power Resources. Thus the new IPR–ISI = IPR + 1/4 of ISI. The values of this variable for 147 countries are given in Appendix 3.2.

The correlation between IPR–ISI and ID-88 (Index of Democratization in 1988) is 0.826, which means that the explained part of the variation is 68 per cent, slightly less than in the case of the Index of Power Resources. Figure 3.2 illustrates the results of regression analysis in which ID-88 is used as the dependent variable and IPR–ISI as the independent variable. The regression line for ID on IPR–ISI crosses the ID level of 5.0 index points approximately at the IPR–ISI level of 7.0 index points. It means that democratization has usually taken place when a country's IPR–ISI value has risen clearly above the IPR–ISI level of 7.0 index points. In other words, when power resources are distributed widely enough (IPR–ISI 7.0 or higher), political systems tend to democratize. We could define the transition level of IPR–ISI as extending from 5.0 to 9.0 index points. Consequently, the countries with IPR–ISI higher than 9.0 should be democracies and those with IPR-ISI below 5.0 should be nondemocracies. Democratization is expected to take place when a country reaches the Index of Power Resources and Structural Imbalance level from 5.0 to 9.0 index points.

The results of regression analysis for nine East European countries are given in Table 3.3. It shows that residuals (the distance between the regression line and the actual value of the Index of Democratization) were negative for all East European countries in 1988 and very negative for Poland and Yugoslavia. Because of its low Index of Power Resources and Structural Imbalance (IPR–ISI) value, Albania was still expected to remain a nondemocracy. The IPR–ISI values of Bulgaria, Czechoslovakia, Hungary, Romania and the USSR were at the transition level of IPR–ISI. In other words, democracy had become possible but was not yet inevitable. The German Democratic Republic, Poland and Yugoslavia were expected to be democracies because their IPR–ISI values were higher than 9.0 (power resources were distributed widely). This means that it would have been possible to predict democratization in these three countries and the feasibility of democratization in five other East European countries on the basis of their IPR–ISI values in 1980.

In addition to the three East European countries, IPR–ISI values were higher than 9.0 for several other nondemocracies in 1988. This group of deviating nondemocracies included Bahrain (10.8), Chile

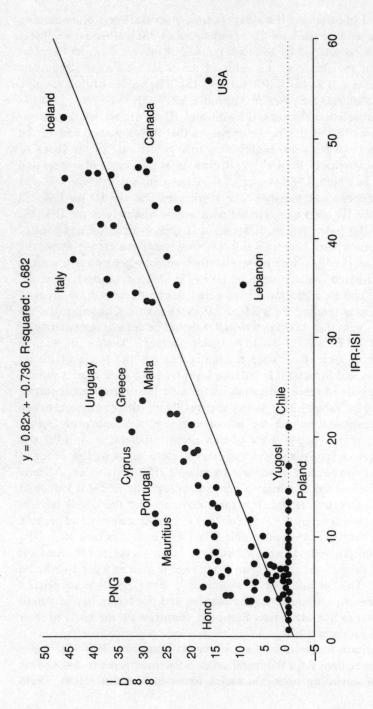

Figure 3.2 The results of regression analysis in which Index of Democratization (ID-1988) is used as the dependent variable and Index of Power Resources and Index of Structural Imbalance (IPR-ISI) as the independent variable in the comparison group of 147 states

Note: PNG = Papua New Guinea.

y = 0.82x + -0.736 R-squared: 0.682

Table 3.3 The results of regression analysis, in which the Index of Democratization (ID-88) is used as the dependent variable and the Index of Power Resources and Structural Imbalance (IPR–ISI) as the independent variable in the comparison group of 147 countries, for nine East European countries in 1988

Country	ID-1988	IPR-ISI	Residual	Predicted ID-88
1 Albania	0	4.4	−2.9	2.9
2 Bulgaria	0	6.9	−4.9	4.9
3 Czechoslovakia	0	7.9	−5.7	5.7
4 German Dem. Rep.	0.1	9.9	−7.3	7.4
5 Hungary	0	7.5	−5.4	5.4
6 Poland	0	14.6	−11.2	11.2
7 Romania	1.6	6.8	−3.2	4.8
8 USSR	0.1	7.9	−5.6	5.7
9 Yugoslavia	0	17.3	−13.4	13.4

(21.1), Fiji (9.3), Iraq (9.5), Jordan (12.8), Kuwait (11.4), Panama (13.6) and Qatar (10.2). Cuba (8.9), Iran (8.4) and the United Arab Emirates (8.9) were quite near this group of highly deviating nondemocracies. These countries will test the explanatory power of IPR–ISI (Index of Power Resources and Structural Imbalance) in the future.

It is reasonable to argue that democratization in Eastern Europe was not merely due to unique historical events and external power resources but also to some particular structural factors, which may have the same significance everywhere. And it would have been possible to predict the existence of a high probability of democratization in Eastern Europe by using, in addition to Index of Power Resources, the new indexes of power resources described here. IPR–ISI may provide a slightly better basis for predicting the prospects of democratization than IPR because it differentiates between countries in which all structural factors are unfavourable for democratization and those in which some structural factors are conducive to democratization. From this perspective, it is interesting to see what happens in the other nondemocracies for which the prospects of democratization, according to this variable, are roughly as good as they were for East European countries in 1980.

PREDICTIONS WITH NEURAL NETWORKS

Tatu Vanhanen's studies have used conventional regression techniques to analyse the socio-economic data with respect to democratization. Recently, new methods of analysis based on 'artificial intelligence' techniques, using neural networks and the ID3 algorithm, have become available, and it has been shown (Garson 1991; Schrodt 1991) that they can often perform better than the standard procedures. Neural networks are designed to learn analogously to the way in which the human brain is thought to learn and thus help to capture the full complexity of the data. They involve the simulation of a network of interconnected 'neurons' or 'nodes' which, when presented with data from outside the network or from other 'neurons', interact, thereby processing that information and producing an output.

Both the new methods are well-suited to the kind of classification problem studied here in which the key question is: given a set of socio-economic data for a country, what level of democracy would we predict for that country? Neural networks,[1] in particular, are very good at giving accurate classifications even with considerable levels of 'noise' in the model. This study mainly relies on the neural network approach, in which data on a given sub-set of the 147 countries is used to train a network in order to make predictions about the remaining countries, though the ability of the ID3 algorithm to pick out salient variables for a classification was used in the early stages.[2] The advantages of the neural network approach may be summarized as follows:

- neural networks are particularly appropriate for problems, such as this one, requiring the recognition of patterns in the data;
- they do not make assumptions about the nature of the data (e.g. interval-level representation, or linear relationships);
- they tend to perform better than standard methods;
- they can cope with missing data;
- eccentric individual input values cannot dominate the analysis.

The neural network method was used to explore Vanhanen's two basic approaches based on the Index of Power Resources (IPR) and the Index of Power Resources and Structural Imbalance (IPR–ISI) respectively. This was done for each approach by dividing the country data into two sets, one (the training set) in which the classification of countries is fixed on the basis of either IPR or IPR–ISI, and the other (the prediction set) for which classifications are unknown. That is, in the first set the countries were grouped into categories according to their level of, say, IPR, and a network was then trained to recognize the patterns of socio-economic variables that are associated with cases in each category of IPR. In other words, the network is in effect told that each country in the training set has a particular potential for democracy (as indicated by the IPR value) and that with this goes a particular pattern of socio-economic variables. The resulting network is then presented with the second set of countries (the prediction set) for which it is expected to predict the category of Index of Power Resources, and thus the potential level of democracy, on the basis of the known socio-economic variables. In principle, it is best to use those cases for training purposes that are regarded as typical of each category; ambiguous and uncertain cases are best either excluded or placed in the second, prediction, set.[3]

The first training set which was constructed consisted of 95 of Vanhanen's 147 countries divided into three levels of democracy according to their IPR value (see Appendix 3.3, pp. 90–2). This produced the predictions for the potential level of democracy in the 45 country prediction set shown in Appendix 3.3. The predictions for nine Eastern European countries in this set are also shown in Table 3.4. The number in each cell of the table may be interpreted as representing how confident the network is that the given case falls in a particular category (with 0 indicating that the case does not fall within a category and 1 indicating that it does).

Table 3.4 The predictions of the neural network for the nine East European countries, trained on 95 countries classified into three categories according to potential for democracy as reflected by their Index of Power Resources (IPR) value

Country	Non-democracy	Transitional	Democracy
Albania	**0.91**	0.10	0.09
Bulgaria	0.12	0.07	**0.92**
Czechoslovakia	0.26	0.03	**0.91**
GDR	0.26	0.03	**0.91**
Hungary	0.10	**0.90**	0.11
Poland	0.10	0.10	**0.90**
Romania	0.10	**0.78**	0.22
USSR	0.26	0.03	**0.91**
Yugoslavia	0.10	0.11	**0.89**

Note: Values of 0.5 or above, which conventionally represent a firm classification, are indicated in bold type.

The results in Table 3.4 seem highly unlikely, predicting democracy for six of the nine countries with only Albania being a nondemocracy. This raises the question of how we should evaluate the results of a neural network. Clearly, we cannot pick and choose the predictions that suit our hypotheses. The set of predictions must be perceived as reasonable and consistent as a whole, and no country should be classified as a nondemocracy that has actually sustained some sort of democracy. While it would be reasonable to accept a classification above the actual level, on the ground that this represents the country's potential (indeed we are investigating whether the socio-economic conditions of the early 1980s can predict levels higher than those actually obtaining at that time), we should also be cautious about

accepting too many such classifications and about implausible predictions (e.g. Albania classified as a democracy). Examination of Table
3.4 and of the complete set of predictions in Appendix 3.3 in the light
of these considerations suggests that the results of this neural network
are not acceptable.

One possible reason for the unsatisfactory nature of the network is
that the three categories devised by Vanhanen are too heterogeneous.
Kimber (1989) has argued that democracy is not a particular state of
existence, but rather a set of principles that are embodied in a regime
to a greater or lesser extent. Given this view that democracy is a matter
of degree, it would make sense at least to refine the categories splitting
the transitional group into two: those whose conditions cannot quite
sustain the highest levels of democracy, and those where a level of
democracy can be sustained somewhat above the very lowest levels.
This enables us also to have two more homogeneous extreme categories.

Using this approach, the process was repeated with IPR values of
0–2.4 (minimal), 2.5–9.9 (intermediate low), 10.0–19.9 (intermediate
high), and 20.0+ (high). The full results may be seen in Appendix 3.4
(see pp. 92–3), while those for the East European countries are also
given in Table 3.5.

The network provides much more plausible predictions, though for
Bulgaria and the USSR, there is no overall classification. This can be
interpreted as a recognition by the network that they are complex cases
which to a degree possess the attributes of more than one category. This
allocation of non-trivial values to several categories may perhaps
represent a potential for regime instability, with social forces pulling
in different directions. This network would seem to suggest that
Romania offers the least prospects of a move to stable levels of
democracy above minimal, with Bulgaria and the USSR (while not
being obviously minimal) as also potentially unstable. The interpretation of the remaining six countries is fairly straightforward, though
Poland is possibly the least stable of those with higher levels of
democracy. Whether we accept these results depends on our view of the
entire set of predictions (see Appendix 3.4). It will be seen that Gambia,
which is a perennial anomaly in the Vanhanen analysis, is also predicted
by this network to have a minimal level of democracy.[4]

Vanhanen has suggested that Index of Power Resources and Structural Imbalance (IPR–ISI) may provide a better basis for predicting
democratization than IPR. In order to test whether a neural network
approach gives support for this view, a further network was constructed
using the four category approach: 0–6.0 (minimal), 6.1–13.9 (intermediate low), 14.0–24.9 (intermediate high), and 25.0+ (high). The

Table 3.5 The predictions of the neural network for the nine East European countries, trained on 93 countries classified into four categories according to their potential level of democracy as reflected by their Index of Power Resources (IPR) value

Country	Minimal	Intermed. low	Intermed. high	High
Albania	0.14	**0.87**	0.09	0.11
Bulgaria	0.14	0.39	0.33	0.23
Czechoslovakia	0.18	0.15	0.07	**0.81**
GDR	0.18	0.15	0.07	**0.81**
Hungary	0.11	**0.90**	0.09	0.10
Poland	0.09	**0.79**	0.05	0.31
Romania	0.30	**0.50**	0.18	0.12
USSR	0.14	0.39	0.33	0.23
Yugoslavia	0.10	0.10	**0.89**	0.11

Note: Values of 0.5 or above, which conventionally represent a firm classification, are indicated in bold type.

Table 3.6 The predictions of the neural network for the nine East European countries, trained on 93 countries classified into four categories representing their potential for democracy as reflected by their Index of Power Resources and Structural Imbalance (IPR–ISI) value

Country	Minimal	Intermed. low	Intermed. high	High
Albania	**0.96**	0.05	0.10	0.10
Bulgaria	0.10	0.09	**0.92**	0.09
Czechoslovakia	0.11	0.13	**0.84**	0.13
GDR	0.11	0.13	**0.84**	0.13
Hungary	0.10	0.19	**0.82**	0.09
Poland	0.09	**0.90**	10.11	0.11
Romania	0.11	**0.90**	0.10	0.10
USSR	0.10	0.09	**0.92**	0.09
Yugoslavia	0.10	**0.89**	0.11	0.10

Note: Values of 0.5 or above, which conventionally represent a firm classification, are indicated in bold type.

complete results for this are shown in Appendix 3.5 (see pp. 94–5), with those for Eastern Europe in Table 3.6.

This network provides less ambiguous predictions than that based on the Index of Power Resources alone, in the sense that countries are more definitely allocated to particular categories. However, the predictions are on balance less plausible. For one thing, there are still a number of anomalies among the other countries in the prediction set (see Appendix 3.5), and the implied ranking of levels of democracy among the East European countries looks somewhat odd.

Overall, what this neural network analysis seems to suggest is that according to the socio-economic data a more than minimal level of democracy can probably be supported in most of the countries of Eastern Europe but that, in terms of more specific predictions, IPR appears to provide a better basis for predicting the potential for democracy in Eastern European countries than does IPR–ISI.

CONCLUSIONS

The results of the alternative analyses presented in this chapter indicate that it would have been possible to make more correct predictions on the chances of democratization in Eastern Europe than what Vanhanen predicted on the basis of the Index of Power Resources if the same data had been combined in a different way (IPR-2 or IPR–ISI) or if a different method of analysis (Kimber's neural network analysis) had been used. Both Kimber's new method of analysis and Vanhanen's alternative IPR-2 (the arithmetic mean of the three sectional indexes) and IPR–ISI produced significantly more correct predictions for East European countries than IPR index values.

The unexpected democratization in Eastern Europe challenged us to reconsider the composition of explanatory variables and to experiment with new methods of analysis. The value of these new findings will be tested in the future by other countries which are still nondemocracies, but for which democratization or the potential for democracy is predicted on the basis of Kimber's new method of analysis or on the basis of Vanhanen's new ways to combine explanatory variables.

Let us briefly summarize the major differences in predictions produced by different methods of analysis. According to Vanhanen's original predictions based on Index of Power Resources (IPR) values in 1980, only Poland and Yugoslavia were expected to democratize, and the seven other countries were expected to remain nondemocracies because of their low Index of Power Resources values. Vanhanen's alternative IPR-2 (the arithmetic mean of the three sectional indexes) predicted democratization for seven East European countries. Only Albania was expected to remain a nondemocracy. Romania was at the transitional level of IPR-2. According to Vanhanen's IPR–ISI, democratization was highly probable in the GDR, Poland, and Yugoslavia, and it had become possible although not yet sure in Bulgaria, Czechoslovakia, Hungary, Romania and the USSR. Only Albania was predicted to remain a nondemocracy. In two of Kimber's analyses, Albania's potential for democracy was minimal and in one case intermediate. The chances of democracy were predicted to be higher than 'minimal' for all other East European countries.

The results of our analyses seem to support the idea that it is possible to make rough predictions of the chances of democracy in particular countries on the basis of socio-economic data, provided that there is a theory which explains why particular socio-economic variables should be related to the degree of democracy. The approximate nature of these predictions represents an indication of the extent to which the socio-economic conditions of the early 1980s could be said to be inimical to democratization and to the extent to which democratization, had it been initiated at that time, could have been expected to be successful.

Significant regime change, of course, requires political leadership. This political activity, however, takes place against a backdrop of socio-economic conditions which limit what is possible and, along with other factors such as the remnants of the political culture of the old regime, influence the long-term stability of the new arrangements. What we hope to have shown here is that, even from the perspective of the early 1980s, the potentiality for democracy can be detected.

APPENDIX 3.1

The operationalization of dependent and independent variables
Two basic political variables, (1) the smaller parties' share of the votes cast in parliamentary and/or presidential elections and (2) the percentage of the total population which actually voted in the same elections, have been used to measure two dimensions of democratization (cf. Dahl 1971), the degree of electoral competition and the degree of electoral participation. The two variables (Competition and Participation) are combined into an Index of Democratization (ID) by multiplying them and dividing the outcome by 100.

Competition and the Index of Democratization (ID) are highly correlated with the arithmetic means of R. D. Gastil's (1988) ratings of political rights and civil liberties. The correlations ranged from −0.811 to −0.902 in the period 1980–7 (see Vanhanen 1991b). Competition and ID were also highly correlated (−0.895 and −0.820) with M. Coppedge and W. Reinicke's (1988) scale of polyarchy in the same group of 147 countries in 1985 (see Vanhanen 1991b). These correlations indicate that different ways of measuring democracy and democratization may lead to more or less similar results.

The same political variables are also used to determine the minimum threshold of democracy, although the selection of threshold values is inevitably arbitrary. In Vanhanen's 1984 study 30 per cent for Competition, 10 per cent for Participation and 5.0 index points for ID were used as threshold values of democracy. The countries above all these threshold values were regarded as Democracies, and the countries below any of them as Non-democracies (see Vanhanen 1984). In a new comparative study (Vanhanen 1990: 32–3) the threshold values of democracy are 30 per cent for Competition, 15 per cent for Participation and 5.0 index points for ID.

Five social variables were used to indicate the distribution of economic and intellectual power resources in Vanhanen's previous comparative study (see Vanhanen 1984). They are: (1) the percentage of urban population (UP), (2) the percentage of nonagricultural population (NAP), (3) the number of students in universities and equivalent degree-granting institutions per 100,000 inhabitants (Students), (4) the percentage of the literate population (Literates), and (5) the percentage share of family farms of the total area of holdings (FF). All five variables are assumed to measure, directly or indirectly, the relative distribution of economic, intellectual and organizational power resources. The first two measure more or less the same phenomenon: occupational diversification of the population. Therefore they were combined into an Index of Occupational Diversification (IOD) by calculating their arithmetic mean. Students and Literates were combined into an Index of Knowledge Distribution (IKD) by calculating their arithmetic mean. For this operation the values of Students were first converted to percentages by taking 1,000 students per 100,000 inhabitants as 100 per cent. Family Farms represent a third dimension of resource distribution. These three variables were combined into an Index of Power Resources (IPR) by multiplying them and dividing the outcome by 10,000. It was assumed that all three dimensions represent crucial power resources and that it may be necessary for a country to reach some minimum level of each variable in order to create favourable preconditions for democracy.

In a later study (Vanhanen 1990: 51–67) a new explanatory variable – (6) the degree of decentralization of nonagricultural economic resources (DDN) – is used to measure the relative distribution of nonagricultural economic power resources. FF and DDN are combined into an Index of the Distribution of Economic Power Resources (DER). This is done by multiplying the value of FF by the percentage of agricultural population and the value of DDN by the percentage of nonagricultural population. After that, the weighted values of FF and DDN are simply added together. The three sectional indexes – IOD, IKD, and DER – are combined into IPR by multiplying them and dividing the outcome by 10,000. It should also be noted that in this new study the values for Students were converted to percentages by taking 5,000 students per 100,000 inhabitants to represent 100 per cent.

APPENDIX 3.2

The values of Index of Democratization (ID-88)), Index of Occupational Diversification (IOD), Index of Knowledge Distribution (IKD), Index of the Distribution of Economic Power Resources (DER), Index of Power Resources (IPR), the arithmetic mean of the three sectional indexes (IPR-2), Index of Structural Imbalance (ISI), and Index of Power Resources and Structural Imbalance (IPR–ISI) for 147 states in 1980

State	ID-88	IOD	IKD	DER	IPR	IPR-2	ISI	IPR-ISI
1 Afghanistan	0	18.5	11.0	45.6	0.9	25.0	13.7	4.3
2 Albania	0	38.5	40.5	0	0	26.3	17.6	4.4
3 Algeria	3.3	47.0	26.5	30.0	3.7	34.5	8.3	5.8
4 Angola	0	31.5	15.5	29.1	1.4	25.4	6.6	3.0
5 Argentina	24.1	84.5	65.0	32.3	17.7	60.7	18.8	22.4
6 Australia	30.9	91.5	71.5	68.9	45.1	77.3	8.6	47.2
7 Austria	36.5	72.5	67.5	69.3	33.9	69.8	1.8	34.3
8 Bahamas	19.3	73.5	52.0	40.7	15.6	55.4	12.1	18.6
9 Bahrain	0	87.5	45.0	10.7	4.2	47.7	26.5	10.8
10 Bangladesh	4.2	13.5	17.5	59.5	1.4	30.2	19.6	6.3
11 Barbados	21.5	63.0	64.5	35.8	14.5	54.4	12.6	17.6
12 Belgium	44.7	84.5	70.5	70.3	41.9	75.1	5.1	43.2
13 Benin	0	34.0	15.5	29.3	1.5	26.3	7.2	3.3
14 Bhutan	0	5.5	11.5	67.9	0.4	28.3	26.4	7.0
15 Bolivia	14.2	41.5	48.5	30.5	6.1	42.2	6.2	7.6
16 Botswana	6.9	18.0	31.0	45.6	2.5	31.5	9.4	4.8
17 Brazil	7.8	65.0	49.5	26.2	8.4	46.9	13.8	11.8
18 Bulgaria	0	65.5	59.0	0	0	41.5	27.7	6.9
19 Burkina Faso	0	14.5	6.0	50.5	0.4	23.7	17.9	4.9
20 Burma	0	37.5	35.0	36.6	4.8	36.4	0.9	5.0
21 Burundi	0	9.0	43.5	51.5	2.0	34.7	17.1	6.3
22 Cameroon	0.4	27.0	25.5	36.7	2.5	29.7	4.6	3.6
23 Canada	28.8	87.5	86.5	59.5	45.0	77.8	12.2	48.0
24 Cape Verde	1.6	32.0	23.0	37.4	2.8	30.8	5.2	4.1
25 Central A. R.	2.1	27.0	17.5	53.5	2.5	32.7	13.9	6.0
26 Chad	0	8.5	24.0	52.0	1.1	28.2	15.9	5.1
27 Chile	0	81.0	59.0	36.4	17.4	58.8	14.9	21.1
28 China	0	26.5	33.5	1.4	0.1	20.5	12.7	3.3
29 Colombia	10.2	71.5	53.0	28.6	10.8	51.0	15.0	14.5
30 Comoros	0.3	23.5	30.0	20.9	1.5	24.8	3.5	2.4
31 Congo	0	55.5	30.0	33.6	5.6	39.7	10.5	8.2
32 Costa Rica	21.2	54.0	70.5	43.7	16.6	56.1	9.6	19.0
33 Cuba	0	71.0	63.5	4.2	1.9	46.2	28.0	8.9
34 Cyprus	31.9	54.0	47.5	71.7	18.4	57.7	9.3	20.7
35 Czechoslovakia	0	76.5	62.5	0.5	0.2	46.5	30.7	7.9
36 Denmark	45.7	88.5	70.0	71.0	44.0	76.5	8.0	46.0
37 Djibuti	0	50.0	10.0	40.0	2.0	33.3	15.6	5.9
38 Dom. Rep.	18.7	47.5	45.5	31.8	6.9	41.6	6.5	8.5

State	ID-88	IOD	IKD	DER	IPR	IPR-2	ISI	IPR-ISI
39 Ecuador	18.3	50.0	72.5	32.2	11.7	51.6	14.0	15.2
40 Egypt	0.7	47.5	38.0	30.0	5.4	38.5	6.0	6.9
41 El Salvador	13.6	45.5	37.5	27.5	4.7	36.8	6.2	6.2
42 Eq. Guinea	1.6	38.0	18.5	23.7	1.7	26.7	7.5	3.6
43 Ethiopia	0	17.5	15.5	12.4	0.3	15.1	1.8	0.7
44 Fiji	0	51.0	44.0	35.2	7.9	43.4	5.5	9.3
45 Finland	38.6	74.5	76.0	73.2	41.4	74.6	1.0	41.6
46 France	27.6	84.5	69.5	71.2	41.8	75.1	6.3	43.4
47 Gabon	0	30.0	27.5	44.3	3.7	34.0	6.9	5.4
48 Gambia	12.7	20.0	10.5	45.0	0.9	25.2	13.2	4.2
49 GDR	0.1	83.5	73.5	2.3	1.4	53.1	33.9	9.9
50 Germany, W.	39.1	90.5	69.5	70.4	44.3	76.8	9.1	46.6
51 Ghana	0	42.5	24.0	48.9	5.0	38.5	9.6	7.4
52 Greece	34.7	62.5	58.5	59.2	21.6	60.1	1.6	21.9
53 Guatemala	6.6	42.0	32.5	28.2	3.8	40.9	7.4	5.6
54 Guinea	0	19.5	16.0	42.6	1.3	26.0	11.0	4.0
55 Guinea-Bissau	0	21.5	10.0	44.4	1.0	25.3	12.7	4.2
56 Guyana	7.6	58.0	50.0	17.4	5.0	41.8	16.3	9.1
57 Haiti	0	30.5	16.0	48.1	2.3	31.5	11.0	5.0
58 Honduras	17.3	36.5	37.0	36.3	4.9	36.6	0.3	5.0
59 Hungary	0	69.0	59.0	1.2	0.5	43.1	27.9	7.5
60 Iceland	46.2	88.0	73.0	79.3	50.9	80.1	5.3	52.2
61 India	16.2	29.5	26.0	58.2	4.5	37.9	13.5	7.9
62 Indonesia	0.8	30.5	37.0	37.7	4.3	35.1	3.0	5.0
63 Iran	4.6	55.5	25.0	41.6	5.8	40.7	10.5	8.4
64 Iraq	0	66.0	31.5	26.0	5.4	41.2	16.6	9.5
65 Ireland	28.0	65.8	65.0	73.4	32.7	67.8	3.5	33.6
66 Israel	35.8	91.0	72.5	58.6	38.7	74.0	11.3	41.5
67 Italy	44.1	79.0	68.0	68.3	36.7	71.8	4.8	37.9
68 Ivory Coast	0	30.5	20.0	48.4	3.0	33.0	10.3	5.6
69 Jamaica	14.6	60.0	54.5	31.0	10.1	48.5	11.7	13.0
70 Japan	25.1	83.5	70.0	62.1	36.3	71.9	7.8	38.2
71 Jordan	0	65.0	45.0	34.2	10.0	48.1	11.3	12.8
72 Kampuchea	0	21.0	24.0	7.4	0.4	17.5	10.2	2.9
73 Kenya	0	18.0	24.5	48.1	2.1	30.2	11.9	5.1
74 Korea, North	0	57.0	65.5	0	0	40.8	27.2	6.8
75 Korea, South	22.9	58.0	62.5	60.7	22.0	60.4	1.6	22.4
76 Kuwait	0	93.0	44.0	10.1	4.1	49.0	29.3	11.4
77 Laos	0	20.0	22.5	27.2	1.2	23.2	2.6	1.8
78 Lebanon	9.5	83.0	68.0	58.8	33.2	69.9	8.7	35.4
79 Lesotho	0	14.0	36.5	52.0	2.7	34.2	13.4	6.0
80 Liberia	7.7	31.5	17.0	36.1	1.9	28.2	7.5	3.8
81 Libya	0	68.0	34.5	14.8	3.5	39.1	19.3	8.3
82 Luxemburg	31.5	87.5	52.0	69.7	31.7	69.7	11.8	34.6
83 Madagascar	8.5	18.5	27.5	49.9	2.5	32.0	12.0	5.5
84 Malawi	0	13.0	18.0	37.7	0.9	22.9	9.9	3.4
85 Malaysia	12.3	40.5	38.0	41.0	6.3	39.8	1.1	6.6

	State	ID-88	IOD	IKD	DER	IPR	IPR-2	ISI	IPR-ISI
86	Mali	0	16.5	7.0	53.5	0.1	25.7	18.6	4.7
87	Malta	30.0	77.5	44.5	60.7	20.9	60.9	11.1	23.7
88	Mauritania	0	20.0	9.0	51.5	0.9	26.8	16.4	5.0
89	Mauritius	27.3	57.5	40.5	41.7	9.7	46.6	7.3	11.5
90	Mexico	14.8	65.5	54.5	34.0	12.1	51.3	11.6	15.0
91	Mongolia	0	51.0	47.0	0	0	32.7	21.8	5.4
92	Morocco	1.0	45.0	20.5	37.1	3.4	34.2	9.1	5.7
93	Mozambique	0	22.5	13.0	31.1	0.9	22.2	6.1	2.4
94	Nepal	0	6.0	14.0	58.1	0.5	26.0	21.4	5.8
95	Netherlands	41.0	85.5	75.0	70.7	45.3	77.1	5.6	46.7
96	New Zealand	29.3	88.0	73.5	69.5	45.0	77.0	7.3	46.8
97	Nicaragua	14.8	55.0	50.0	17.0	4.7	40.7	15.8	8.6
98	Niger	0	12.5	5.5	52.9	0.4	23.6	19.5	5.3
99	Nigeria	0	33.5	19.0	41.2	2.6	31.2	8.2	4.6
100	Norway	37.1	72.5	69.0	71.6	35.8	71.0	1.4	36.1
101	Oman	0	22.5	10.5	34.8	0.8	22.6	8.1	2.8
102	Pakistan	12.2	37.5	15.0	33.7	1.9	28.7	9.2	4.2
103	Panama	0	59.5	64.0	24.9	9.5	49.5	16.4	13.6
104	Papua N.G.	32.8	18.0	21.5	53.0	2.1	30.8	14.8	5.8
105	Paraguay	3.5	45.0	51.0	16.1	3.7	37.4	14.2	7.2
106	Peru	15.3	65.0	57.5	25.6	9.6	49.4	15.8	13.5
107	Philippines	17.0	45.0	69.0	42.9	13.3	52.3	11.1	16.1
108	Poland	0	63.5	65.5	24.2	10.1	51.1	17.9	14.6
109	Portugal	27.1	52.5	51.5	41.0	11.1	48.3	4.9	12.3
110	Qatar	0	79.0	35.5	15.5	4.3	43.5	23.8	10.2
111	Romania	1.6	51.5	57.5	4.2	1.2	37.7	22.4	6.8
112	Rwanda	0	7.0	25.0	60.2	1.1	30.7	19.6	6.0
113	Saudi Arabia	0	53.5	19.0	29.2	0.3	33.9	13.1	3.4
114	Senegal	4.4	25.5	15.0	41.1	1.6	27.2	9.3	3.9
115	Sierra Leone	0.1	28.5	13.0	49.5	1.8	30.3	12.8	5.0
116	Singapore	19.9	99.0	51.0	29.5	14.9	59.8	26.1	21.4
117	Solomon Is.	15.7	12.0	28.0	57.3	1.9	32.4	18.6	6.5
118	Somalia	0	25.0	3.5	50.0	0.4	26.2	15.9	4.4
119	South Africa	2.8	60.5	30.0	17.1	3.1	35.9	16.4	7.2
120	Spain	28.9	78.5	65.0	63.4	32.3	69.0	6.4	33.9
121	Sri Lanka	16.3	37.0	46.0	57.5	9.8	46.8	7.1	11.6
122	Sudan	11.7	24.0	11.5	44.6	1.2	26.7	11.9	4.2
123	Surinam	7.0	66.0	39.0	11.1	2.9	38.7	18.4	7.5
124	Swaziland	0	20.5	34.5	27.5	1.9	27.5	4.5	3.0
125	Sweden	36.4	91.0	74.0	65.3	44.0	76.8	9.5	46.4
126	Switzerland	22.9	76.5	63.0	71.2	34.3	70.2	4.8	35.5
127	Syria	0	51.0	42.0	29.6	6.3	40.9	7.5	8.2
128	Tanzania	1.0	15.5	33.5	38.6	2.0	29.2	9.1	4.3
129	Thailand	5.3	19.5	57.0	56.2	6.2	44.2	16.5	10.3
130	Togo	0	26.0	18.0	47.2	2.2	30.4	11.2	5.0
131	Trinidad & T.	15.1	52.5	53.0	31.3	8.7	45.6	9.5	11.1
132	Tunisia	0	55.5	28.5	31.5	5.0	38.5	11.3	7.8

State	ID-88	IOD	IKD	DER	IPR	IPR-2	ISI	IPR-ISI
133 Turkey	15.0	46.5	40.0	50.5	9.4	45.7	3.8	10.3
134 Uganda	0	14.0	26.5	52.4	1.9	31.0	14.3	5.5
135 USSR	0.1	73.0	69.5	0	0	47.5	31.7	7.9
136 UAE	0	78.5	31.0	10.2	2.5	39.9	25.7	8.9
137 UK	33.2	94.5	64.5	69.3	42.2	76.1	12.3	45.3
138 USA	16.7	87.5	99.5	60.0	52.2	82.3	14.9	55.9
139 Uruguay	38.2	86.0	59.5	40.4	20.7	62.0	16.0	24.7
140 Venezuela	18.7	82.5	62.5	26.4	13.6	57.1	20.5	18.7
141 Vietnam	0	24.0	44.0	5.0	0.5	24.3	13.1	3.8
142 Yemen, North	0	17.5	5.5	37.0	0.4	20.0	11.3	3.2
143 Yemen, South	0	39.0	22.0	10.0	0.9	23.7	10.2	3.4
144 Yugoslavia	0	52.5	64.0	46.6	15.7	54.4	6.4	17.3
145 Zaïre	0.4	30.0	28.5	41.1	3.5	33.2	5.3	4.8
146 Zambia	0.9	38.0	35.5	41.4	5.6	38.3	2.1	6.1
147 Zimbabwe	8.3	32.0	35.5	25.9	2.9	31.1	3.5	3.8

APPENDIX 3.3

Neural network predictions for 45 countries (socialist hegemonic group plus Vanhanen's anomalies), trained on a set of examples in which cases were classified into three categories representing their potential for democracy as reflected by their Index of Power Resources (IPR) value. The corresponding prediction using Vanhanen's method is given in the right-hand column

Country	Minimal	Intermediate	High	Vanhanen
Afghanistan	**0.91**	0.09	0.10	Minimal
Albania	**0.91**	0.10	0.09	Minimal
Angola	0.11	**0.89**	0.09	Minimal
Argentina	0.10	0.09	**0.91**	High
Benin	0.10	**0.92**	0.08	Minimal
Bulgaria	0.12	0.07	**0.92**	Minimal
Burkina Faso	**0.91**	0.09	0.10	Minimal
Chile	0.10	0.11	**0.89**	High
China	**0.90**	0.09	0.10	Minimal
Congo Republic	0.10	**0.91**	0.09	Intermed.
Cuba	0.12	0.07	**0.92**	Minimal
Czechoslovakia	0.26	0.03	**0.91**	Minimal
Ethiopia	**0.91**	0.09	0.10	Minimal
Gambia	**0.91**	0.09	0.10	Minimal
GDR	0.26	0.03	**0.91**	Minimal
Guinea	**0.89**	0.11	0.10	Minimal
Hungary	0.10	**0.90**	0.11	Intermed.
Iraq	0.10	**0.85**	0.15	Intermed.
Jamaica	0.10	0.11	**0.89**	High

Country	Minimal	Intermediate	High	Vanhanen
Jordan	0.10	**0.91**	0.08	High
Kampuchea	**0.90**	0.09	0.10	Minimal
Korea, North	0.10	**0.67**	0.33	Minimal
Korea, South	0.10	0.10	**0.90**	High
Laos	**0.89**	0.11	0.10	Minimal
Lebanon	0.10	**0.89**	0.11	High
Libya	0.10	**0.91**	0.09	Intermed.
Mexico	0.10	0.09	**0.91**	High
Mongolia	0.09	**0.90**	0.10	Intermed.
Mozambique	**0.91**	0.09	0.10	Minimal
Panama	0.10	0.10	**0.90**	High
Papua New Guinea	**0.89**	0.11	0.10	Minimal
Philippines	0.10	0.11	**0.89**	High
Poland	0.10	0.10	**0.90**	High
Romania	0.10	**0.78**	0.22	Minimal
Singapore	0.10	0.14	**0.86**	High
Solomon Islands	**0.91**	0.09	0.10	Minimal
Somalia	0.11	**0.89**	0.09	Minimal
Tanzania	**0.91**	0.09	0.10	Minimal
Turkey	0.10	**0.89**	0.11	High
Uganda	**0.89**	0.11	0.10	Minimal
USSR	0.26	0.03	**0.91**	Minimal
Uruguay	0.10	0.14	**0.86**	High
Vietnam	**0.90**	0.14	0.07	Minimal
Yemen PDR	**0.91**	0.08	0.10	Minimal
Yugoslavia	0.10	0.11	**0.89**	High

Original Training set (102)

Minimal (IPR 0–2.9)
Bangladesh, Bhutan, Burundi, Cape Verde Is., Chad, Comoros, Djibuti, Equatorial Guinea, Guinea-Bissau, Kenya, Liberia, Madagascar, Malawi, Mali, Mauritania, Nepal, Niger, Oman, Pakistan, Paraguay, Rwanda, Saudi Arabia, Senegal, Sierra Leone, Sudan, Swaziland, United Arab Emirates, Yemen Arab Republic.

Intermediate (IPR 3.0–9.3)
Algeria, Bahrain, Bolivia, Botswana, Brazil, Burma, Cameroon, Central African Republic, Dominican Republic, Egypt, El Salvador, Gabon, Ghana, Guatemala, Guyana, Haiti, Honduras, India, Indonesia, Iran, Ivory Coast, Kuwait, Lesotho, Malaysia, Morocco, Nicaragua, Nigeria, Qatar, South Africa, Sri Lanka, Surinam, Syria, Thailand, Togo, Tunisia, Zaïre, Zambia, Zimbabwe.

High (IPR 9.3+)
Australia, Austria, Bahamas, Barbados, Belgium, Canada, Colombia, Costa Rica, Cyprus, Denmark, Ecuador, Fiji, Finland, France, FR Germany, Greece, Iceland, Ireland, Israel, Italy, Japan, Luxemburg, Malta, Mauritius, Netherlands, New Zealand, Norway, Peru, Portugal, Spain, Sweden, Switzerland, Trinidad & Tobago, UK, USA, Venezuela.

Basic prediction set (45)

A. Socialist Hegemonic States
1 Eastern Europe
Albania, Bulgaria, Czechoslovakia, GDR, Hungary, Poland, Romania, USSR, Yugoslavia.
2 Other
Afghanistan, Angola, Benin, Burkina Faso, China, Congo Republic, Cuba, Ethiopia, Guinea, Iraq, Kampuchea, North Korea, Laos, Libya, Mongolia, Mozambique, Somalia, Tanzania, Yemen PDR, Vietnam.

B. Vanhanen anomalies
Argentina, Chile, Gambia, Jamaica, Jordan, South Korea, Lebanon, Mexico, Panama, Papua New Guinea, Philippines, Singapore, Solomon Islands, Turkey, Uganda, Uruguay.

APPENDIX 3.4

Neural network predictions for 45 countries (socialist hegemonic group plus Vanhanen's anomalies), trained on a set of examples in which cases were classified into four categories representing their potential for democracy as reflected by their IPR value. The corresponding prediction using Vanhanen's method is given in the right-hand column

Country	Minimal	Intermed. low	Intermed. high	High	Vanhanen
Afghanistan	**0.90**	0.10	0.10	0.10	Minimal
Albania	0.14	**0.87**	0.09	0.11	Minimal
Angola	0.11	**0.89**	0.10	0.10	Minimal
Argentina	0.09	0.10	0.10	**0.91**	Int.high
Benin	**0.90**	0.09	0.09	0.10	Minimal
Bulgaria	0.14	0.39	0.33	0.23	Minimal
Burkina Faso	**0.90**	0.10	0.10	0.10	Minimal
Chile	0.10	0.10	**0.89**	0.11	Int.high

Country	Minimal	Intermed. low	Intermed. high	High	Vanhanen
China	**0.92**	0.08	0.11	0.10	Minimal
Congo Republic	0.08	**0.92**	0.10	0.11	Int.low
Cuba	0.14	0.39	0.33	0.23	Minimal
Czechoslovakia	0.18	0.15	0.07	**0.81**	Minimal
Ethiopia	**0.90**	0.10	0.10	0.10	Minimal
Gambia	**0.89**	0.11	0.10	0.10	Minimal
GDR	0.18	0.15	0.07	**0.81**	Minimal
Guinea	**0.89**	0.11	0.10	0.10	Minimal
Hungary	0.11	**0.90**	0.09	0.10	Minimal
Iraq	0.10	**0.89**	0.11	0.10	Int.low
Jamaica	0.11	0.09	**0.91**	0.09	Int.high
Jordan	0.11	**0.81**	0.07	0.24	Int.high
Kampuchea	**0.83**	0.17	0.09	0.10	Minimal
Korea, North	0.35	0.35	0.11	0.26	Minimal
Korea, South	0.11	0.09	0.11	**0.89**	High
Laos	**0.90**	0.10	0.11	0.10	Minimal
Lebanon	0.11	**0.59**	0.05	**0.57**	High
Libya	0.11	**0.90**	0.09	0.11	Int.low
Mexico	0.10	0.10	**0.89**	0.11	Int.high
Mongolia	0.28	**0.59**	0.12	0.15	Minimal
Mozambique	**0.89**	0.11	0.10	0.10	Minimal
Panama	0.10	0.10	**0.89**	0.11	Int.low
Papua New G.	0.10	**0.91**	0.10	0.09	Minimal
Philippines	0.09	0.30	0.38	0.33	Int.high
Poland	0.09	**0.79**	0.05	0.31	Int.high
Romania	0.30	**0.50**	0.18	0.12	Minimal
Singapore	0.11	0.10	0.11	**0.90**	Int.high
Solomon Islands	0.10	**0.91**	0.10	0.09	Minimal
Somalia	**0.90**	0.11	0.10	0.10	Minimal
Tanzania	0.11	**0.89**	0.11	0.10	Minimal
Turkey	0.12	**0.89**	0.10	0.10	Int.low
Uganda	**0.89**	0.11	0.10	0.10	Minimal
USSR	0.14	0.39	0.33	0.23	Minimal
Uruguay	0.11	0.10	0.11	**0.90**	High
Vietnam	**0.90**	0.11	0.11	0.09	Minimal
Yemen PDR	0.11	**0.90**	0.09	0.11	Minimal
Yugoslavia	0.10	0.10	**0.89**	0.11	Int.high

APPENDIX 3.5

Neural network predictions for 45 countries (socialist hegemonic group plus Vanhanen's anomalies), trained on a set of examples in which cases were classified into four categories representing their potential for democracy as reflected by their Index of Power Resources and Structural Imbalance IPR–ISI value. The corresponding prediction using Vanhanen's method is given in the right-hand column

Country	Minimal	Intermed. low	Intermed. high	High	Vanhanen
Afghanistan	0.21	**0.79**	0.10	0.10	Minimal
Albania	**0.96**	0.05	0.10	0.10	Minimal
Angola	**0.90**	0.10	0.10	0.10	Minimal
Argentina	0.10	0.10	0.11	**0.90**	Int high
Benin	0.03	**0.97**	0.09	0.13	Minimal
Bulgaria	0.10	0.09	**0.92**	0.09	Int low
Burkina Faso	0.11	**0.90**	0.11	0.10	Minimal
Chile	0.10	0.10	**0.91**	0.09	Int high
China	**0.95**	0.06	0.10	0.10	Minimal
Congo Republic	**0.86**	0.18	0.08	0.10	Int low
Cuba	0.10	0.09	**0.92**	0.09	Int low
Czechoslovakia	0.11	0.13	**0.84**	0.13	Int low
Ethiopia	**0.91**	0.10	0.11	0.10	Minimal
Gambia	0.10	**0.91**	0.10	0.10	Minimal
GDR	0.11	0.13	**0.84**	0.13	Int low
Guinea	0.10	**0.91**	0.10	0.10	Minimal
Hungary	0.10	0.19	**0.82**	0.09	Int low
Iraq	0.09	**0.91**	0.11	0.10	Int low
Jamaica	0.10	0.11	**0.90**	0.10	Int low
Jordan	0.09	**0.93**	0.10	0.11	Int low
Kampuchea	**1.00**	0.00	0.10	0.11	Minimal
Korea, North	0.13	0.08	**0.91**	0.09	Int low
Korea, South	0.10	0.11	**0.89**	0.11	Int high
Laos	**0.91**	0.10	0.10	0.10	Minimal
Lebanon	0.09	0.47	0.07	**0.64**	High
Libya	0.11	**0.90**	0.10	0.10	Int low
Mexico	0.10	0.10	**0.91**	0.09	Int high
Mongolia	0.14	**0.84**	0.12	0.11	Minimal
Mozambique	**0.91**	0.09	0.11	0.10	Minimal
Panama	0.10	0.10	**0.91**	0.09	Int low
Papua New Guinea	**0.90**	0.11	0.10	0.10	Minimal
Philippines	0.10	**0.83**	0.11	0.15	Int high
Poland	0.09	**0.90**	0.11	0.11	Int high
Romania	0.11	**0.90**	0.10	0.10	Int low
Singapore	0.11	0.10	**0.89**	0.11	Int high
Solomon Islands	**0.90**	0.11	0.10	0.10	Int low
Somalia	**0.90**	0.11	0.11	0.11	Minimal

Country	Minimal	Intermed. low	Intermed. high	High	Vanhanen
Tanzania	**0.90**	0.10	0.11	0.10	Minimal
Turkey	**0.89**	0.13	0.10	0.10	Int low
Uganda	**0.91**	0.09	0.11	0.10	Minimal
USSR	0.10	0.09	**0.92**	0.09	Int low
Uruguay	0.11	0.10	**0.89**	0.11	Int high
Vietnam	**0.86**	0.11	0.15	0.10	Minimal
Yemen PDR	**0.91**	0.09	0.10	0.10	Minimal
Yugoslavia	0.10	**0.89**	0.11	0.10	Int high

NOTES

1 For descriptions of the new methods used in this analysis, see Garson 1991; Kimber 1991b; Schrodt 1991.
2 For further details, see Kimber 1991a.
3 Further details on how the two categories were constructed may be found in Kimber 1991a. The countries in the two sets are listed in Appendix 3.3 The data used was that published in Vanhanen 1989. Since then Vanhanen has made slight refinements to the data set for his 1990 study on which his analysis here is based, but the differences are not thought to affect the comparison between the two approaches.
4 Kimber has suggested that a satisfactory set of predictions can be obtained by training a network on a set of countries which have been classified subjectively into four levels of democracy. See Kimber 1991a.

BIBLIOGRAPHY

Coppedge, M., and Reinicke, W. (1988) 'A scale of polyarchy', in R. D. Gastil (ed.) *Freedom in the World. Political Rights & Civil Liberties 1987–88,* New York: Freedom House.
Dahl, R. A. (1971) *Polyarchy. Participation and Opposition,* New Haven and London: Yale University Press.
Garson, G. D. (1991) 'Comparing expert systems and neural network algorithms with common multivariate procedures for analysis of social science data', *Social Science Computer Review* 9: 399–434.
Gastil, R. D. (1988) *Freedom in the World. Political Rights & Civil Liberties 1987–1988,* New York: Freedom House.
Kimber, R. (1989) 'On democracy', *Scandinavian Political Studies* 12: 199–219.
—— (1991a) 'Predicting democracy in Eastern Europe', Paper presented at the workshop on Democratization in Eastern Europe at the ECPR Joint Sessions of Workshops, University of Essex, 22–28 March.
—— (1991b) 'Artificial intelligence and the study of democracy', *Social Science Computer Review* 9: 381–98.
Schrodt, P. A. (1991) 'Prediction of interstate conflict outcomes using a neural network', *Social Science Computer Review* 9: 359–80.

Vanhanen, T. (1984) *The Emergence of Democracy. A Comparative Study of 119 States, 1850–1979*, Commentationes Scientiarum Socialium, vol. 24, Helsinki: The Finnish Society of Sciences and Letters.
—— (1989) 'The level of democratization related to socioeconomic variables in 147 states in 1980–85', *Scandinavian Political Science Review* 12: 95–127.
—— (1990) *The Process of Democratization. A Comparative Study of 147 States, 1980–88*, New York: Crane Russak.
—— (1991a) 'Structural imbalance as an explanation for the collapse of hegemonic regimes in Eastern Europe', Paper presented at the ECPR Joint Sessions of Workshops, 22–29 March, at the University of Essex, UK.
—— (1991b) 'Construction and use of an Index of Democratization', Paper presented at a meeting of experts on social development indicators in Rabat, 8–11 April.

Part II
Emerging party systems and institutions

4 Building party systems after the dictatorship

The East European cases in a comparative perspective

Maurizio Cotta

TRANSITIONS TO DEMOCRACY AND THE REBIRTH OF PARTIES

When the crisis of a nondemocratic regime arises, and the transition to democracy starts unravelling, two main questions are at stake. The first is whether democracy will succeed, i.e. whether the instauration of democratic institutions is followed by consolidation of the new regime.[1] The second is what type of democracy will be adopted and what will be the peculiar features of the new political system. This means on the one hand what type of institutional framework – parliamentary versus presidential, majoritarian versus consensus, etc. (Lijphart 1984) – will prevail; on the other hand what configuration of political actors will emerge during the transition and become relatively crystallized in the course of the first years. A major aspect is obviously which parties and what kind of party system will develop.

The two questions are strictly linked in the real process of democratic transitions. Suggestions that different institutional arrangements (for instance a parliamentary constitution versus a presidential one) or different configurations of the party system can play a crucial role in determining the success of the democratic transition have been at the centre of older and more recent discussions (Linz 1978; Lijphart, *et al.* 1990; Morlino 1986b; Pridham 1990). At the same time, it is pretty clear that the transition process and the way it develops are bound to affect the specific institutional choices and the moulding of the new political actors.

The two questions, which are analytically distinguishable, can be used as the starting point for two different research perspectives. In the following pages I will concentrate on certain aspects of the perspective suggested by the second question (what parties and party systems emerge out of the democratic transition) and leave aside the other one.[2]

There is no need to spend time justifying the relevance for the quality of the new democracy of which parties and what kind of party system will emerge out of the transition. There are good reasons to pay attention to this aspect since pluralistic democracy is, to our best knowledge, strictly identified with the existence of a fairly well-structured party system (Sartori 1987: 148 ff.), and with the ability of the latter to assert its role *vis-à-vis* other potential actors (as the military, interest groups, etc.) and to perform effectively the crucial democratic functions. More specifically the party system and its stabilization seem to play an important role in the consolidation of a new democracy (Morlino 1986b; Pridham 1990). Finally, the shape and composition of the party system must be considered a significant factor affecting the policies of governments (Wilensky 1981; Castles 1982; von Beyme 1984). Indeed, even a cursory survey of Western European countries where transitions to democracy have taken place in the past (Austria, France, Germany and Italy after the Second World War; Greece, Portugal and Spain in the 1970s) shows rather clearly that the party variable (and this means both the characteristics of party units and the nature of the party system) has made for significant differences in all the fields mentioned above.

The demise of communist regimes in Central and Eastern Europe, and the transitions to pluralist democracy now under way all at the same time in about twenty countries (or successor countries where larger units have broken apart), offers the political scientist a fascinating addition of empirical cases for exploring the processes of building competitive party systems. Comparatists, normally faced with the well-known problem of having too few cases and too many variables (Lijphart 1971), now have to deal with a bounty of cases. The advantages of the increase in the number of empirical cases available, however, risk being offset by an even greater increase of potentially relevant variables if the cases are too heterogeneous. To reduce the heterogeneity of cases, and to make comparisons between the new cases and the older and better known cases of Western Europe more fruitful, it is probably wise to concentrate on a subgroup of post-communist transitions: those that are taking place in countries that have had some previous democratic or proto-democratic experiences. It is useful to remember that Western European transitions have been not just 'democratizations' but 're-democratizations'. This is the case also for some of the post-communist cases but not for all (the Soviet Union and most of its successor states do not share this characteristic[3]). This aspect is particularly relevant for the discussion about the birth of parties. In re-democratization cases parties had existed during the first democracy (or proto-democracy) before being outlawed by the nondemocratic regime. This immediately raises the problem of the legacies of the past and how meaningful they are.

I will concentrate here on the role that continuity and discontinuity with the past play in the making of the party systems of new democracies. And I will try to identify similarities and differences existing between the new Eastern European cases and the older Western European ones. A note of caution is in any case required. The definition and crystallization of a new party system always requires a certain number of years.[4] In Western European cases a sufficiently long period of time has elapsed after the transition; we are able therefore to evaluate the end results of the process. In Eastern Europe the first steps have taken place, but the process is far from concluded and we can still expect significant changes to happen in the years ahead. We have therefore to find a middle way between an explanation of what already exists and conjectures about the future.

BIRTH AND DEVELOPMENT OF PARTY SYSTEMS: A ROKKANIAN PERSPECTIVE

The general theme of the formation and transformation of party systems has received a good deal of attention in the past and again in more recent years. Before discussing the special problems of our cases it is worth while to recall the central points of that debate. In this field the name of Stein Rokkan, with his ambitious effort to elaborate a theoretical scheme for explaining the genesis of parties and the long-term development of party systems, occupies a particularly important place. His model is notably interesting both on methodological grounds for the fruitful blending of analytical instruments of the social sciences with those of the historical approach, and on substantial grounds for the relations it establishes between the development of party systems, societal transformations and democratization processes (Daalder 1980; Flora 1980). Although the validity of part of his views – and in particular of the so-called 'freezing proposition' (Lipset and Rokkan 1967) – has been questioned in recent years, no other theoretical model of comparable breadth has been put forward.

Rokkan's model, to put it briefly, has two main facets. The first is the attempt to explain the creation of parties as the result of cleavage lines that were generated by the effects of the great 'revolutions' taking place during the processes of state and nation building. The breeding ground for European parties has been the great conflicts (and the political alignments and alliances that go with them) between centre and peripheries, state and Church, primary and secondary economy, workers and capitalists, that were produced by these revolutions (Lipset and Rokkan 1967; Rokkan 1970). It must be said that Rokkan does not attempt to connect these cleavages to each specific party but rather to categories of parties (conservative, liberal, agrarian, Christian, etc.). That means also that the correspondence between cleavage lines and specific parties can be stronger or weaker. For instance, more than one socialist party could represent the workers' side of the class cleavage. This obviously leaves space for adding other explanatory variables in order to make sense of the specific configuration of a party system and can be seen as a relaxation of the determinism of the theory. How and with what results different layers of conflict are superimposed on each other plays an important explanatory role here. The emergence of a new cleavage line with its specific contrapositions affects previous alignments determining new alliances and may produce a restructuring of the previous party system (Lipset and Rokkan 1967: 36ff.). How these alliances are formed, which of the old parties are able to survive and which not, are obviously crucial questions for understanding the final shape of a party system.

The second point concerns the development over time of parties and party systems. Rokkan starts from an empirical finding – the fact that in Europe political alignments and party systems of the 1960s reflect to a great extent those of the twenties (Lipset and Rokkan 1967: 50–1). The interpretation he suggests is that once the full extension of the suffrage has been attained, leaving no more space to significant extensions of the 'support market', already existing parties find themselves in a particularly strong position to reject attempts by new parties to enter the political arena (Lipset and Rokkan 1967: 51). Political alignments tend therefore to remain frozen in spite of all the changes that may affect society.

At the centre of Rokkan's analysis (both when the discussion focuses on the creation of parties and when it deals with their ability to last over a long time) are the processes of political mobilization. The major difference between the creative phase of parties and the phase of continuity has to do with the different conditions under which political mobilization operates before and after the threshold of mass politics. The first phase is characterized by an expanding support market, since the full extension of the suffrage has not yet been reached: the political orientations of the new sections of the citizenship that are admitted (or win entrance) in the political system are determined by the great conflicts that split society during that period. The mobilizing potential of such conflicts favours the establishment of strong political affiliations. In turn the strong mass organizations of parties that develop during that period will reinforce the stability of these political loyalties. After the stage of mass politics has been reached the mobilization of voters is fundamentally under the control of existing parties. As a consequence little space is left for innovations in the party system. Or, to be more accurate, change will be channelled essentially through the established parties rather than via the creation of new ones.

Rokkan's theses, and in particular the freezing proposition, have come under discussion during the last decade, and it has become fashionable to speak of the 'unfreezing' of European party systems (see Pedersen 1979, 1983; Maguire 1983; Dalton, Flanagan and Beck 1984; Inglehart 1984; Shamir 1984, for example). There is more than one point at stake in this discussion. Some are just factual points. Was Rokkan correct when he found continuity for the period 1920–65? And then, if Rokkan was correct for 1920–65, have things changed after that and has stability given way to instability in party alignments? But others are of a more theoretical nature; if the new facts are true does that imply that Rokkan's theory was wrong or, at least, that its validity is limited to a special historical period? And then, are the explanatory variables that have to be introduced to explain change contradictory or compatible with Rokkan's perspective? It is not the place here to discuss in a detailed way the somewhat contradictory results of this discussion. On the factual side, evidence of a somewhat increased rate of change can indeed be found, starting with the 1970s for certain European countries. But in a more long-term perspective the view that volatility and discontinuity have prevailed is unwarranted as was thoroughly proved by Bartolini and Mair (1990). For the more recent trends of change two main explanations are proposed: (1) fundamental changes in the value systems of voters (from materialist to post-materialist values) (Inglehart 1984); and (2) a decline of party as such, as a consequence of the emerging of new instruments of political communication and mobilization (television being the first and foremost) (Dalton, Flanagan and Beck 1984: 460). Both explanations are based upon factors that allegedly derive from transnational phenomena, and are to some extent related to a globally determined developmental chronology rather than to internal national evolutions. For these reasons it is particularly interesting to pay some attention to these points in the analysis of the new democratizations in Eastern Europe that are taking place exactly during the era of post-materialism and television.

From our point of view it is worth mentioning the fact that the whole discussion about change and continuity has had as its central focus European countries with an uninterrupted democratic history. For the other countries the analysis has been generally confined to periods of democratic continuity. Lipset and Rokkan mention some of the 'discontinuous' cases, such as France, Germany and Italy, calling to the attention the 'striking . . . continuities in the alternatives . . . [as well] as the disruptions in their organizational expressions' (Lipset and Rokkan 1967: 52–3). But they do not discuss the problems of these countries more specifically. Twenty years later, however, we must give due consideration to this category of countries which has greatly expanded. Indeed more than half of the European political units (not to mention countries of other geographical areas) have experienced during this century one or more democratic breakdowns, and have finally reverted to democratic institutions only after an authoritarian or totalitarian phase of variable length which has involved the suppression of parties (apart from the ruling one).

To what extent can the general discussion about continuity and change of political alignments and party systems be applied to the more complicated developmental patterns of these countries? It is easy to see that countries that have experienced a regime discontinuity raise some very specific problems. In the countries that have avoided a democratic breakdown there is a fairly clear distinction between two historical phases: one that sees the successive creations of new parties and the other that is dominated by continuity and limited adaptation over time of the party system. The specific problems of the two different historical periods may be treated more or less separately. In the other group of countries the two problems are more strictly interconnected. In these countries, the problem of the birth of parties (which specific parties are created and succeed; what global configuration the party system takes, etc.) opens up when transition to democracy begins after the crisis of the nondemocratic regime. But the problem of the birth of new parties is coupled with the problem of continuity with the previous democratic experience of the country and with the parties existing at that time. The point is that these transitions to democracy are not just democratizations but re-democratizations. Are the parties born with the transition to democracy really new, or are they at least to some degree a continuation of old democratic parties? What space is taken in the new party system by the old parties (or their successor organizations) and what is left to really new parties? These questions require an answer. To explain the new parties and the new party system we have thus to explain also the weight of continuity (or discontinuity) with the past. There is a certain paradox in saying that while in 'continuous' countries (the problem of) the birth of parties antedates (the problem of) continuity, in 'discontinuous' countries the opposite is true: the (problem of the) birth of parties (during re-democratization) comes after (the problem of) continuity.

Discontinuous countries also require more specific attention to a problem that is latent in the discussion about party system continuity. Does continuity (and, vice versa, discontinuity) refer to basic political alternatives (a working-class party versus a bourgeois party, etc.) or rather to specific organizational expressions of these alternatives (i.e. a well-identified socialist party versus a similarly defined conservative or liberal party)? The point is much more relevant in the countries we are discussing because organizational expressions have been obviously disrupted by the nondemocratic period.

In spite of all these qualifications the Rokkanian model offers important suggestions from which to start understanding the rebirth of pluralist party systems after transitions to democracy.

A TWO STEPS EXPLANATORY MODEL

In order to understand the specific problem of discontinuous countries – i.e. how the legacy of the past affects the birth of the new democratic party system – I suggest adopting an explanatory model based on two steps. The first step deals with the conditions affecting the probable survivals from the past. Depending on a number of factors that will be discussed in the next pages we may expect greater or lesser amounts of persistence of the old parties. This is bound to leave a smaller or greater amount of political space for new parties. At this point – and this is the second step of the explanatory model – we have to explain the new additions that are introduced alongside that larger or smaller pre-existing basis of continuity. Depending on the nature of the first stage the second may be rather tightly 'confined' (within the boundaries of a basic continuity with the past) or, on the contrary, rather open (because little of the past survives to condition the new choices). I will accordingly develop my discussion in two parts. The first seeks to explain the weight of the legacies of the first democratic experience; the second to explain the emergence of the new in the transition process.

Although this sequence (from past to present) may seem obvious, one should not completely discard the possibility of a 'backward' effect: if the creation of new parties proves difficult for reasons of its own and new parties are therefore weak, the influence of the past might be enhanced and, *faute de mieux,* the re-emergence of the old parties favoured. 'Forward' and 'backward' perspectives should probably complement each other.

With regard to the cases considered (although not systematically analysed) in the following pages, it must be admitted that comparing the group of Central and East European countries that have just completed the process of transition to democracy, together with Western European countries that have undergone the same process in a more distant past, raises a few problems. We must obviously be aware of the peculiarities of the two groups of countries. Post-communist countries of Central and Eastern Europe have some common background properties (more or less the same type of nondemocratic experience; state control of the economy; an unparalleled history of subjugation of civil society to political power, etc.) that are not shared by the other countries. It would be wrong however to emphasize only the similarities among these countries; we should not forget that their political experiences before communism had been rather diversified (Rothschild 1974; Seton-Watson 1986), and that in spite of the transnational homogeneity of the communist model certain important aspects of that regime, such as the degree of its institutionalization, legitimacy, control over society, etc., were affected by specific national situations.

Western European cases are an even more diversified group. Among a number of potentially significant dimensions of variation we should remember at least the timing of re-democratization and, strictly linked to it, the political context in which this process developed. The timing of re-democratization discriminates neatly between two groups of countries. The group of countries (Austria, France, Germany, Italy) where transition to democracy took place during or immediately after the Second World War, and the group of countries (Greece, Portugal, Spain) that saw the breakdown of authoritarian regimes during the 1970s. In the first group the international political context (war defeat, external occupation, new international alignments) played a crucial role; in the second group internal politics was the dominant factor. Significant differences also emerge when we look at the features of the first democratic experience, at the nature and the length of the nondemocratic regime, and at the peculiarities of the transition to democracy.

The balance of similarities and differences between and within the two groups of countries offers an extremely interesting field of research for developing and testing hypotheses about the creation and development of party systems under the special conditions of 'discontinuous' countries. Given the already mentioned fact that in Central and Eastern European cases the building of the new party systems is far from being concluded, because too few years have elapsed after the fall of the communist regime, we can now elaborate hypotheses about the meaning of the first steps that they have taken.

THE FIRST STEP: EXPLAINING CONTINUITY
(DISCONTINUITY) WITH THE PAST

What factors may have affected the ability of the first democratic experience, and more precisely of its party system, to survive? In the Rokkanian model, as mentioned before, once full democratic mobilization has been reached political alignments (and party systems) tend to become stable because the political market has been monopolized (through mechanisms of socialization and loyalty as political identification, but also through mechanisms of exclusion) by parties created before or during the transition to democratic mass politics (Lipset and Rokkan 1967). The space for new parties is pre-empted and continuity consequently prevails. The point to be discussed is to what extent discontinuous countries with their special developmental conditions deviate from this model.

There are in fact a number of factors, at work in our cases, that seem potentially relevant because of their effects upon the ability of parties to control mass mobilization and the support market. Such factors can be seen as conditions setting limits to the maximum of continuity the original Rokkanian proposition would have predicted.

The first condition is directly related to the political turning-point proposed by Rokkan in his analysis of continuity – i.e. the universalization of (male) suffrage and the achievement of mass mobilization. If during the first democratic experiment this threshold has not been fully reached we should expect less continuity with that period. The fundamental condition put forward by Rokkan to explain continuity has not come into being. Some sections of the population will still be 'virgin' to political mobilization when the post-authoritarian democracy is installed. On this basis we can formulate the first hypothesis:

H.1 The less complete the extension of the suffrage during the first democratic experience and/or the less complete the mobilization of the mass electorate the greater the chances of a weak continuity (and vice versa).

To elaborate Rokkan's reasoning on the role of the organizational aspect in connecting political mobilization with the stabilization of political alternatives and of party systems, we may add the following hypothesis that takes into account the specific role of parties:

H.2 The lower the degree of institutionalization of parties and the degree of partyness of political life during the first democratization the weaker the chances of continuity.

But the ability of the first democratic experience, together with the party system it produced, to persist over time should not be linked exclusively to its original strength. We must not forget that in the countries we are discussing democracy reached crisis at a certain point and was finally destroyed. We must therefore look at this destructive process for its impact upon the party system.

A first aspect to be mentioned is that during the first democratic experience a decline of certain parties or even of larger political 'areas' (for instance the old bourgeois area) of the party system may have already begun. The reason may be that certain (older) parties had not been able to adapt to the new political conditions created by universal suffrage. We could therefore suggest the next hypothesis:

H.3 To the extent that sections of the party system have undergone a significant decline already during the first democratic experience the chances of continuity are diminished.

Next, the transition process leading to the nondemocratic regime deserves some careful attention. Precisely during that phase things happen that are relevant for the ability of the old parties to survive. The support to the establishment of the nondemocratic regime given by some for the parties that had previously participated in the democratic game is a case in point. Such behaviour by parties that do not share fully the goals of authoritarian actors originates from a mixture of factors: the hope to save democracy in the end through nondemocratic means, the fear of revolution, the competitive outbidding and pressures from extremist parties, etc. In such situations loyalty to the democratic regime often gives way to what Linz has called semi-loyalty (1978: 36–7). In many European countries, in fact, the 1920s saw a shift towards semi-authoritarian positions of bourgeois parties because of their fears concerning leftist militancy on one side and the pressure of rightist radicalism on the other. And after the Second World War in Eastern Europe some parties have been 'captured' in a somewhat similar way in the communist take-overs. After the fall of the non-democratic regime the parties that have been involved in its rise will share the negative stigma of the regime. From this derives:

H.4 Whenever parties of the first democratic regime have been involved in supporting (at least initially) the authoritarian take-over their chances of revival after the fall of this regime will be weaker; the overall chances of continuity of the old party system will be consequently reduced.

The impact of the nondemocratic regime is the next factor to be considered. By its anti-pluralistic nature the nondemocratic regime exerts during its lifetime an obviously negative effect upon the persistence of the old party system. Parties are banished from public life and their leaders and members are more or less severely repressed. The negative impact of this period upon the chances for the old parties being resurrected after the demise of the nondemocratic regime should be linked to its duration and to its specific character. And both the elite and the mass dimension of political life will be affected. The length of the authoritarian interruption seems relevant from our point of view for its potential effects upon the linkages between voters and parties: the longer the interruption of democratic life the weaker will become old partisan identifications and potentially stronger the cohorts of new voters that were never socialized by the old parties. But also the ability of party elites to survive and preserve party traditions and images will be affected. If the authoritarian regime is short, old elites (unless physically eliminated) will be able to make a comeback. Beyond a certain duration of the nondemocratic regime their ranks will be necessarily curtailed. After forty years it is highly improbable that any top member of the old elite could play a very significant role. We can therefore add this hypothesis:

H.5 The longer the nondemocratic regime the weaker the continuity with the democratic past.

But the destructive effects of the nondemocratic regime are not only produced by the mere fact of its duration. Its qualitative aspects and particularly its 'intensity' seem especially relevant. There are indeed significant differences among nondemocratic regimes concerning their willingness and ability to erase and transform the pre-existing socio-political 'landscape'. Differences in this field between 'rightist' and 'leftist' regimes, between authoritarian and totalitarian regimes, etc., are well known (Linz 1975; Fisichella 1987). The impact of nondemocratic regimes should not be seen only in 'negative' terms like the destruction of older political alignments and linkages. There is also a 'positive' side: under that regime new patterns of political behaviour, new alignments and the potential for new coalitions (for instance against the regime) may develop. For all these reasons we could say that:

H.6 The 'stronger' the nondemocratic regime (i.e. the greater its mobilizing potential, the more extensive its social impact, the deeper its institutionalization, etc.) the lesser the chances of continuity with the past.

The formulation of this series of hypotheses helps to specify different variables that seem potentially relevant for building an explanatory model of continuity (and discontinuity) with the first democratic experience. Obviously it would be difficult to test the impact of each variable individually – not only because of the limited number of cases, but also because some variables are not entirely independent from the others.[5] For all these reasons the best way is probably to use a more synthetic approach by building a comprehensive factor based on all the variables. We will have a strong discontinuity factor when all (or at least a majority) of the variables point in the direction of discontinuity, and a strong continuity factor when the opposite is true. A weak democratic past with limited mass mobilization and a low degree of partyness, the crisis of democratic parties climaxing already during that phase, a high degree of involvement of some of the original parties in the authoritarian take-over, and a prolonged and very strong nondemocratic regime would leave little space for the re-emergence of the old party system. The opposite conditions would instead make continuity with the past much more probable. There will also be intermediate cases where some of the variables point in one direction and others in the opposite or where their values are median.

If we turn now to the empirical cases, Western European countries seem indeed to offer some confirmation of these hypotheses. Although an attempt to order them in terms of the degree of discontinuity between the pre-authoritarian and the post-authoritarian party systems necessarily involves certain problems, the fit with the results expected from our explanatory model is not too bad. If continuity and discontinuity are evaluated by the ability of the parties of the first democratic experience to re-emerge after the fall of the nondemocratic regime and by the extent to which both their electoral strength and their weight in the governmental processes are preserved, there is little doubt that on the continuum between lowest and highest discontinuity Austria should be placed near the lower end and Portugal near the higher end. And between these cases we could place in an order of increasing discontinuity Germany (Weimar to Bonn), Italy, and Spain.

In the Austrian case the extremely high degree of continuity[6] corresponds rather well to the strong institutionalization of parties in the first democracy, to the short duration of the nondemocratic period, to the relatively low 'intensity' of that regime (at least in its autochthonous phase). The only factor not consistent with this picture is the strong involvement of one of the major parties of the first democracy (the Christian Social party) in the authoritarian take-over.[7] At the other extreme the Portuguese case – with a pre-authoritarian phase characterized by limited franchise and very weak parties (a proto-democracy rather than a true democracy), an ongoing decay of the same parties in the years preceding the *coup d'état* (Wheeler 1978), a very long authoritarian period – has most of the factors playing for discontinuity. The only factor which could have played in the other direction – the limited intensity of the authoritarian regime – was probably offset by the other factors. In fact the post-Salazar party system bears little relation with that of the beginning of the century.[8]

Countries like Germany and Italy occupy a more intermediate position: important elements of continuity with the past (the main one to be mentioned is the renewed or even increased weight of the Christian Democratic and working-class parties) are balanced by significant changes (affecting in particular the old bourgeois right).[9] This should not come as a surprise given the combination of explanatory factors that point in the direction of continuity (high level of institutionalization of mass politics and strong organized parties particularly in Germany, and to a somewhat lesser extent in Italy; relatively short duration of the nondemocratic period) and of factors favouring discontinuity (significant involvement of certain parties in the ascent to power of the nondemocratic regime, extreme or rather high intensity of this regime). Spain, with a weak and unstable party system during the Second Republic, with a large involvement of parties (of the right) in the authoritarian take-over, with a very long nondemocratic period, has as expected a lesser degree of continuity with the past than Germany and Italy (Linz 1967, 1978). However, the degree of continuity with the past is greater in Spain than in Portugal, which might be explained by the more advanced stage of democratization and mass politics reached in the interwar years by Spain compared to Portugal.[10]

If we turn now to the Central and Eastern European countries we can ask how these factors have operated and what can be their consequences in the process of rebirth of parties after the fall of communism. A preliminary point that has to be stressed when answering these questions is that their developmental path has been particularly complex. The first democratization phase (which in a number of these countries coincided also with the gaining of independent statehood from crumbling multinational empires[11]) came to an end in the interwar years and was first followed by rightist nondemocratic regimes of different types (Rothschild 1974; Seton-Watson 1986);[12] and then, after the Second World War, by the communist regime. But a short-lived re-democratization (in most cases with one round at least of more or less pluralistic elections) was squeezed in the mid-1940s between the two nondemocratic experiences.[13] The problem of continuity is

therefore more complicated than in other countries. Given the short
duration of the democratic experience of the 1940s the discussion of
these cases should be based primarily on the interwar experience. This
is not to say that the 'second' democratic attempt should be entirely
forgotten, but that it should be used to provide further elements for
evaluating how strong were the roots of the original party system and
its ability to survive over time.

Comparing Central and Eastern European countries as a group with
'discontinuous' countries of Western Europe shows rather clearly that
almost all the conditions limiting the possibility of continuity with past
democratic experiences and with the old parties are stronger in the
former than in the latter group. As we have seen, limiting conditions
operate to a greater or lesser extent in all the countries of the Western
group, but none of these countries is so heavily affected by all of them.

We may start with a brief discussion of the single factors. In Central
and Eastern European cases (as previously stated we leave aside Soviet
Russia and its successor states here), democratic experiences following
the First World War had generally been rather unstable and had not been
characterized by very strong parties. The role of personalistic leadership with authoritarian tendencies had often played an important role
and had frustrated the emergence of well-developed party systems. The
main exception is Czechoslovakia (and, if we include it in the group,
East Germany for which the democratic past is obviously Weimar's
Germany), where a fairly strong and stable party system survived
until 1939 (Mamotey 1973; Bosl 1979). With the exception again of
Czechoslovakia, the short years of democratic and parliamentary life
saw in most cases clear signs of decay of the parties that had initially
had a pre-eminent role (Rothschild 1974). To this should be added
numerous cases of the involvement of significant parties in the rise to
power of the authoritarian regimes of the interwar period as well as in
the communist take-overs after the Second World War.[14] In all the
countries the weight of the nondemocratic interruption has been
particularly heavy. The first reason is its length: to the approximately
forty years of communist rule have to be added the periods of variable
length under rightist authoritarian regimes (and in some cases also
under externally controlled occupation regimes). The second reason
derives from the nature of communist rule. Its totalitarian or quasi-
totalitarian aspects are especially relevant. The depth of destruction of
the old system went well beyond the elimination of opposition parties:
a full-scale assault was launched against traditional class structures and
organizations, professional associations, religious and cultural institutions. To this should be added also the extended mobilization efforts

and the importance of the new political and social structures created by the regime. All this suggests that old alignments and linkage systems should face great problems in re-emerging.

From these observations, albeit extremely general and synthetic, our expectations are that these countries will be rather clearly located near the discontinuity extreme of the continuity/discontinuity continuum. On the basis of the first step of the explanatory model the new party systems now 'under construction' in Central and Eastern Europe should bear little relation to those of the past. If we consider Czechoslovakia, Hungary and Poland this expectation is fulfilled. In fact a look at the first electoral results indicates that the weight of old parties is generally weak and in no case can they be counted among the largest parties.

In Czechoslovakia, only the Christian Democratic Party and the Slovak National Party among significant parties could be related in some ways to parties of the interwar years; in 1990 they jointly won approximately 16 per cent of the vote at the national level, and in 1992 even less.[15] In Hungary the Christian Democrats and the Smallholders Party totalled 18 per cent of the vote (Korosenyi 1991). In Poland the great victory of Solidarity in the first election round of 1989 left practically no space to the resurgence of old parties. And the many new parties that were able to win representation in the election of 1991 were more the result of the 'explosion' of Solidarity and of the conflicts within its leadership than directly linked to older political traditions.

But in the other countries the picture is less clear. In Bulgaria electoral results are difficult to interpret because most opposition forces ran in a unified front: the Union of Democratic Forces. Within that front (36 per cent of the vote in 1990 and 34 per cent in 1991) a prominent place was initially occupied by two parties (the Petkov Agrarian Union and the Social Democratic Party) that defined themselves as the continuation of pre-war parties (Ashley 1990). What their specific electoral weight was in the global result of the coalition is difficult to evaluate however. In any case continuity with the past seems seriously weakened by the fact that a broad coalition has taken the place of the individual parties. The Romanian case is also rather peculiar. On one side the main political forces not linked to the communist regime derive at first from pre-war parties. That is the case for the National Liberal Party, the National Peasants Party, and other minor groups. But these parties were confined by the first elections to the role of a weak opposition (the strongest of them reaching only 7 per cent of the vote). The overwhelming victory went in 1990 to the National Salvation Front, a political formation that in many ways can be seen as a new incarnation of the Communist Party. And in the following elections

(1992) a broad coalition of opposition (the Democratic Convention of Romania) displaced the traditional parties as the main contender of the two wings of the National Salvation Front. But neither the old nor new parties seem able to grasp the leadership of the transition from the hands of the (restyled) communist elites.

East Germany seems at first the most clear exception to the weakness of old parties; the elections of 1990 for the *Volkskammer* are won by parties (CDU, SPD and League of Free Democrats) which could be considered the continuation of the parties of the Weimar period and of the short democratic interlude of the 1940s. There are good reasons however to judge this apparent continuity with the past as spurious; the anomalous result of East Germany is the consequence of the process of assimilation of East German parties to the contemporary party system of Western Germany rather than of the strength of autochthonous party traditions. If there is continuity with the past it is not a direct one but one transmitted 'through' the political history of the Bundesrepublik.

We can summarize these first findings by saying that in Eastern Europe, at least on the basis of the first electoral results, pre-Communist Party systems do not provide the basic structure for the new party systems of the post-communist era. Their legacies are on the whole marginal.[16] This distinguishes them clearly from some at least of the Western European cases (Austria, Germany, Greece, Italy) where the opposite was true. In order to explain the new party systems of Eastern Europe and their characters we should rather look to the next step of the explanatory model, i.e. to factors related to other phases of the political development of these countries.

THE SECOND STEP: THE FACTORS BEHIND THE NEW PARTIES

The weaker the thrust of continuity of past democratic experiences the greater should be the space left for innovation, for the creation of new political groups. In some way we can conceive the political arena as an empty space that has to be filled. In our search for the factors that could explain the configuration and institutionalization of the new party systems we should look to other aspects of the political transformations that went on in these countries.

Firstly, it must be pointed out that the establishment of a new democracy is not only the resumption of the older democratic political course (the aspect discussed so far), but also the deliverance from the nondemocratic regime. This means that there is another 'legacy problem'. The nondemocratic regime does not simply disappear but leaves more or less significant consequences. What happens to the ruling party of that regime (where there was one) is particularly important from our point of view. The new democracy may have to face the survival of a political force linked with the previous regime. The problem will be all the more relevant when the previous regime had enjoyed strong support, at least among certain sections of the population, when the party had a strong mass organization and when the demise of the nondemocratic regime was not produced by a complete collapse or by a destruction from outside. A continuous transition (Morlino 1986a), with the old ruling party able to control, at least to some extent, the turn of events, would seem to provide the most favourable conditions for some degree of survival of that party in the original version, or more probably with a refurbished image (a new name, new leaders, etc.). In some way the two factors evoked by Rokkan – mobilization efforts and organizational continuity – are at stake here. We can therefore formulate the following hypothesis:

> *H.7* The stronger the support basis of the ruling party of the nondemocratic regime, and the more continuous the transition, the greater the chances for such a party to survive as a significant political actor under the democratic regime.

From the point of view of these conditions the old ruling parties of East European countries are generally in a better position than those of Western Europe. In Eastern Europe the Communist Party has been the foundation and the keystone of nondemocratic regimes wherever they have emerged, and the transition to democracy has been to some degree at least continuous. In Western Europe the two favourable factors are never combined. Where the nondemocratic party had had a strong role in the old regime (Italy and even more Germany) the regime collapse was, because of international conditions, complete and the transition discontinuous. Where transition was continuous, most clearly in Spain, the authoritarian party was in any case a very weak political creature. In other cases (Austria, Greece, Portugal, Vichy France) there was not even a real party. All this being said we should not forget differences inside the Eastern group. It is sufficient to mention the fact that some of the communist countries had had to face serious political crises (Poland 1956, 1970, 1980–1; Hungary 1956; Czechoslovakia 1968), which can be seen as a sign of a relatively weak popular legitimation of these regimes and of their ruling parties (Grilli di Cortona 1989).

The results of the first free elections lend some support to this hypothesis. While in no case in Western Europe did parties of the old regime obtain a meaningful following,[17] in all the countries of the East

European group they are able to survive as significant parties. There are however significant differences of strength even in this group. There is a first subgroup of countries – 'Eastern Germany', Czechoslovakia, Hungary and Poland – where communist parties or their successor parties have become minority parties (within the 10 to 15 per cent range of votes); in a second subgroup – Romania, Bulgaria, Serbia – they have managed, at least initially, to maintain a much larger electoral following and even a dominant political role. It is easy to see that the divide between the two subgroups follows rather neatly the differences mentioned before in the degree of legitimation and internal strength of the communist regimes.

The nondemocratic period is relevant in another way. During that period an illegal opposition often develops. The 'dissenters', particularly when the nondemocratic regime has had a long life, may have little direct experience of the old democracy. But through their challenges to the nondemocratic regime they gain some kind of political training and popular prestige. If they have not been wiped away completely by repression they can become the nucleus of the new democratic elite. When the regime crisis becomes more acute because of internal or external problems the conflict between regime and dissent may produce a significant amount of popular mobilization (and an even larger area of unexpressed political support for the new opposition). To some extent at least we have at work the factors that in a Rokkanian perspective should provide the basis for new political alignments and parties. We can expect therefore that during the transition to democracy opposition movements become important building blocks for the making of the new party system. We can therefore formulate the following hypothesis:

> *H.8* The more significant and large the popular basis of the opposition movements under the nondemocratic regime (or during the process of its displacement), the greater the chances that such movements and their leaders will play a leading role in shaping the democratic party system.

But in order to understand the role that the 'opposition born under the dictatorship' may play in the new party system we should not forget the other side of the picture. The special features this opposition tends to have may produce significant problems once democracy is at work. The dominant goal to overthrow the regime requires from opposers the need to put aside political differences and gives a special value to unity of action. The pressure for unity is further reinforced by the moral component which generally plays a crucial role in this opposition.

Opposition to the nondemocratic regime tends therefore to take the form of unified fronts.[18] Problems arise once the old regime is overthrown and competitive political life begins. Unity of action must now give way to pluralistic competition. If the front as such had not played a very strong part in the transition to democracy, and/or it was a loosely unified confederation of political groups, it will be more easy to put it aside. The building of a party system along pluralistic lines will not find obstacles here. The parties of the opposition front regain their freedom of action and new parties are created outside that group. But if the opposition front played a dominant role in the fight against the old regime and was highly unified the development of a pluralistic party system may be a more troublesome process. At first the front may try to define itself as something different from a party. Moreover there is little space left outside the front; so in the end if pluralism must develop it must arise from an internal split of the front. Another possibility of course is that the front remains united and dominates the new politics but that would not be compatible with democracy. We can therefore add this hypothesis:

H.9 The stronger and more unified the opposition front to the nondemocratic regime the greater the difficulties for a pluralistic party system being established quickly.

Empirical cases provide some support to the last two hypotheses. With regard to the first one the examples of France and Italy show that parties taking an active part in the Resistance against fascist regimes and Nazi occupation were rewarded with electoral success and acquired a central role in the new party systems. There is also some counter evidence: in Spain the Communist Party, which had undoubtedly had a significant role in mobilizing an opposition in the last years of the Franco regime, did not reap great electoral benefits from it.[19] In Central and Eastern Europe opposition movements against the communist regime play an important role in the first steps at least of the creation of the democratic political system. Where the opposition was stronger and contributed in a crucial way to the fall of the old regime the new party system derives more closely from those movements.

Poland, Czechoslovakia and Hungary offer some interesting evidence. The three countries can be easily rank-ordered by the strength of opposition movements. Poland is obviously first on this dimension. Solidarity, for its ability to mobilize a very large mass following in the 1980s and to bring the communist regime almost to its knees, had been by far the strongest of opposition movements in Eastern Europe. It was not a surprise therefore when at the beginning of democratic life it gained almost a monopoly of electoral preferences. As a result the new party system seemed at first to develop like a *de facto* one party system. At some distance the Czech and Slovak twin opposition movements – Civic Forum and Public Against Violence – acquired a central role but far less than a monopoly in the first steps of the Czechoslovak party system.[20] In Hungary, where the opposition had played a much more limited role in overturning the regime the first democratic elections were not fought by a unified opposition front but rather by different political movements that acted as parties.[21] The three countries show also that where a strong and unified opposition movement existed the establishment of a pluralistic party system follows a more difficult course than in other cases. At first only weak parties can develop outside the opposition movement; later pluralism will develop out of rancorous splits from the old opposition front. Such a process may not be easily conducive to strong parties, as the troubled breakdown of Solidarity in Poland seems to show. The process has been easier where, as in Western Europe, opposition fronts were cartels of parties that had (and kept) an autonomous identity, and could therefore resume their freedom of action once the nondemocratic regime had disappeared.

Political movements that rely for their identity mainly on the past role of opposition to the non-democratic regime necessarily face a problem of adaptation once the 'enemy' has disappeared (or has been reduced to a small and marginalized successor party). The themes that dominate the political debate and agenda change drastically in a matter of months. Choices in the fields of democratic institutions, of economic reconstruction, of international alliances take the place of the struggle for political freedom. The need to find new bases of support therefore becomes urgent. An important question is whether in the first years of the new democracy old or new conflicts can acquire, because of their breadth and depth, the potential of creating stable cleavages and a large-scale political mobilization. The general hypothesis from which to start is the following:

H.10 The new parties will develop on the basis of conflicts that have the potential for sustaining a broad and durable political mobilization.

The question therefore is what conflicts can play this role in the new democracy. Our attention should go first of all to the great 'structural' conflicts that have produced the party systems of continuous countries. Among them the socio-economic cleavage has a special place. Its influence has been the strongest and most homogeneous on European party systems producing large working-class parties in almost all the countries (Lipset and Rokkan 1967). We should also expect its impact to be significant in the making of the new party systems after the restoration of democracy. This is because the persistent importance of this cleavage favours continuity with the past democratic experience and with the working-class parties already existing at that time, or because it offers the basis for the establishment of new ones when they had not been significant before the dictatorship. In fact, in all Western European cases after the transition to democracy, strong working-class parties have taken an important place in the reborn party systems. In some cases, as in Austria and Germany, they could revive strong traditions of the first democracy. In other countries such traditions had been weaker. But even in Portugal where the Socialist Party had played practically no role before Salazar, this party became one of the important actors after the fall of the dictatorship.

The importance of this cleavage obviously derives from the capitalistic structure of societies. In Eastern Europe, because of the radical transformation of the socio-economic structure under the communist regime, we should expect a rather different situation. The abolition of the market economy and of private ownership of the means of production, resulting in the destruction of the capitalistic bourgeoisie, takes the wind from the sails of the socio-economic cleavage (workers vs owners) in post-communist democracies. We may therefore formulate the following hypothesis:

H.11 Working class parties will have an important role in the new party systems except where the nondemocratic regime produced a large-scale state control of the economy.

Czechoslovakia, Hungary and Poland seem to lend support to the hypothesis. Socialist parties have fared very poorly in the first elections and have not become significant political players.[22] It is true however that in other Eastern European countries socialist parties have had greater success. But it is not difficult to find the special reasons for that. In Eastern Germany the large electoral following of the SPD had to do more with the 'imitation' of the West German party system, with the organizational support coming from the brother party of the West, than with the intensity of the socio-economic cleavage in that country. As for Bulgaria and Romania, the electoral victories of the Socialist Party and of the Salvation Front, parties which to some extent could be defined as working-class parties, can be explained more by the ability of the old communist ruling parties to survive in a new form, thanks to the peculiarities of the transition rather than to the weight of the class cleavage.

If these are the initial results we should not discount the possibility that in the future socio-economic conflicts will play a greater role in the political life of Eastern Europe. We can reasonably expect, however, that they will follow a somewhat different course than in Western Europe. For some time at least the main conflicts should originate from the dismantling of state ownership and centralistic controls and from the reconstruction of a more decentralized market economy. That process will pit a growing private sector against a retreating public sector: risk-oriented against security-dependent groups of the population rather than working class against bourgeoisie. Whether such conflicts will produce well-structured cleavage lines and provide a stable basis for competing parties is a difficult question. There are some chances, however, that rather than fostering the growth of social democratic parties along Western lines they might ensure the survival of the refurbished communist parties campaigning on the advantages of the old state economy with the security it guaranteed (to those willing to comply), or the birth of populist parties.

What can be the role of other Rokkanian cleavages such as the centre/ periphery or the Church/state ones? And what, consequently, are the chances of ethnic and regionalist or of Christian Democratic parties? Perspectives for the first type of cleavages and parties appear rather favourable after the fall of nondemocratic regimes. Very often these regimes have, because of their centralistic inclinations, adopted repressive policies *vis-à-vis* ethnic groups and suppressed associations and parties connected with them; but, leaving aside exceptional cases of total elimination, the probability that in spite of everything these ethnic identities will have survived is significant. Repression may have even strengthened their autonomist orientations. In the new democracy such groups will have both the motivation for establishing political parties – as the instruments for obtaining back their autonomy – and the social bases for doing it. The empirical evidence shows in fact that in the countries where ethnic diversities were significant, parties based on these identities have quickly and successfully re-emerged in the transition to democracy. Spain is the most important case for Western Europe: regionalistic parties have soon acquired a relevant and stable role in the new party system.[23] As for Eastern Europe, it has become apparent that wherever national minorities exist, autonomist or even secessionist parties rapidly bloom. To what extent parties based on such principles can be accommodated within democratic life or will produce the breakdown of multi-ethnic countries is the major question at stake here (Di Palma 1990).

Less easy to evaluate is the role of the religious cleavage. Various factors complicate the picture. On one side relations between the

Church and the nondemocratic regimes have been far from homogeneous across countries and over time. They have indeed gone from
the strong support of sections of the German Lutheran Church for the
Nazi regime and of the Catholic Church for the Franco regime (of the
first decades), to the increasing detachment of the same Catholic Church
from the Spanish dictatorship in the 1970s, to the brutal suppression of
the Church under the communist regimes. But beside this, one should
also add the important changes in the degree of secularization occurring
in the time-span during which the individual transition processes are
scattered. Where the two factors add together, i.e. where the support of
the Church to the nondemocratic regime has been more explicit and the
process of secularization has reached a more advanced stage at the time
of the transition to democracy, there should be less space for confes-
sional parties in the new party systems. Cases like Spain and (albeit not
so clearly) Portugal, where in spite of the past importance of the
religious/secular cleavage Christian Democratic parties have gained
little weight in the new democratic party systems, seem in line with
those expectations. On one side the support given by the Church to the
two authoritarian regimes had been substantial; on the other side the
transition processes have taken place at a period of time when processes
of secularization had severely weakened the Catholic Church all over
the world.

In other cases the two factors are at odds. In the Austrian, German
and Italian cases, in spite of some greater or lesser support given by the
Church to the nondemocratic regimes (particularly in the founding
years), Christian Democratic parties could manage a very successful
comeback in the new democracy. The less advanced secularization of
the 1940s, and perhaps also the fact that other political forces (like
conservatives and liberals) had been even more heavily involved in the
old regime, could perhaps explain those results. A bit more astonishing
is what seems to be happening in Eastern Europe. Because of the
significant role of the Church in the opposition to the communist
regimes many had expected a success for Christian Democratic parties.
On the contrary, this did not materialize. Even in a country like Poland,
where the role of the Church in the opposition to the communist regime
had been particularly strong (also through the unambiguous support
given to the Solidarity movement), no large party with a religious basis
has developed after the dissolution of Solidarity.[24] The explanation for
these unexpected results might perhaps be found in a combination of
factors. The advanced secularization of society, the fact that the
extreme anticlerical policies of the communist regimes have seriously
weakened the legitimation of secularist positions (which had been

politically relevant in the interwar period), and the large popularity acquired by the Church may have paradoxically created a situation where the relevance of issues relating to the religious/secular cleavage is limited and the need for sections of the population to rally behind a religiously defined party is weak.

Summing up the three important cleavages that have contributed most to the structuring of party systems in Europe only one, for the time being at least, seems bound to play a role in the making of the new party systems of Eastern Europe. Structural factors therefore appear much less 'confining' than in most Western European cases.

TENTATIVE CONCLUSIONS

At the end of this analysis of the different factors that seem relevant for the rebuilding of the pluralistic party system after the fall of nondemocratic regimes we may formulate some tentative conclusions. The constellations of conditions at work when the new party systems of discontinuous countries start developing can be extremely varied. The weight of old democratic traditions, of factors connected with the nondemocratic period, and finally of the socio-political conditions existing at the moment of the transition to democracy, change significantly from country to country.

To simplify this picture we can imagine a continuum stretching between two extreme poles. At one pole there are situations which we might describe as 'tight conditions'. Because factors of continuity with the first democratic past are strong and/or structural conditions existing at the time of transition define clear cleavages, the making of the new party system takes place within a strictly 'confined' track. At the other extreme there are situations of 'open conditions'. The past has left only weak legacies and present conditions do not provide clear structural bases for strong alignments. When such a situation applies, the making of the new party system is much more difficult to predict. Idiosyncratic and situational factors – like institutional choices (concerning electoral systems or parliament–executive relations) made during the transition; leaders' personalities; specific issues appearing on the political agenda; success or lack of it in solving economic problems; or even external influences – can play a much stronger role. Since these factors are much more volatile than the others the chances that weaker parties and more unstable party systems will develop are greater.

On this continuum Eastern European cases seem generally bound to to be placed, compared to most Western cases, nearer to the 'open' than to the 'tight' pole. The combinations of factors that work in this direction have been discussed in these pages. Perhaps to these should also be added some of the transnational factors that the comparative discussion about the decline of parties has evoked. The timing of the transitions makes them more relevant in Eastern Europe than in other countries.

There is already some empirical evidence about the effects of such an 'open' situation: the most striking is the dramatic 'atomization' of the Polish party system during 1991. Czechoslovakia soon followed with a radical restructuring of the original party system taking place in 1992. We can reasonably expect that in many of these countries further significant transformations of the party systems will take place in the next years. Any conclusion about these party systems has necessarily to be tentative.

NOTES

1 The distinction between instauration and consolidation is common in the discussion about transitions (see Morlino 1986a and 1986b for a thorough analysis of these concepts).
2 The other perspective is touched on in other chapters of this book.
3 Baltic states are a case apart since they have had between the wars a period of democratic life (although in the end failed) (von Rauch 1970; Linz 1978: 70).
4 The length may vary from country to country: for example in Italy the process starts in 1943 and is concluded in 1953; in Germany it develops between 1949 and 1953; in Spain between 1976 and 1982. Austria is perhaps the only exception: the new party system becomes crystallized almost immediately.
5 Certain variables can in fact influence the effects of others. This may be the case of the variables considered in the first three hypotheses *vis-à-vis* the following ones. If a fairly structured party system did not exist during the first democratic experience, the next variables, whatever their values, will not be able to do very much for the continuity of the old party system, because from the start there will be little to be perpetuated.
6 The two dominant parties of the interwar years make a successful comeback (with some changes in their names) in the Second Republic. Their electoral weight is practically unchanged: their average combined share of the vote was 84 per cent in the 1920s and 88.5 per cent in the 1940s (Mackie and Rose 1982).
7 The negative effect of the participation of the Catholic Party in the authoritarian experience was probably weakened by the fact that with the *Anschluss* an externally controlled Nazi regime took the place of autochthonous authoritarianism.
8 The parliamentary scene before Salazar was dominated by rather weak and personalistic bourgeois parties like the Republican Party, often dividing itself into rival groups, and the Nationalist Party. These parties had no successors in the new democracy.

9 The decline of the traditional right parties, which before fascism and Nazism had a crucial role in the political system, is a common feature of Italy and Germany. On the other hand, in both cases Christian Democratic parties managed not only to survive but to increase their influence by dramatically gaining from the crisis of the bourgeois right (in Italy the rise was from 20 per cent of the PPI in 1921 to 35 per cent of the DC in 1946; in Germany, from a Zentrum vote oscillating between 11 and 13 per cent in the Weimar republic to the CDU–CSU 31 per cent in 1949 and 45 per cent in 1953). As for working-class parties the increased weight coincided with the opposite organizational developments: a monopoly of this area by the Social Democratic Party in Germany, fragmentation in two and later three or more parties in Italy.

10 The Socialist Party and some of the regionalist parties in the Basque country and in Catalonia are the most significant signs of continuity with the past.

11 That was the case of Poland, Czechoslovakia, Hungary, Yugoslavia and the Baltic countries.

12 A partial exception is Czechoslovakia where, in Slovakia, the democratic regime gave way to an internal authoritarianism, but in the Czech part of the country came to an end only with external occupation by Germany.

13 In Czechoslovakia the elections of 1946, and in Hungary those of 1945 and to a lesser degree those of 1947, can be considered fairly free elections; much less free were the elections of 1945 and 1946 in Bulgaria, the elections of 1947 in Poland, and the elections of 1946 in Romania (Seton-Watson 1950).

14 Rightist authoritarianism of the interwar years was generally supported by 'national coalitions' which included some of the major parties (or at least factions of them). The main examples were: in Poland after 1926 the BBWR (Nonpartisan Bloc for Cooperation with the Government) which saw the convergence of 'converts from all the earlier political orientations in Poland' (Rothschild 1974: 59); in Hungary the government bloc (called the Christian and Bourgeois Party of Small Landowners and Agrarians) which fused Nationalists and Small Landowners (Seton-Watson 1986: 190); in Romania the Front of National Rebirth (1938); in Bulgaria the Democratic Concord which in the twenties included Populists, Democrats, Radicals and obtained even the collaboration of Social Democrats (Rothschild 1974: 342 ff.). As for the communist take-overs after the Second World War significant components of the leadership of Social Democratic, bourgeois, agrarian and other parties were through different means coopted in the process (Seton-Watson 1950; Fejto 1952; Hammond 1977).

15 The Christian Democrats obtained (for the Chamber of the People of the Federal Parliament) 8.7 per cent of the vote in the elections of 1990, in the Czech lands and 6 per cent in 1992; in Slovakia 19 per cent in 1990 and 9 per cent in 1992. The Slovak National Party had (in Slovakia) 11 per cent in 1990 and 9 per cent in 1992. The social democratic parties, which also could be related to older political traditions, did not pass the threshold of representation in 1990, but obtained nearly 8 per cent in the Czech lands in 1992 and 5 per cent in Slovakia.

16 I have not discussed in this context the communist parties which in most cases had existed in the first democratic experiments. These parties are a special case compared to other 'old parties'; because of their dominant role

during the nondemocratic regime it is more relevant to discuss them where the legacies of that period will be taken into account.

17 In Italy the Neo-Fascist Party obtained only 2 per cent of the vote in the 1948 elections (and 5.8 per cent in 1953); in Germany extreme right lists did not even reach 2 per cent of the vote in 1949. In Spain the explicitly Francoist lists were a conspicuous failure (they obtained only 0.5 per cent in 1977 and 2.1 per cent in 1979). Things would be different if one included Alianza Popular (AP) in the count because of its leadership which was largely derived from Francoist elite; that party, however, defined its political identity in different terms. In Greece the military dictatorship had not created a party; however, to some extent the National Front could be seen as linked to the old regime; in 1977 it had a comparatively good result (6.8 per cent), but subsequently disappeared.

18 There are obviously cases when this does not happen and the opposition is internally divided; in such cases, however, the opposition will be ineffective. This is what happened in the first years of the Pinochet regime in Chile; only later, did a general unity among opposition parties give the opposition the opportunity to play a crucial role in the downfall of the military regime.

19 The same could be said for one of the anti-fascist parties in Italy. The left liberals of the Action Party, although very active during the Resistance, were practically wiped away by the ballot.

20 In the elections of 1989 Solidarity gained all seats of the Senate where elections were completely open, and 160 of the 161 available seats in the other chamber. In the Czechoslovak elections of 1990 Civic Forum and Public against Violence had together a little less than the absolute majority (46.6 per cent of the vote).

21 The fact that one was named Forum, as in Czechoslovakia, was but a formal aspect, a residuum of the past. In fact, the National Forum acted as a party, competing with other opposition movements (like the Free Democrats or the FIDESZ).

22 In Czechoslovakia a Socialist and a Social Democratic party did not even win representation in the first freely elected parliament (together they accounted for only 5.2 per cent of the vote). The Communist Party, on the other hand, obtained 13.6 per cent of the vote. In 1992 the Social Democrats were a little more successful; they reached nearly 8 per cent in the Czech lands and nearly 5 per cent in Slovakia. In Hungary the Social Democratic Party scored 3.6 per cent, and two 'socialist' parties derived from the Communist Party obtained a joint total of 14 per cent.

23 Italy also could be mentioned, although on a much more limited scale due to the smaller size of its minorities. The small French-speaking minority in the Aosta Valley and the German-speaking group in South Tirol have sustained their nationally weak but locally dominant parties after the fall of fascism.

24 Only a number of small 'Christian democratic' parties unable to unite in a common political formation have emerged with the elections of 1991. In Czechoslovakia and Hungary Christian democratic parties also exist, but they are small and have a marginal role in the new party system.

BIBLIOGRAPHY

Ashley, S. (1990) 'Bulgaria', *Electoral Studies* 9: 312–18.

Bartolini, S., and Mair, P. (1990) *Identity, Competition and Electoral Availability*, Cambridge: Cambridge University Press.

Beyme, K. von (1984) *Parteien in westlichen Demokratien*, Munchen: Piper.

Bosl, K. (ed.) (1979) *Die erste Tschechoslowakische Republik als multinationaler Parteienstaat*, München: Oldenbourg Verlag.

Castles, F. (ed.) (1982) *The Impact of Parties*, London: Sage.

Daalder, H. (1980) 'Stein Rokkan: dallo studio del caso norvegese all'analisi comparata', *Rivista Italiana di Scienza Politica* 10: 343–68.

Dalton, R. J., Flanagan, S. C., and Beck, P. A. (1984) 'Political forces and partisan change', in R. J. Dalton, S. C. Flanagan, and P. A. Beck (eds) *Electoral Change in Advanced Industrial Democracies: Realignment or Dealignment?* Princeton: Princeton University Press.

Di Palma, G. (1990) 'Aquaria and fish soups. Totalitarianism, civil society, transitions', Unpublished manuscript, Ferrara University.

Fejto, F. (1952) *Histoire des Democraties Populaires: 1945–1952*, Paris: Editions du Seuil.

Fisichella, D. (1987) *Il totalitarismo*, Firenze: La Nuova Italia Scientifica.

Flora, P. (1980) 'Il macro-modello dello sviluppo politico europeo di Stein Rokkan', *Rivista Italiana di Scienza Politica* 10: 369–435.

Grilli di Cortona, P. (1989) *Le crisi politiche nei regimi comunisti*, Milano: Angeli.

Hammond, T. (ed.) (1977) *The Anatomy of Communist Takeovers*, New Haven: Yale University Press.

Inglehart, R. (1984) 'The changing structure of political cleavages in western societies', in R. J. Dalton, S. C. Flanagan and P. A. Beck (eds) *Electoral Change in Advanced Industrial Democracies: Realignment or Dealignment?* Princeton: Princeton University Press.

Korosenyi, A. (1991) 'Complexity of political formations in 1990', in S. Kurtan, S. Peter and L. Vass (eds) *Magyarorszag Politikai Evkoenyve 1991*, Budapest: Oekonomia Alapitvany.

Lijphart, A. (1971) 'Comparative politics and the comparative method', *American Political Science Review* 65: 682–93.

—— (1984) *Democracies. Patterns of Majoritarian and Consensus Government in Twenty-One Countries*, New Haven: Yale University Press.

——, Linz, J.J., Valenzuela, A., and Godoy, O. (1990) *Hacia una democracia moderna: la opcion parlamentaria*, Santiago: Ediciones Universidad Catolica de Chile.

Linz, J. J. (1967) 'The party system of Spain: past and future', in S. M. Lipset and S. Rokkan (eds) *Party Systems and Voter Alignments: Cross National Perspectives*, New York: The Free Press.

—— (1975) 'Authoritarian and totalitarian regimes', in F. I. Greenstein and N. W. Polsby (eds) *Handbook of Political Science. Vol. III: Macropolitical Theory*, Reading: Addison-Wesley.

—— (1978) 'Crisis, breakdown, and reequilibration', in J. J. Linz and A. Stepan (eds) *The Breakdown of Democratic Regimes*, Baltimore: The Johns Hopkins University Press.

Lipset, S. M., and Rokkan, S. (1967) 'Cleavage structures, party systems, and voter alignments: an introduction', in S. M. Lipset and S. Rokkan (eds) *Party Systems and Voter Alignments: Cross National Perspectives*, New York: The Free Press.

Mackie, T. T., and Rose, R. (1982) *The International Almanac of Electoral History*, London: Macmillan.

Maguire, M. (1983) 'Is there still persistence? Electoral change in Western Europe, 1948–1979', in H. Daalder and P. Mair (eds) *Western European Party Systems,* London: Sage.

Mamotey, V. S. (1973) *A History of the Czechoslovak Republic*, Princeton: Princeton University Press.

Morlino, L. (1986a) 'Democratic establishments. A dimensional analysis', in E. Baloyra (ed.) *Comparing New Democracies: Dilemmas of Transition and Consolidation in Mediterranean Europe and the Southern Cone*, Boulder: Westview.

—— (1986b) 'Consolidamento democratico: definizione e modelli', *Rivista Italiana di Scienza Politica* 16:197–238.

Pedersen, M. (1979) 'The dynamics of European party systems: changing patterns of electoral volatility', *European Journal of Political Research* 7: 7–26.

—— (1983) 'Changing patterns of electoral volatility in European party systems, 1948–1977: explorations in explanation', in H. Daalder and P. Mair (eds) *Western European Party Systems*, London: Sage.

Pridham, G. (ed.) (1990) *Securing Democracy: Political Parties and Democratic Consolidation in Southern Europe*, London: Routledge.

Rauch, G. von (1970) *The Baltic States: the Years of Independence*, London: Hurst.

Rokkan, S. (1970) *Citizens, Elections, Parties*, Oslo: Universitetsforlaget.

Rothschild, J. (1974) *East Central Europe between the Two World Wars*, Seattle: University of Washington Press.

Sartori, G. (1987) *The Theory of Democracy Revisited*, Chatham: Chatham House Publishers.

Seton-Watson, H. (1950) *The Eastern European Revolution*, London: Methuen.

—— (1986) *Eastern Europe between the Wars, 1918–1941*, Boulder: Westview Press.

Shamir, M. (1984) 'Are Western party systems "frozen"? A comparative dynamic analysis', *Comparative Political Studies* 17: 35–79.

Wheeler, D. L. (1978) *Republican Portugal. A Political History 1910–1926*, Wisconsin: The University of Wisconsin Press.

Wilensky, H. L. (1981) 'Leftism, catholicism and democratic corporatism: the role of political parties in recent welfare state development', in P. Flora and A. J. Heidenheimer (eds) *The Development of Welfare States in Europe and North America*, New Brunswick: Transaction Books.

5 The founding electoral systems in Eastern Europe, 1989–91

Kimmo Kuusela

As more and more countries of the world are turning into constitutional democracies, the effects of electoral systems on politics remain a subject of justifiable interest in the discipline of political science. Indeed, it has been highlighted by such system transformation. Currently, the most obvious target for electoral system designing is Eastern Europe, where all countries embarked on free or at least partially free parliamentary elections after the communist regimes collapsed in 1989. It is important to look at these early electoral systems for their formative influence on the new multi-party systems.

The study of electoral systems has traditionally regarded Eastern Europe and the Soviet Union as typical examples of no-choice elections, in which people can only approve or disapprove a candidate presented by the ruling party. Various functions of such 'elections' have been suggested, such as legitimation, communication between regime and citizenry, and a means of political mobilization and socialization (White 1985: 225–6). Now that most East European countries have held their first – and some even their second – post-communist-rule multi-party elections, it is time we took a look at how they have coped with the problem of choosing an electoral system. The choice is not simple, given the great variety of methods used in Western democracies during the history of electoral systems.

One general feature of the changes made to electoral practices in Eastern Europe after transition began was a shift away from the majority allocation rule, which was a universal system under the non-competitive elections, toward more proportional procedures, except in the Soviet Union, where the parliamentary elections of 1989 were only partially free. This is not a surprising trend, since proportional representation of parties would obviously be meaningless in a one-party system. Also, one has to bear in mind that the elections in Eastern Europe before the Second World War were proportional and that nowadays only English-speaking and British-influenced countries elect their parliaments on a plurality or majority basis.

Yet many East European states have not given up another rule characteristic of communist regimes, namely the requirement that unless the voter turnout in a constituency exceeds 50 per cent the elections are invalid, and a new round of voting must be held within two weeks. Despite the common features, the end result was that all these states produced electoral systems different from each other, and none of them is a straight imitation of any Western democratic polity.

THE SOVIET UNION

The first experiment with competitive elections in the Soviet Union was made at the local elections of 1987, in which more than one candidate was presented to the voter in about 1 per cent of the constituencies. President Mikhail Gorbachev found the effects of the experiment so beneficial that he recommended a substantial renewal of the electoral system (White 1990: 60).

The new electoral law was part of the constitutional reconstruction of the Soviet state. It was approved on 1 December 1988 to be used on 26 March 1989 for electing the Soviet Union's restyled parliament, the Congress of People's Deputies. The balloting required a voter to indicate a preference by crossing the names of candidates he or she did not favour; in cases where only one name was on the ballot, crossing it out indicated a vote against the sole candidate. Each voter cast votes on separate ballots for two candidates, one of whom stood in one of 750 'territorial' constituencies organized to represent roughly equal numbers of voters, and the other in one of 750 'national-territorial' constituencies organized to give representation to all the Soviet Union's numerous ethnic groups. The remaining 750 deputies were elected during March by 32 all-union 'social organizations', including the Communist Party, trade unions, the Leninist Young Communist League (*Komsomol*), cooperative organizations and professional unions (*Keesing's* 1989: 36486, 36512).

Under the new law the right to nominate candidates was extended to voters' meetings of 500 or more in addition to the Communist Party and other public organizations, but a candidate's endorsement by voters' meetings did not guarantee him/her a place on the ballot on 26 March, since candidate lists would now be reviewed by the Communist Party-dominated Central Electoral Commission, which was empowered to strike off names in constituencies where there were two or more candidates (*Keesing's* 1989: 36401). As the final result of the selection, from a total of 7,558 nominees – among whom were an unidentified number of multiple proposals – that had initially been put forward for selection as constituency candidates only 2,899 candidates remained. Only one candidate stood in 399 constituencies, two candidates in 952 constituencies and three or more candidates in 149 constituencies (Brunner 1990: 42).

After the first round of elections, 1,226 of the 1,500 constituency seats had been filled. In 76 constituencies, where no candidate from a list of three or more had received the required absolute majority, a run-off between the two best-placed candidates was held on 2 April or 9 April. In the remaining 195 constituencies, enough voters had crossed out either the name of a single candidate, or the names of both of the two candidates, to prevent the emergence of a victor with the necessary absolute majority, and the whole process of nominating and selecting candidates had thus to begin again. In these constituencies, as in three Armenian constituencies in which the elections were invalid because voting turnout was less than 50 per cent, and in one constituency where the elected deputy died after the election, fresh elections were held on 14 May (Brunner 1990: 42–3).

It is not possible to estimate the effects of the USSR's electoral system on party representation, because the Communist Party was the only political party operating nationwide. An estimated 85 per cent of the constituency candidates were Communist Party members. The central focus of interest in analyses of the congress election results was instead on the defeats that were suffered by party and state leaders at all levels.

POLAND

In Poland the round table talks which had begun on 6 February 1989 between the authorities and the outlawed Solidarity trade union led to comprehensive reforms, including the constitutional amendments on 7 April. A new bicameral National Assembly was created comprising as its lower house the 460-seat *Sejm* (the former unicameral legislature) and as its upper house a new 100-seat Senate. Direct elections for the two houses, which were planned to sit for simultaneous four-year terms, took place in two rounds on 4 and 18 June (see Table 5.1). In the *Sejm* elections, contests for 65 per cent of the seats were restricted to candidates from the then-ruling Polish United Workers' Party (PZPR), and from its traditional coalition partners, the United Peasants' Party (ZDL) and the Democratic Party (SD), or from three lay Roman Catholic organizations; while the remaining 35 per cent were contested

Table 5.1 The Polish election results of 4 and 18 June 1989

Party or group of MPs	Seats	Seats %
Polish United Worker's Party (PZPR)	173	37.6
Opposition (Solidarity Citizens' Committee)	161	35.0
United Peasant's Party (ZSL)	76	16.5
Democratic Party (SD)	27	5.9
Christian Associations (CHSS + PZK)	13	2.8
Progressive Catholic (PAX)	10	2.2
Total	460	100.0

Sources: Raina 1990: 114–15; Lewis 1990: 93–9; Gambarelli and Holubiec 1990: 30.
Note: Turnout (first ballot) 62.1 per cent, (second ballot) 25.9 per cent.

by candidates from opposition or independent groups, and were all won by the Solidarity Citizens' Committee (the electoral platform of the recently relegalized Solidarity trade union). The Senate seats were all filled by completely free balloting, and all but one were won by Solidarity candidates (*Keesing's* 1990: 37733).

The electoral system for the *Sejm* election was as follows: (1) 35 seats were predetermined for a national list of unopposed candidates. Voters were able to reject any or all of the candidates on this list by crossing out their names. To be elected a candidate needed 50 per cent of the vote. (2) 425 seats were allocated to 108 districts. District magnitude varied from 2 to 5, but the contest was effectively a system of majority in single-member districts, because there was a separate list of candidates exclusively for each individual seat, and within each list a voter could either vote for one candidate or reject all candidates on a list. If no candidate received 50 per cent of the vote in the first round, a second election was held after two weeks between the two leading candidates on a first-past-the-post basis (Opolska and Owen 1989: 1).

In the 100-seat Senate election district magnitude was 2, except for Warsaw and Katowice, which both returned 3 senators. In two-member districts voters could either vote for one or two candidates or reject all candidates. In three-member districts a combination of three candidates was also allowed. To become a senator on the first round of the election, a candidate had to have his name uncrossed on at least half of the valid votes. As in the Soviet Union's elections, a preference for a candidate was indicated by striking out the names of non-preferred candidates. The number of candidates on the second round was, at a maximum, twice the number of seats remaining to be filled after the first ballot (Opolska and Owen 1989: 26–7).

A total of 558 candidates ran for the Senate and 1,760 for the *Sejm*.

Many non-Solidarity candidates did not identify themselves openly with any political organization. Nearly all of the Solidarity candidates were elected with outright majorities on the first round. The second round was contested on a first-past-the-post basis by the two leading candidates in 295 *Sejm* seats and eight Senate seats. On a 'national list' of 35 unopposed candidates from the approved parties, a total of 33 candidates failed to win the required 50 per cent of the vote in the first round. Hence electoral regulations were amended by drawing up a new slate of candidates, with two candidates contesting each of the 33 seats (*Keesing's* 1989: 36723).

Poland's first fully free parliamentary elections on 27 October 1991 witnessed a remarkable proliferation of parties. A total of 29 groups received seats in the *Sejm* (see Table 5.2). It was widely assumed that this was caused by an extremely proportional electoral system. But the result was not very proportional, since 'the total deviation from proportionality' (D) was as high as 12.4 per cent. The theoretical range of D is from 0 to 100. For example in Finland D was only 5.7 per cent

Table 5.2 *Sejm* elections in Poland, 27 October 1991

Party	Votes (%)	Seats	Seats (%)
Democratic Union	12.3	62	13.5
Democratic Left Alliance (ex-communists)	12.0	60	13.0
Catholic Action	8.7	49	10.7
Polish Peasant Party (ex-allies of communists)	8.7	48	10.4
Confederation for an Independent Poland	7.5	46	10.0
Central Alliance	8.7	44	9.6
Liberal Democrats	7.5	37	8.0
Peasant Solidarity	5.5	28	6.1
Trade Union Solidarity	5.1	27	5.9
Beer-Lovers	3.3	16	3.5
German Party	1.2	7	1.5
Christian Democracy	2.4	5	1.1
Labour Solidarity	2.1	4	0.9
Party of Christian Democrats	1.1	4	0.9
Polish Western Union	0.2	4	0.9
Union of Political Realism	2.3	3	0.9
Party X	0.5	3	0.7
Movement for Silesian Autonomy	0.4	2	0.4
Democratic Party	1.4	1	0.2
Democratic–Social Movement	0.5	1	0.2
Others	8.6	9	2.0
Total	100.0	460	100

Sources: Professor Jacek Mercik, letter to the author, November 1991; *Keesing's* 1991: 38536; Millard 1991–2: 73; Webb 1992: 167.
Note: Turnout 43.2 per cent. Valid votes 40.8 per cent of the electorate.

in the 1991 *Eduskunta* elections. On the other hand, *D* may sometimes overstate the disproportionality of elections with many parties. The general formula for *D* is

$$D = (1/2) \Sigma \mid s_i - v_i \mid$$

where Σ = summation over all parties involved, s_i = fractional or per cent seat share of i-th party, and v_i = fractional or per cent votes share of i-th party (Taagepera and Shugart 1989: 104–5). The fragmentation of the parliament was essentially caused by the voters, not by the system, which can also be seen from the fact that in the simultaneous Senate elections (see Table 5.3), which were conducted by plurality rule in two and three member districts with a total of only 100 seats, even more parties (31) won seats than in the *Sejm* elections. If the plurality rule is applied in multimember districts, as in Poland, the number of seat-winning parties is likely to be even lower than with single member districts. This holds in a setting where the voters vote for as many candidates as there are seats to be filled in a district. Thus, only by incorporating into law a legal threshold of a minimum nationwide vote share could the number of seat-winning parties have been reduced. The problem is that the choice of the height of the threshold cannot be based upon any general principle.

Knowledge of Poland's October 1991 electoral law draws on the

Table 5.3 Senate elections in Poland, 27 October 1991

Party	Seats
Democratic Union	21
Trade Union Solidarity	11
Catholic Action	9
Central Alliance	9
Polish Peasant Party	7
Liberal Democrats	6
Peasant Solidarity	5
Democratic Left Alliance	4
Confederation for an Independent Poland	4
Party of Christian Democrats	3
National Electoral Committee	1
German Party	1
Christian Democracy	1
18 local parties, 1 seat each	18
Total	100

Sources: Professor Jacek Mercik, letter to the author, November 1991; *Keesing's* 1991: 38536.
Note: Turnout 43.2 per cent. Valid votes 41.7 per cent of the electorate.

English translation of that law (*Act of June 28, 1991* . . .; *Act of May 10, 1991* . . .). In the elections to the *Sejm*, 391 out of 460 seats were filled with a method akin to Finland's electoral system, i.e. a voter casts a vote for one candidate, and the personal votes are added to determine the total number of votes for each party. There is a proportional allocation of seats among parties, and a plurality rule for allocating seats to individual candidates within parties. The mathematical formula used in Poland in the proportional allocation was the method of largest remainders with simple quota (or Hare quota). The number of electoral districts was 37. The range of the magnitude of the districts was from 7 to 17, with an average of 10.6.

As many as 70 political parties presented their lists of candidates, and the number of candidates was altogether 6,980. To gain a nomination, a list of candidates had to be supported by at least 5,000 signatures of voters residing in a given constituency. If this was achieved in at least five districts, or if the list had collected at least 50,000 signatures in any one district, the party was allowed to register a list of candidates in all the other districts as well. For the organizations of national minorities the criteria were less stringent: 5,000 signatures in two districts or 20,000 signatures in one district.

The next problem was the nomination of national lists of candidates. These candidates too had to be chosen from the group of persons that had already been registered as candidates in the districts. A party could form a national list only if it had registered a district list in at least five districts; while for national minorities, registering in one district was sufficient. Yet another rule provided that in order to be allowed to participate in the distribution of national seats, a party had to have gained seats in at least five districts or obtained at least 5 per cent of the votes cast for all the lists in all districts.

The method for allocation of the national seats was the one used in Scandinavia, namely the modified Sainte-Laguë (divisors 1.4, 3, 5, 7, . . .). The order of candidates on the national lists was predetermined by the parties, but before starting the distribution of seats to candidates the candidates who had already been elected from the district lists were deleted from the national list; and thus the candidates who had not won enough support from the voters were given a second chance. This type of system of adjusting seats differs from the compensatory seat principle used in nationwide allocation in Denmark and Sweden. In Poland's method the nationwide seats are allocated without regard to who got how many seats in the districts. The effect is like adding another 69-seat district to the normal districts (Taagepera and Shugart 1989: 126–41).

The electoral system in Poland's senate elections in October 1991 was similar to the one in the 1989 elections, except that there was no option for a second round of election.

EAST GERMANY

The first completely free and secret election in the still separate East Germany was held on 18 March 1990 (see Table 5.4). It was also the first free election during the process of democratization in Eastern Europe. The task of a voter was no longer a negative one: instead of crossing out the names of the candidates he or she did not like, a voter now simply marked a party for which he or she voted. The names of the candidates did not appear on the voting form.

Table 5.4 The results of the *Volkskammer* elections in the GDR, 18 March 1990

Party	Votes (%)	Seats	Seats (%)
Christian Democratic Union (CDU)	40.8	163	40.8
Social Democrats (SPD–DDR)	21.9	88	22.0
Democratic Socialists (PDS)	16.4	66	16.5
German Social Union (DSU)	6.3	25	6.3
League of Free Democrats (BFD)	5.3	21	5.3
Alliance '90 (New Forum etc.)	2.9	12	3.0
Democratic Peasants' Party (DBD)	2.2	9	2.3
Green Party/Ind. Women's Union	2.0	8	2.0
Democratic Awakening (DA)	0.9	4	1.0
National Democratic Party (NDPD)	0.4	2	0.5
Democratic Women's League (DFD)	0.3	1	0.3
Action Alliance United Left (AVL)	0.2	1	0.3
Others	0.5	0	0.0
Total	100	400	100

Sources: Hyde-Price 1990: 4; *Keesing's* 1990: 37301.
Note: Turnout 93.4 per cent. Valid votes 92.9 per cent of the electorate.

The country was divided into 15 electoral districts corresponding to the country's 15 administrative regions. The number of seats in each district varied from 13 to 45, determined by the population in each case. To ensure proportionality and representation, even for parties polling a small fraction of the vote across the country, a first count was made on a country-wide basis according to the so-called Hare–Niemeyer system, which is the same as the traditional Hare system but differently formulated. Afterwards a second constituency-by-constituency count was made. There was no legal threshold of 5 per cent of nationwide votes, as in West Germany (*Keesing's* 1990: 37301; Hyde-Price 1990: 3).

These rules, together with the large size (400 seats) of the *Volks-kammer*, contributed to a very high degree of proportionality in the election results. The total deviation (*D*) from perfect PR was only 0.6 per cent. Compared with 48 countries' national elections in 1980s, only Greenland (0.2 per cent) had a lower value of Deviation from proportionality (Taagepera and Shugart 1989: 106–7).

HUNGARY

There was some degree of choice available for Hungarian voters already in the 1985 parliamentary election, with a compulsory minimum of two candidates per district and a voters' right to nominate their own candidates in competition with the official Patriotic People's Front list (HNF). However, all candidates had to pledge themselves to the HNF political programme. The electoral reform also introduced a national list of 35 candidates without opposition, nominated by the HNF (Racz 1989: 39).

The 1989 law on parliamentary elections provided for a rather complicated mixed system of proportional representation and single-member constituencies. Of the 386 members, 176 were to be elected from single-member local constituencies called 'individual seats', where results were decided either by an absolute majority in the first round, or in a second round, to which candidates would proceed if they finished in the top three or obtained over 15 per cent of the vote (see Table 5.5). The turnout had to be at least 50 per cent of the electorate in the first round. If the required turnout was not achieved, a valid election in the second round required a turnout of over 25 per cent, and the candidate with the most votes won (Batt 1990: 8; Szendrei 1990: 6; *Keesing's*, 1990: 37325). But voters were handed two voting slips at the polling station; 152 seats were to be elected on a proportional basis from 20 multi-member county and metropolitan electoral districts. The district magnitude varied from 4 to 28, with an average magnitude of 7.6.

The requirement of a turnout of over 50 per cent for a valid election in the first round, and similarly of 25 per cent in the second round, also applied to each of these regional districts. The parties submitted their regional lists of candidates in order of preference. The voters could only vote for a party, not for a candidate. Parties polling less than 4 per cent of the vote calculated from the regional votes over the country as a whole could not obtain seats in the regional districts even if in any particular district they had won over 4 per cent. The seats in the regional districts were allocated to parties according to the Droop quota/largest remainder procedure, except that a seat could not be gained with a

Table 5.5 Seats and votes won by parties in the 176 single-member constituencies in Hungary, 1990 (first round 25 March; second round 8 April)

Party	Seats	Seats (%)	First round votes (%)
Hungarian Democratic Forum (HDF)	114	64.8	23.9
Alliance of Free Democrats (AFD)	35	19.9	21.7
Independent Smallholders' Party (ISP)	11	6.3	10.7
Independent Candidates	6	3.4	6.9
Christian Democratic Peoples' Party (CDPP)	3	1.7	5.8
AFD/*Fidesz* (joint deputy)	2	1.1	0.6
Hungarian Socialist Party (HSP)	1	0.6	10.1
Federation of Young Democrats (*Fidesz*)	1	0.6	4.7
Agrarian Alliance	1	0.6	2.8
Agrarian Alliance/*SZFV* (joint deputy)	1	0.6	0.3
AFD/*Fidesz*/CDPP (joint deputy)	1	0.6	0.1
Others	0	0.0	12.4
Total	176	100	100.0

Sources: *Parlamenti Választások 1990;* Mackie 1992: 326.
Note: Turnout (first ballot) 65.0 per cent. Valid votes (first ballot) 62.8 per cent of the electorate, (second ballot) 45.9 per cent.

remainder smaller than two-thirds of the quota (Batt 1990: 8–9; Szendrei 1990: 6; *Act No. XXXIX of 1989*: 41–3).

These surplus votes, together with the votes for unsuccessful candidates in single-member constituencies, were transferred to a third level of allocation, that of national seats, according to the party affiliation of the candidates. The parties had presented separate lists of candidates for these originally 58 seats. In the final allocation, the number of regional seats not filled due to the two-thirds rule mentioned above was added to the number of seats obtainable on the national list, so the final number of national seats was raised to 90, and the number of regional seats respectively reduced to 120. If a party failed to win the 4 per cent minimum of the county votes, it was also barred from taking part in the allocation of national seats. The distribution of seats on the national level took place according to the Hare quota. Such a quota is computed by dividing the total number of votes by the number of deputies to be elected. A Droop quota, which was used on the county level, is slightly more favourable to large parties. It is calculated by dividing the number of votes by the number of seats to be filled plus one (Batt 1990: 10–11; *Act No. XXXIV of 1989:* 41–2).

There was yet another difference between the rules of county seats and national seats. On the county level each party list was first given as many seats as the whole number, which resulted when the number of its votes was divided by the quota. If all the seats were not distributed, the number of 'unused votes' was computed for each list. The lists were ranked in descending order according to the number of unused votes. They were awarded one seat each from the top of this ranking up to two-thirds of the quota. For the national seats the second phase of the process was different, since if vacant seats remained after the whole quotas had been subtracted from each party's vote share, the total number of remaining votes was divided again by the number of vacant seats. The division resulted in a new number of votes required for obtaining a seat. The filling-up of mandates was carried on under the new quota and the remaining votes in decreasing order until all seats were filled up, and the calculation repeated if needed (Hylland 1990: 24; *Act No. XXXIV of 1989*: 41–3).

This system of allocating the remaining seats used in the national level of Hungary's elections is unknown in the literature of electoral studies. It does not seem to make much sense either. For example, in a hypothetical election (from Taagepera and Shugart 1989: 23), in which there are five seats to be filled and the vote distribution among parties is 48.5–29–14–7.5–1, the quota is 100/5 = 20 per cent. The largest party gets two seats for 2 x 20 = 40 per cent, and the remainder is 48.5–40 = 8.5. The second largest party is allocated one seat, and the remainder is 29–20 = 9 per cent. The other parties have mere remainders at this stage: 14 per cent, 7 per cent and 1 per cent. Two seats remain to be distributed. Now, according to the Hungarian electoral law, 'the number of . . . surplus votes shall be divided by the number of vacant mandates. The division results in a new number of votes required for obtaining a mandate' (*Act No. XXXIV of 1989*: Annex No. 4, Par.III/6). The sum of the surplus votes is 8.5 + 9 + 14 + 7.5 + 1 = 40 per cent, which divided by 2 is the same 20 per cent as the original quota. Obviously, a proper allocation of seats is impossible by this procedure.

The results of the majority seats' election were very disproportional. Total deviation from PR was 42.1 per cent, a figure which is higher than in any of the 48 countries' recent elections listed in Taagepera and Shugart (1989: 106–7).

A closer resemblance to perfect PR was of course achieved in the distribution of regional seats by the modified PR allocation rule. Yet the deviation from proportionality (D) was 18.1 per cent, which is also a relatively high value. Factors causing this disproportionality were: (1) the legal threshold of 4 per cent of nationwide votes, (2) the two-thirds rule in remainder distribution, (3) the Droop quota as a formula for the allocation of seats to parties, (4) because district magnitude was only 4 seats in the smallest districts, and (5) because the psychological effect

Table 5.6 Regional, national and total votes and seats in Hungary, (first round) 25 March and (second round) 8 April 1990

Party	Regional seats (%)	Regional votes (%)	National seats	Total seats	Total seats (%)	Total votes (%)
HDF	33.3	24.7	10	164	42.5	24.3
AFD	28.3	21.4	23	92	23.8	21.6
ISP	13.3	11.7	17	44	11.4	11.2
HSP	11.7	10.9	18	33	8.5	10.5
Fidesz	6.7	9.0	12	21	5.4	6.8
CDPP	6.7	6.5	10	21	5.4	6.1
Independent	0	0	0	6	1.6	3.5
AFD/*Fidesz*	0	0	0	2	0.5	0.3
Agrarian	0	3.1	0	1	0.3	3.0
SZFV/Agrarian	0	0	0	1	0.3	0.1
AFD/*Fidesz*/CDPP	0	0	0	1	0.3	0.1
Others	0	12.8	0	0	0	12.5
Total	100.0	100	90	386	100.0	100.0

Sources: *Parlamenti Választások 1990*; Batt 1990: 10–11; Mackie 1992: 326.
Note: Turnout (regional election) 65.1 per cent. Valid votes (regional election) 62.8 per cent of the electorate.

might not work in a first election: people have not yet had opportunities to see that a vote for a small party can be ineffective.

The allocation of national seats somewhat further reduced disproportionalities, but the final results (see Table 5.6) still showed a considerable bonus to the largest party, HDF, which received a 42.5 per cent share of the total seats with 24.3 per cent of the total vote (total vote includes votes cast in the first round of the individual seats' election plus party list votes cast in the regional districts). Total deviation from PR, calculated from total seats and votes, was 21.2 per cent, which is quite large for a system aiming at some proportionality. On the other hand, the result made it possible to form a majority coalition government relatively quickly.

ROMANIA

The two chambers of the Romanian parliament – the National Assembly and the Senate – were elected on 20 May 1990. In the elections, 387 seats were contested in the National Assembly (see Table 5.7) and 119 in the Senate (see Table 5.8). The total number of National Assembly seats was brought up to 396 by the allocation of a further nine seats to national minority organizations that were registered at the time the electoral law was adopted but failed to win representation through the regular electoral process (Shafir 1990: 29; *Keesing's* 1990: 37741).

Table 5.7 National Assembly election results in Romania, 20 May 1990

Party	Votes (%)	Seats	Seats (%)
National Salvation Front	66.3	263	68.0
Hungarian Democratic Union of Romania	7.2	29	7.5
National Liberal Party	6.4	29	7.5
Ecological Movement of Romania	2.6	12	3.1
Christian Democratic National Peasants' Party	2.6	12	3.1
Romanian Unity Alliance	2.1	9	2.3
Agrarian Democratic Party	1.8	9	2.3
Romanian Ecologist Party	1.4	8	2.1
Romanian Socialist Democratic Party	1.1	5	1.3
Romanian Social Democrat Party	0.5	2	0.5
Democratic Group of the Centre	0.5	2	0.5
Democratic Party of Labour	0.4	1	0.3
Free Exchange Party	0.3	1	0.3
Party of the National Reconstruction of Romania	0.3	1	0.3
Free Democratic Youth Party	0.3	1	0.3
Democratic Forum of the Germans of Romania	0.3	1	0.3
'Bratianu' Liberal Union	0.3	1	0.3
Democratic Union of the Romanies of Romania	0.3	1	0.3
Others	5.4	0	0
Total	100.0	387	100

Source: Mackie 1992: 331.
Note: Turnout 86.2 per cent. Valid votes 79.7 per cent of the electorate.

The electoral system for both chambers was a PR one based on 41 multi-seat districts, which were geographically the same as the counties plus the Bucharest municipality. The district magnitude in the National Assembly election ranged from 4 to 15 for the county districts and it was 39 in Bucharest. Average magnitude was 9.4. In the Senate election the range of magnitude was from 2 to 4 in the counties, and Bucharest had 14 senators, while the average magnitude was 2.9 (Hylland 1990: 25).

Elections in any constituency were valid only if at least half the eligible voters plus one cast their votes. If turnout was lower than that, new elections were to be held within two weeks, using the same lists of candidates. For the second round, no minimum number of voters was stipulated. However, a second round was not needed in any constituency, since more than 86 per cent of the electorate voted in the elections (Shafir 1990: 30; *Keesing's* 1990: 37441).

Distribution of lower house seats took place as follows. In the first stage, seats were allocated to parties and other lists of candidates in

Table 5.8 Senate election results in Romania, 20 May 1990

Party	Votes (%)	Seats	Seats (%)
National Salvation Front	67.0	92	77.3
Hungarian Democratic Union of			
Romania	7.2	12	10.1
National Liberal Party	7.1	9	7.6
Christian Democratic National Peasants'			
Party	2.5	1	0.8
Ecological Movement of Romania	2.5	1	0.8
Romanian Unity Alliance	2.2	2	1.7
Agrarian Democratic Party	1.6	0	0
Romanian Ecologist Party	1.4	1	0.8
Romanian Socialist Democrat Party	1.1	0	0
Other parties and independents	7.4	1	0.8
Total	100.0	119	100

Sources: *Keesing's* 1990: 37442; Gallagher 1991: 90; Deletant 1990: 25.
Note: Valid votes 81.1 per cent of the electorate.

each constituency according to a simple Hare quota, which is the number of votes that results when the total number of valid votes in the constituency is divided by the number of deputies to be elected. Each list of candidates received a number of seats equal to the result of dividing the number of votes for the respective list by Hare quota. Within lists, seats were awarded to candidates appearing on top of a list in a predetermined order. Voters had no opportunity to influence the order of candidates within a list (*Juridical Regulations . . .* 1990: 16).

Full quota allocation in constituencies was followed in the second stage by a d'Hondt allocation in the national level, using remainder votes from the first stage. In the absence of a legal vote share threshold for small parties, this system of nationwide distribution of remaining votes is favourable to small parties, because small parties that received no constituency seats at the first stage account for a disproportionately large fraction of the remainder votes (Hylland 1990: 28; Taagepera and Shugart 1989: 132). The third stage was for determining to which constituencies the seats won by parties in the second stage should be assigned. The rules at this stage become rather complicated. Hylland (1990: 29) comments on them by saying: 'I have tried to understand the text, but I have not succeeded. I doubt that it gives a precise algorithm for how to perform the distribution.'

The National Assembly election results (see Table 5.7) showed support for the prediction of small parties' success, but the total deviation from proportionality was still 5.7 per cent because of the large number of very small parties. The landslide victory of the ruling

142   *Emerging party systems and institutions*

National Salvation Front was not much amplified by the mechanics of the electoral system.

The electoral system for the 119 Senate seats was identical to the Assembly system, but remainder votes were not computed nationally. Instead, the remaining seats were distributed according to the descending weight of the parties' remaining votes at the constituency level. The consequence of a small district magnitude and of the lack of nationwide compensation was a larger disproportionality (D = 13.8 per cent) than in the Assembly election. Here the National Salvation Front's 67 per cent vote share was translated into 77 per cent of the seats (see Table 5.8).

CZECHOSLOVAKIA

Czechoslovakia's first free and secret general election since 1946 was held on 8–9 June 1990. The elections at federal level were for 300 seats in the federal assembly – 150 in the Chamber of the People and 150 in the Chamber of Nations (see Table 5.9). In the Chamber of the People, 101 seats were reserved for the Czech Republic and 49 for the Slovak Republic; in the Chamber of Nations each republic had 75 seats. Parties had to exceed a 5 per cent threshold of votes in either the Czech Lands or Slovakia in order to win seats. The same proportional representation system applied to elections to both chambers (*Keesing's* 1990: 37542).

The apportionment of seats to districts was not based on the

Table 5.9 Czechoslovakia's federal election results, 8 and 9 June 1990

Party	Chamber of People Votes (%)	Seats	Seats (%)	Chamber of Nations Votes (%)	Seats	Seats (%)
Civic Forum & Public Against Violence	46.6	87	58.0	45.9	83	55.3
Communist Party of Czechoslovakia	13.6	23	15.3	13.7	24	16.0
Christian and Democratic Union & Christian Democratic Movement	12.0	20	13.3	11.3	20	13.3
Movement for Self-Governing Democracy & Society for Moravia and Silesia	5.4	9	6.0	3.6	9	6.0
Slovak National Party	3.5	6	4.0	6.2	7	4.7
Coexistence	2.8	5	3.3	2.7	7	4.7
Others	16.1	0	0	16.6	0	0
Total	100.0	150	100	100.0	150	100.0

Sources: *Keesing's* 1990: 37542–3; Mackie 1992: 320.
Note: Turnout 96.3 per cent. Valid votes 95.0 per cent of the electorate.

population, but on the total number of valid votes cast (*Law on Elections* . . . 1990: 12). This may have contributed to a very high turnout (96.3 per cent), but as Taagepera and Shugart (1989: 18) point out, it is 'against the rule of "one person, one vote" – regardless of whether one makes use of one's vote'. Lists of candidates could be presented only by political parties. Within each political party, the candidates received the seats allocated to the party according to the order printed on the ballot. However, if at least one-tenth of the total of voters casting a valid vote for the respective party in the electoral district used the right to a preference vote, the candidates who received a preference vote from more than 50 per cent of those voters were moved to the top of the list. The voter was allowed to express a preference for candidates by circling the numbers of a maximum of four candidates listed on one ballot. This could be more accurately defined as an application of approval voting, since the personal votes were of equal weight and not truly preferential (*Law on Elections* . . . 1990: 9, 12).

The distribution of seats to parties started at the district level with a full quota allocation, using the Droop quota (the total number of valid votes in a district divided by the number of seats to be allocated plus one). A Droop quota is smaller than a Hare quota, which means that more seats can be allocated by full quotas. As a result of this first stage, 137 of the 150 seats had been allocated in both chambers (*Law on Elections* . . . 1990: 12; *Složení Federálního* . . . 1990).

As in Hungary and Romania, so also in Czechoslovakia: the remainder seats after district allocation were transferred to the national level (Republic level in the case of Czechoslovakia). The need for such a complication is questionable. If the aim is to increase proportionality, it could be done more simply (e.g. by using a Hare quota on the district level instead of a Droop quota). The former treats small and large parties equally, while the latter gives a slight advantage to larger parties. The average district magnitude (12.5) would have been large enough to give all parties a fair representation even without the aggregate-level compensatory allocation of remainder seats (*Law on Elections* . . . 1990: 12, appendix).

What was good in Czechoslovakia's remainder distribution rules was that they avoided the problems of Hungary's and Romania's rules. The parties nominated a separate list of candidates for the national seats, which means that there was no need to redistribute these seats between districts, as in Romania, although it could also lead to some imbalance in the number of deputies per district. Also, the description of quota allocation was followed by a largest remainder rule, which ensured that all seats could be allocated (unlike in Hungary) (*Law on Elections* . . . 1990: 13).

The main reason for deviations from proportionality was the 5 per cent threshold. When calculated on the basis of only those parties which surpassed the threshold, total deviation from proportionality in the Chamber of the People election was only 2.5 per cent, but on the basis of all votes it was 16.4 per cent. The vote shares of parties in the Chamber of Nations election were roughly equal to those of the Chamber of the People election, with a D of 18.1 per cent.

BULGARIA

Democratic elections to Bulgaria's unicameral National Assembly were held on 10 and 17 June 1990. The electoral law provided for two separate systems which were both used to elect 200 seats of the total of 400 seats (see Table 5.10). Every voter had two votes. There were 200 single-member districts and 28 multi-member districts with an average magnitude of 7.1. In order to win a seat in a single-member district, a candidate had to receive at least 50 per cent of the vote in the first round of the election. Otherwise a second election was held with the two candidates who had the most votes in the first round. A second round was also to be held if voter participation in the first round was less than 50 per cent (*Keesing's* 1990: 37543; *Loi Electorale* . . . 1990: 1, 24).

The other half of the legislature was elected by proportional representation. Only parties receiving at least 4 per cent of valid votes in all multi-member constituencies could win seats through the proportional part of the election. The rules for allocating the PR seats were not prescribed in the electoral law, but were instead to be determined by the Central Electoral Commission, which chose the d'Hondt system (*Keesing's* 1990: 37544; *Loi Electorale* . . . 1990: 24–5; Crampton 1990: 34).

The 4 per cent threshold did not have much effect on proportionality since the parties below 4 per cent received together only about 2 per cent of the vote. Total deviation from proportionality in the PR part of the election was only about 2.3 per cent. When the majority election seats are added, the deviation grows to about 6 per cent, which is still a reasonable value. (The vote shares in the majority election have not been published. I assume that they were approximately similar to those of the PR election.)

In Bulgaria's second free elections on 13 October 1991 (see Table 5.11), the electoral system had been clarified by abandoning the single-member districts and reducing the size of the parliament to 240 seats (sources for these elections: Owen 1991; Dr Nicolay Stanoulov, letter to the author, December 1991). Parties submitted a separate ranked list

Table 5.10 Election results in Bulgaria, 10 and 17 June 1990

| Party | PR election | | | | Majority election | | | Total |
	Votes (%)	Seats	Seats (%)	Seats	Seats (%)	Seats	Seats (%)	Seats (%)
Bulgarian Socialist Party	47.2	97	48.5	114	57.0	211	52.8	
Union of Democratic Forces	36.2	75	37.5	69	34.5	144	36.0	
Bulgarian Agrarian People's Union	8.0	16	8.0	0	0	16	4.0	
Movement for Rights and Freedoms	6.0	12	6.0	11	5.5	23	5.8	
Fatherland Union	*	0	0	2	1.0	2	0.5	
Bulgarian Social Dem. Party	0.1	0	0	1	0.5	1	0.3	
Fatherland Party of Labour	0.6	0	0	1	0.5	1	0.3	
Independents	*	0	0	2	1.0	2	0.5	
Others	1.9	0	0	0	0	0	0	
Total	100.0	200	100.0	200	100.0	400	100	

Sources: Keesing's 1990: 37544; Mackie 1992: 319.

Notes: *Did not stand in the proportional election for party electoral lists. Turnout (majority election, first ballot) 90.8 per cent, (PR election) 90.6 per cent, (majority election, second ballot) 84.1 per cent. Valid votes (PR election) 87.6 per cent of the electorate.

Table 5.11 Parliamentary election in Bulgaria, 13 October 1991

Party	Votes (%)	Seats	Seats (%)
Union of Democratic Forces	34.4	110	45.8
Socialists (ex-communists)	33.1	106	44.2
Movement for Rights and Freedoms			
(Turkish party)	7.6	24	10.0
Others	24.9	0	0
Total	100.0	240	100.0

Source: Dr Nicolay Stanoulov, letter to the author, December 1991.
Note: Turnout 83.9 per cent. Valid votes 81.6 per cent of the electorate.

of candidates to those of the 31 districts in which they wanted to participate, but all the seats were allocated by the d'Hondt method to parties according to their nationwide vote shares. The districts were used only to distribute regionally, also utilizing the d'Hondt rule, the seats each party had already won on the basis of national results. This rule has obviously been borrowed from the Federal Republic of Germany, where the *Länder* perform a similar role. As in Czecho-slovakia, the regional representation is determined by the number of votes, not by the size of population.

This time the effect of the 4 per cent threshold was more profound than in 1990, as only three parties gained seats, and 24.9 per cent of the total vote went to parties that failed to win any seats. Because of the nationwide seat distribution, the seat-winning parties got almost exactly a proportional share of the seats when the votes for other parties are excluded from calculation. The total deviation from proportionality was the same as the share of 'wasted' votes, i.e. 24.9 per cent, which is very high. There were altogether 38 parties contesting, of which seven received a vote share ranging from 1 to 4 per cent.

ALBANIA

Albania's first free multi-party elections were held on 31 March 1991 followed by a second round of voting on 7 and 14 April (see Table 5.12). Participation rates reached higher levels than in any other country which had embarked on democratic elections. In the first round, it was 98.7 per cent, and even in the second round – when only 18 seats were at stake – 96.6 per cent cast their votes. The votes were translated into seats by the method of two-round majority in 250 single-member districts. The ruling communist Albanian Party of Labour (PLA) obtained 56.2 per cent of the vote in the first round. On the level of seats, with 67.6 per cent the PLA won a two-thirds majority in the

Table 5.12 Albania's election results, 31 March 1991, and 7 and 14 April 1991

Party	Votes (%)	Seats	Seats (%)
Albanian Party of Labour (PLA)	56.2	169*	67.6
Democratic Party (DP)	38.7	75	30.0
Omonia (ethnic Greeks)	0.7	5	2.0
National Veterans' Committee	0.3	1	0.4
Republican Party	1.8	0	0
Ecology Party	n/a	0	0
Agrarian Party	0.1	0	0
Party of National Unity	n/a	0	0
Women's Union	n/a	0	0
Trade unions	n/a	0	0
Youth Union	n/a	0	0
Democratic Front	n/a	0	0
17 independent candidates	n/a	0	0
Total	100	250	100.0

Sources: Szajkowski 1992: 160; *Keesing's* 1991: 38106, 38160.
Notes: *Including 19 contested jointly with the Democratic Front, the Youth Union, the trade unions and the Women's Union. Turnout (first ballot) 98.9 per cent, (second ballot) 96.6 per cent.

People's Assembly, which would empower it to change the Constitution without the support of other parties. There was a strong regional polarization between urban centres and rural areas, as the PLA took about 90 per cent of the seats in villages and small towns, whereas its main rival, the Democratic Party, won 94 per cent of the seats in the cities. Therefore, the total deviation from proportionality was only 12.8 per cent, which is not very high for a majority electoral system (*Keesing's* 1991: 38106, 38160; Szajkowski 1992: 159–60).

CONCLUSIONS

All the East European countries held free or at least partially free parliamentary elections within a short time after the fall of the communist regimes. The latter had favoured majority-type elections, whereas the new leaders introduced various forms of proportional representation. Hungary and Bulgaria adopted a mixture of majority and proportional allocation rules in their first elections. In East Germany, Czechoslovakia, Romania, and in 1991 also in Bulgaria, all the seats were distributed proportionally. The parliamentary elections of 1989 in the Soviet Union and 1991 in Albania were to a lesser extent a shift toward competitive elections. Therefore, the electoral systems in those countries did not change as radically as elsewhere. Yugoslavia's experiments with free elections did not include national level elections in the period 1989–91. It remains to draw some lessons from these early experiences with constitutional democracy.

It seems that the electoral systems in Poland, Hungary, Romania, Czechoslovakia and Bulgaria (and East Germany's 1990 electoral law) all supplied a framework that guarantees a reasonable connection between the parties' support among the voters and their representation in the elected body. However, Hungary, Czechoslovakia, and Bulgaria needed perhaps to consider striving for a closer approximation to perfect PR – although such changes could make the parliamentary situation more unstable. On the other hand, regime stability might be threatened also if many small social segments were to be excluded by the electoral system. Therefore in the former Soviet Union and Albania a shift from single-seat plurality to some form of PR is to be recommended. The rules that require a second round of voting if the turnout does not exceed 50 per cent should be abolished. All empirical evidence shows that the turnout tends to be lower in the second round.

Another aspect that clearly called for reform is the excessive complexity of the East European systems. The improvement achieved by multi-level remainder distribution, for instance, can be only marginal. Proportional representation itself does not necessarily have to be a very complex system. In particular, it might be desirable to simplify Hungary's electoral system. The idea of the dual voting system did not live up to expectations, because the vast majority of voters favoured the new large parties on both their voting slips, and personalities were a secondary consideration (*Fact Sheets on Hungary (2)* 1990). However, it would be difficult to change these rules, because the leading party in the governing coalition, Hungarian Democratic Forum, was so well served by the current electoral system.

There is no need to create a mixed system of majority and proportional rules in order to give voters more influence on the choice of persons than is possible in a pure closed party-list PR. A better choice would be, for example, the system that is currently used in Finland. Poland's electoral reform prior to the October 1991 elections was a clear move in that direction. Also the Czechoslovakian system had some similarities with the Finnish system but lacked its simplicity. In the Finnish system a voter gives one vote to one candidate. The vote is counted for both the candidate and the party he or she represents. The order of candidates within each party list is determined by the number of votes they have received. Consequently, there is simultaneously a proportional election between parties, and a plurality election within each party.

Evidently, the problems identified here are not merely technical for they can have significant political consequences in these new and still fragile democracies. Conventional wisdom says that there is a linear trade-off between fair representation and political stability: if you want political stability, choose a plurality electoral system, but if you appreciate more fair representation, choose proportional representation. The evidence from the founding elections of Eastern Europe does not give support to such an interconnection, since proportional representation in Eastern Europe has not generated any visible effects on the durability of cabinet coalitions. In contrast, introduction of a plurality electoral system in the context of the founding elections can involve unexpected consequences. (As in Algeria's 1991 elections, which were cancelled after the first round, when parties realized that the winning party might unilaterally change the whole political system.) No doubt, Eastern Europe will continue to be a rich field for students of electoral systems in the years to come.

BIBLIOGRAPHY

Act No. XXXIV of 1989. On the Election to the Members of Parliament (Hungary's electoral law).
Act of June 28, 1991. On Election to the Sejm of the Republic of Poland. Officially published in the Law Journal of the Republic of Poland (*Dziennik Ustaw Rzeczypospolitej Polskiej*) 1991: no. 59, item 252.
Act of May 10, 1991. On Election to the Senate of the Republic of Poland. Officially published in the Law Journal of the Republic of Poland (*Dziennik Ustaw Rzeczypospolitej Polskiej*) 1991: no. 58, item 246.
Batt, J. (1990) 'The Hungarian general election', *Representation* 29: 7–11.
Brunner, G. (1990) 'Elections in the Soviet Union', in R. K. Furtak (ed.) *Elections in Socialist States,* Hemel Hempstead: Harvester Wheatsheaf.
Crampton, R. (1990) 'The Bulgarian elections of 1990', *Representation* 29: 33–5.
Deletant, D. (1990) 'The Romanian elections of May 1990', *Representation* 29: 23–6.
Fact Sheets on Hungary (2) (1990) Budapest: Ministry of Foreign Affairs.
Gallagher, T. (1991) 'Romania: the disputed election of 1990', *Parliamentary Affairs* 44: 79–93.
Gambarelli, G., and Holubiec, J. (1990) Power indices and democratic apportionment, (photocopied).
Hyde-Price, A. (1990) 'The Volkskammer elections in the GDR, 18 March 1990', *Representation* 29: 2–4.
Hylland, A. (1990) *The Romanian Electoral Law of 1990: Discussion and Comments,* Working Paper, Sandvika: Norwegian School of Management.
Juridical Regulations on the 20th of May 1990 Bucharest: Provisional Council of National Union.
Keesing's Record of World Events (1989–91).

150   *Emerging party systems and institutions*

Law on Elections to the Czechoslovak Federal Assembly (1990) Prague: Orbis.
Lewis, P. (1990) 'Non-competitive elections and regime change: Poland 1989', *Parliamentary Affairs* 43: 90–107.
Loi Electorale de l'Assamblee Constituante de Bulgarie (1990) (Bulgaria's electoral law), Paris: Centre d'Etudes Comparatives des Elections.
Mackie, T. T. (1992) 'General elections in Western Nations during 1990', *European Journal of Political Research* 21: 317–32.
Millard, F. (1991–2) 'Poland: the 1991 parliamentary election', *Representation* 30: 72–5.
Opolska, H., and Owen, B. (eds) (1989) *La Loi Electorale Polonaise 7 avril 1989*, Paris: Centre d'Etudes Comparatives des Elections.
Owen, B. (1991) 'The Electoral System at Work in the Election, October 13, 1991 – Bulgaria', National Democratic Institute Pre-Election Fact-Finding Mission to Bulgaria, 8–13 September, and NDI–NRI Election Observer Mission, 13 October. Research Report.
Parlamenti Választások 1990, Politikai Szociológiai Körkép. MTA Társadalomtudományi Intézet. (Hungary's Election Results).
Raina, P. (1990) 'Elections in Poland', in R. K. Furtak *Elections in Socialist States*, Hemel Hempstead: Harvester Wheatsheaf.
Racz, B. (1989) 'The parliamentary infrastructure and political reforms in Hungary', *Soviet Studies* 41: 39–66.
Shafir, M. (1990) 'The electoral law', *Report on Eastern Europe*, May 4, 28–31.
Slození Federálního Shromázdení CSFR Mandáty Pridelené Podle Stran Ve Volbách V Roce 1990 (Czechoslovakia's election results).
Szajkowski, B. (1992) 'The Albanian election of 1991', *Electoral Studies* 11: 157–61.
Szendrei, T. (1990) '34th time lucky. How the election works', *The Hungarian Observer* 3: 6–7.
Taagepera, R., and Shugart, M. (1989) *Seats and Votes. The Effects and Determinants of Electoral Systems*, New Haven and London: Yale University Press.
Webb, W. L. (1992) 'The Polish general election of 1991', *Electoral Studies* 11: 166–70.
White, S. (1985) 'Non-competitive elections and national politics: the USSR Supreme Soviet elections of 1984', *Electoral Studies* 4: 215–29.
—— (1990) 'The elections to the USSR Congress of People's Deputies March 1989', *Electoral Studies* 9: 59–66.

6 The emergence of multi-party systems in East-Central Europe
A comparative analysis

Paul Lewis, Bill Lomax, and Gordon Wightman

INTRODUCTION: POST-COMMUNIST CONDITIONS FOR DEMOCRACY

In the light of existing analysis and theoretical discussion, political parties stand in an intimate relationship with modern democracy (Powell 1982: 7). The formation of independent, competitive parties must accordingly be seen as a critical aspect of contemporary processes of democratization. The emergence of effectively operating multi-party systems (with an emphasis on the systematic and orderly character of the relations obtaining between the parties) should, further, be understood as a major feature of the consolidation of new democracies and establishment of the conditions for their continuing development (Pridham 1990: 4). Party formation and the emergence of multi-party systems seem to offer the best prospects for political development and progress towards democracy.

It is, however, by no means sure at any stage that parties will be able to find solutions to the central problems of political development (Weiner and LaPalombara 1966: 435). Even if such prospects do open up satisfactorily for the post-communist countries of East-Central Europe (comprising in this context Czechoslovakia, Hungary and Poland), party formation, progress in party development and the emergence of multi-party systems may well be lengthy processes, hastened or retarded by the cultural and historical background of individual nations, accompanying aspects of social and political change, and specific conditions of the early phase of democratization. While the collapse of communist dictatorship in Eastern Europe was rapid (or at least had the appearance of so being), democratization and the emergence of multi-party systems are likely to be more protracted processes.

In the pre-1939 period only Czechoslovakia had a functioning democratic system and even then there was dissatisfaction about the absence of self-government for the Slovak population. While the democratic traditions of Eastern Europe are not that weak in comparison with recently democratizing countries in Africa, Asia, Latin America – or even perhaps Southern Europe, they are certainly different from those of Western Europe. Moreover, the divergent experiences of authoritarian rule, Nazi occupation and communist dictatorship that Czechoslovakia, Hungary and Poland underwent for a period of more than half a century have been such as to make it impossible for them to plug into previously established patterns of representative government and political participation. International conditions have mixed implications for ongoing processes – the attractions of democratic values within contemporary global society and the growing influence of the European Community certainly contribute to the strength of democratic currents in Eastern Europe. But attempts to switch to a capitalistic, market-based economy and to encourage industrial modernization – resulting in recession, inflationary pressures (particularly acute in the case of Poland), rising unemployment and growing social inequalities – risk producing forces which fit uneasily with the progress of democratization processes and may promote sentiments which are difficult to accommodate within the partially formed institutions of democratic government.

All these factors exert a significant influence on contemporary prospects for the development of democracy and the emergence of multi-party systems. But the processes that gained momentum during the growth of opposition to communist rule and the forces that came into prominence during this phase also play a significant part. They shaped the specific forms that emerged during the retreat of the Soviet-sponsored authorities and then played a leading part in the early stages of democratization in Eastern Europe. The role of the social movement – Solidarity in Poland (which was, above all, the regional model for opposition to the visibly crumbling communist power in Eastern Europe and its institutional successors), *Neues Forum* in the German Democratic Republic, Civic Forum and the Public Against Violence in Czechoslovakia and The Union of Democratic Forces in Bulgaria – was identified with a specific kind of political force and was perceived to act as a characteristic basis for the early stages of post-communist rule.

This was less evident in Hungary where popular energies were presented with greater opportunities for self-expression in terms of economic enterprise and private activity during the last stages of communist rule. The political opposition also developed closer relations with communist authorities and the political establishment. In general, however, such movements – easily identifiable with the recently highlighted new social movements in the West – were regarded as a major feature of East European democratization and often perceived as a characteristic component of its specific path of political development and democratic evolution. Such social movements met the needs of the moment in a number of ways. Developing outside and in opposition to the bureaucratized power structures, which spread through and across the different levels and facets of the communist system, the movements provided a focus for the resentments and aspirations of society in relation to the agencies of the state, clearly subject to the dictates of the party and its specialized apparatus of power.

They served to integrate those who shared the widespread disillusionment with and antipathy towards communist authority, and provided a distinctive vehicle for the expression of political opposition whose form as well as content was quite different from that of the political establishment and incumbent power-holders. They were effective in conveying the distaste increasingly felt for the objectives and methods employed in the exercise of communist power, and they channelled the spirit of 'anti-politics' that encapsulated the revulsion felt against the Soviet-backed dictatorship (Konrad 1984; Havel 1988). A characteristic indication of this was the decision of the Citizens' Committees, set up in Poland to contest the 1989 election, not to extend their reach beyond the Solidarity organization to include the relatively small political groups and proto-parties already in existence (Barany and Vinton 1990: 196–7).

But it should also be recognized that in various ways the form and ethic of the social movements reflected some of the characteristics of the power-structures their activity and spirit were so set against. These were not wholly conducive to processes either of party formation or the development of multi-party systems. They rested, to varying degrees, on relatively undifferentiated forms of organization and represented an inclusive form of alternative political authority. Solidarity was criticized for its monolithic form and for embodying a near-universal opposition to communist authority that mirrored the general Marxist-Leninist claims to overall leadership. Their attachment to anti-politics, embodying religious, ethical, and national sentiment, was also in practice not so far removed from the opposition of communist officials and the resistance of Marxist-Leninism to pluralism, the institutionalized expression of social conflict and the operation of the democratic politics established in the West. It was the latter, however, and the pattern of Western-style multi-party politics that was so generally admired by the anti-communist opposition.

Communist power was obviously identified with that of the state, but it could well be argued that the dictatorship of the communist party was as much one over the state (conceived as a legal, constitutional form) as over society and its discrete groups (Schapiro 1972). The implicit values underlying East European movements in terms of their rejection of formal politics and doubts about the nature of state authority flowed from the ready identification of communist power with that of the state in general. These were, however, at the outset rarely contrasted with the normative underpinnings of Western pluralism and conditions of the modern democracy they also sought to establish, but such tensions soon became evident and exerted an influence on the institutional development of the post-communist systems. The tendency of the movements to adopt a general form and develop an inclusive form of organization was also linked with their aim, and often effective capacity, to express the hopes and feelings of society as a whole against Communist Party-state power.

But this impressive aim and, on occasion, achievement of representing society as a whole against communist power reflected as much a process of transcending the particular forms of society, its actual structures and forms of division, as of articulating its specific interests and of pursuing the achievement of concrete objectives. It was sometimes a symbolic expression of national and religious sentiment (most notably in the archetypal emergence of Solidarity in 1980) and at others more a commitment to universal values like human rights and environmental protection. Rarely did it involve anything like a process of representation in any way related to the expression and pursuit of social interests observed in developed Western democracies. Yet representation may be regarded as the critical innovation of the modern age that has made democracy a practicable form of rule and effective as a basis for government under contemporary conditions (Dahl 1989: 28–30). Its emergence in symbolic form within the framework of the social movement rather than as a pragmatic articulation of group interest was a further factor distancing the East European oppositions from the practice of Western democracy.

The very forces that contributed to the success of the opposition in Eastern Europe and to the collapse of communist power were marked by features, then, that occupied a highly problematic position with regard to democratization and suggested that East-Central European conditions might produce some particular problems for the emergence of multi-party systems of the West European type. The current of antipolitics, the tendency of the new social movements to mirror the inclusive political fronts set up by the Communist Party, their antagonism to state authority, and inclinations to strive in political action for

broadly conceived symbolic expression rather than group representation, all seem in some ways to point as much back to the practices
and structures of traditional Soviet-style communism as forward to the
processes of modern democracy and the structures of Western pluralism.

The initial stages of the transition to democracy also served to
strengthen the association of the post-communist situation with characteristics of Marxist-Leninist politics in terms of the central role
played by elites. While broad social movements seemed to be the
characteristic mode in Eastern Europe for the mobilization and expression of discontent and the articulation of opposition, the critical
junctures of regime transition and the mechanisms of power transfer
remained very much within the domain of elite politics. If some East
European countries increasingly took on the appearance of fractured
systems during the 1980s, the opening of round-table negotiations –
first in Poland and then in Hungary and Czechoslovakia – adopted the
classic form of 'overarching cooperation at the elite level' identified as
the essential characteristic of consociational democracy (Lijphart 1968:
17, 21). It is not, indeed, unusual for it to be argued that democratization
is invariably an elite-based process (Huntington 1984) – but it also
carries the threat of reinforcing tendencies that stand in some tension
with more general principles of mass democracy.

In these respects Hungary stood very close to Poland in its experience
of elite confrontation followed by negotiation and accommodation as
the initial phase of political democratization. It was the small group
which had made up the Democratic Opposition since the 1970s, which
became the basis for the Alliance of Free Democrats (SZDSZ: founded
in November 1988), and significant forces within the reformist wing of
the Hungarian Socialist Workers' Party (MSZMP: disbanded in October
1989) who led the way to elite accommodation and joint commitment
to reform in September 1989. Other groups also entered the process,
pre-eminent among them the Hungarian Democratic Forum (MDF),
whose organization had been founded earlier than that of the Free
Democrats in September 1987 and which drew on the established
traditions of Hungarian populism. But it was only prior to the historic
free elections of March 1990 that, as Glenny puts it, 'the slumbering
bear of Hungarian populism awoke from its hibernation and the MDF
conquered all in sight' (Glenny 1990: 80).

The initial transition to democracy had thus been very much a matter
of elite negotiation in both countries. Of course, in distinction to
Hungary, Poland had seen the emergence of a highly significant mass
movement in the form of Solidarity during the summer of 1980. But by
the time prospects for effective democratization began to emerge in

1988 Solidarity had for some years, following the repression of the union during the period of martial law and the official suspension of its activities, effectively lost the capacity to act as a social movement (Staniszkis 1989). When the opportunity for negotiation again presented itself, its representatives acted in combination with leading figures from reformist circles in the Communist Party as members of a relatively restricted opposition elite rather than as leaders of a multi-million strong movement. Nevertheless, once the negotiations bore fruit and the opportunity to participate in elections with even a limited scope for democratic choice emerged, Solidarity again gathered massive support and the active allegiance of the great majority of the population.

Like Hungary and Poland, the initial transition to democracy in Czechoslovakia was the outcome of elite negotiation but the context of those negotiations was very different from those of Czechoslovakia's neighbours. Opposition to the communists remained very much weaker than in Poland and Hungary and neither the one movement with long roots dating back to the late 1970s, the human rights group Charter 77, nor the numerous independent initiatives that began to surface in the late 1980s appeared strong enough to challenge a regime that remained opposed to any real departure from neo-totalitarian rule. The emergence of broader political movements – Civic Forum in Prague and the Public Against Violence in Bratislava – came rather late, two days after the brutal police attack on student marchers on 17 November 1989 that also set in train ten days of popular protest that toppled the communist regime.

In the political vacuum that was created by the resignation of the Communist Party leadership on 24 November, the stronger cards proved to lie in the hands of the representatives of those two movements than with the surviving members of the political establishment, led initially by the then Prime Minister Ladislav Adamec. If the initial outcome of round-table negotiations in early December between Adamec and representatives of the opposition appeared to be the establishment of a caretaker government in which the communists retained a dominant role, the degree to which power had in fact shifted to their opponents was made clear with the election of Alexander Dubcek, leader of the Communist Party in 1968 but no longer a member of that party, as chairman of the Federal Assembly on 28 December, and of Václav Havel as Czechoslovak president the following day. In practice, the communists' position was weaker than their initial tenure of ten of the twenty-one posts in the new Government of National Understanding indicated. On the one hand, they were deprived of key ministries such as those of Finance, Foreign Affairs and the Interior, and on the other the loyalty to the party of some of their representatives, notably the Prime Minister Marián Calfa, was to prove short-lived. Power in effect had shifted to representatives of the new political movements which were to take on tasks that might not be generally understood to be appropriate to new social movements: those of guiding the processes of formal democratization and preparing the way for parliamentary elections.

In so far as the founders of Civic Forum saw it initially as a transitional force formed to defeat the communist regime rather than as a permanent feature of the political scene, its survival until the end of 1990 was somewhat surprising, as Havel himself noted in an interview published in *Lidové noviny* (7 December 1990). At least some of the explanation for that must lie in the continuing commitment to a broadly based movement and antipathy towards traditional party structures shared by Havel and his 'inner circle' of colleagues from the dissident movement whose influence remained very strong indeed within Civic Forum until after the June elections (Mezník 1992; Glenny 1990: 46). Preference for a more hierarchical party structure and a more precisely defined programme than was possible in a movement as disparate and loosely organized as Civic Forum was, however, to make itself felt in the autumn of 1990. In that respect, experience in Czechoslovakia was to conform with a pattern observable more widely in Eastern Europe whereby the processes and organizations which occupied the central place in the early stages of East European democratization were, then, by no means always ones that might be anticipated to lead the subsequent process of democratization or, in particular, to foster the formation of political parties and facilitate the emergence of multi-party systems. They did, nevertheless, provide many of the particular characteristics of the beginnings of the transition to democracy and influenced the conditions under which the processes of post-communist development were to take place. The rest of this chapter charts the early stages of democratization in East-Central Europe in terms of the beginnings of post-Communist Party formation, the first free elections and early stages of the emergence of multi-party systems.

HUNGARY

Amongst the countries of East-Central Europe, it was Hungary that saw the earliest development of party organization. At the same time, its transition from communism followed a peaceful and gradual course, described by some observers as a 'negotiated revolution' (Bruszt 1990). As a result of this, Hungary might today appear to have the best chances among the three post-communist countries of East-Central Europe of developing and consolidating democratic political institutions and a pluralistic, multi-party system. And yet, as will be shown, the development of the new party system shows some disturbing signs about progress towards viable political pluralism and in particular about parties as societal actors.

The new political parties began to form in 1987 and 1988, the first of them emerging from the opposition milieux of the final decade of the Kádár regime. The semi-clandestine opposition groups that had existed in Hungary since the late 1970s, running unofficial seminars, publishing *samizdat* literature and organizing occasional protests against violations of human rights, gradually came above ground following Mikhail Gorbachev's accession to power in March 1985 in the Soviet Union. On 14–16 June 1985, a remarkable gathering took place in the village of Monor to the south-east of Budapest to discuss the future of Hungary and its place in the modern world. Among the 45 present were leading spokespersons of the country's populist writers – including Sándor Csoóri and István Csurka, major figures of the dissident democratic opposition including György Konrád and János Kis, and representatives of the reform wing of the Hungarian Socialist Workers' Party (HSWP) like Ferenc Kósa and László Lengyel. The Monor gathering brought together, perhaps for the first and last time, representatives of the three main political forces that were to set the pace of change during the next five years.

The unity of Monor was, however, short-lived and the chasm it sought to bridge too wide. When a similar meeting was held at Lakitelek two years later on 27 September 1987 to set up a Hungarian Democratic Forum, the proceedings were opened by the leader of the HSWP's reform wing, Imre Pozsgay, but, with the exception of the writer György Konrád, representatives of the democratic opposition had been deliberately excluded (Lengyel 1991: 238). Nevertheless it would be a misrepresentation of this meeting to see it as the founding body of Hungary's present ruling party, the Democratic Forum, as not only many reform communists and HSWP members, but also future supporters of the Free Democrats, the Young Democrats, and the Smallholders' Party were also present. Nor was the mood of the meeting that of the Christian and nationalist conservatism that has come to characterize the Democratic Forum since late 1989 – indeed, neither the Forum's future leader and prime minister József Antall, nor the leader of its parliamentary caucus, Imre Kónya, were present.

However, Hungary in the 1980s was the scene not only of political opposition groups but also of broader social movements. The beginning of the decade had seen the emergence of independent peace groups campaigning for disarmament in the East as well as West and, although they had been firmly repressed, they had represented one of the first consciously non-political strivings for the development of an autonomous civil society. In 1984 the ecological issue came to the fore with the formation of a Danube Circle to mobilize opposition to the building of a massive hydro-electric plant at Gabcíkovo-Nagymáros on the Danube. Another issue which raised public concern was the fate of the Hungarian minority in Transylvania at a time when Romanian leader Ceausescu was implementing his policy of bulldozing Hungarian villages into the ground.

The first new forms of political representation to emerge sought to build on these social movements, and avoided the shape of traditional political parties. On 30 March 1988 an independent student organization, the Association of Young Democrats, was formed and rapidly grew to become a generational movement calling for radical change (Bozóki 1992). In the same spirit, on 1 May 1988, activists of the democratic opposition launched a Network of Free Initiatives which sought to promote and assist democratization at all levels of society. This mood did not last for long, however, and on 13 November 1988 an internal coup by the 'hard-core' of the democratic opposition transformed the Network into a more politically oriented body, renamed the Association of Free Democrats. Autumn 1988 and the beginning of 1989 saw the reformation of the so-called 'historic' or 'nostalgia' parties that had existed before the communists came to power, the most important of which were the Smallholders' Party, the Social Democratic Party and the Christian Democratic People's Party. Yet these parties, in particular the first two, were plagued by internal rifts both between personalities and different generations of party leaders that lost them much of the public support they hoped to gather (Kiss and Kovács 1991).

Finally, 1988 and 1989 saw the rising challenge to Károly Groz's leadership of the HSWP from the growing movement of reformists within the party led by Imre Pozsgay. But despite pressure from his more radical supporters, Pozsgay failed to provide the leadership that many of them sought and held back from breaking away to form an independent social-democratic party. When he and his colleagues finally came to disband the HSWP in October 1989 and form a new Hungarian Socialist Party, time had already run out for the reform communists who had let history pass them by (Lomax 1991).

October 1989 – October 1990 was the year of party politics and election campaigns, but it was not a year for the development of democratic politics or new forms of political representation. On the contrary, if anything, the increased activity of the parties in fact served to demobilize society, weaken the parties' own bases of support and to foster a growing discontent with, and alienation from, the new political system and the new parties (Arató 1990). This was partly a result of the parties themselves not being, in any sense, mass organizations. Although they campaigned and mobilized society to remove the old order – the communist regime – they did not serve either to represent interests or to articulate programmes and ideologies. By the end of the year a consensus would arise amongst the population to the effect that there had not been any real change of system, merely an alternation of elites.

The general election of March–April 1990 was fought in two rounds under a system that elected 50 per cent of members of parliament from individual constituencies and 50 per cent under proportional representation from county and national lists, with a 4 per cent minimum required for any party to enter the parliament. In the first round, voting for party lists, on a 63 per cent poll, the Hungarian Democratic Forum came first with 24.73 per cent of the votes, closely followed by the Free Democrats with 21.39 per cent. The Smallholders gained 11.73 per cent, the Socialist Party 10.89 per cent, the Young Democrats 8.95 per cent, and the Christian Democrats 6.46 per cent; 15.85 per cent of votes were cast for parties, including the Social Democrats and the reconstituted HSWP, that failed to clear the 4 per cent threshold to enter the parliament. In the first round of voting for individual constituencies, the results were fairly similar, with 24.03 per cent of the votes cast for the Democratic Forum, 22.17 per cent for the Free Democrats, 10.56 per cent for the Smallholders, 10.33 per cent for the Socialists, 5.77 per cent for the Christian Democrats, 5.12 per cent for the Young Democrats, and 22.02 per cent for other parties and independents.

In the second round of voting in individual constitutencies, on a lower poll of 44 per cent, the Forum increased its vote to 41 per cent and, together with the Smallholders and the Christian Democrats who had won a further 10.95 per cent and 3.73 per cent respectively, was able to form a government supported by a majority of voters, and with an even more comfortable majority in parliament. Yet, despite what many commentators have suggested, there was no major swing away from the Free Democrats towards the Democratic Forum between the first and second rounds. On the contrary, the combined vote for the two liberal parties held steady and in fact showed a slight increase, with 31.04 per cent of votes cast for the Free Democrats and 2.37 per cent for the Young Democrats, whereas the Forum benefited from the votes for its partner parties where they were unable to stand candidates in the second round, and from mopping up most of the votes of those who had supported parties that failed to win 4 per cent in the first round (Körösényi 1990; Moldován 1990; Szoboszlai 1990).

Despite the clear majority commanded by the Forum-led centre-right coalition, the government still had a problem. When the new constitutional proposals had been drawn up during the course of the Tripartite Talks of 1989, the then opposition parties had feared that the communists might still cling on to power. They had then sought to limit the powers of the executive by arguing for a strictly ceremonial presidency, for most changes in the law and the Constitution to require a two-thirds majority in parliament, and for parliament to have strong powers for the impeachment of ministers.

Having won the election, the Forum's leader and new prime minister, József Antall, now sought a deal with his former rivals. The presidency was offered to the highly respected Free Democrat writer Arpád Göncz in return for the Free Democrats dropping the two-thirds requirement for all but the most 'basic laws' and agreeing to the institution of a 'constructive vote of no-confidence', whereby votes of no-confidence can only be brought against the prime minister – and only then if his replacement is named. Perhaps more significant than its content was the fact that this pact was made between the party leaders without their first consulting their parties' leading organs or, in the case of the Forum, its coalition partners (Kurtán, Sándor and Vass 1991: 428–9).

The spring election had only effected change at the very top of the political system. The real 'spring cleaning' was expected to come in the autumn with the local government elections, which were seen as an opportunity for the wholesale replacement of the *nomenklatura* that would complete the change of regime. Originally, the Democratic Forum expected to benefit from its position as the party of government to complete its victory and establish total domination of the political system. However, the opposite happened. The government had by now lost much of its early popularity and the liberal parties swept the board, winning control of Budapest and almost all the county towns, the largest gainers being the Young Democrats who almost doubled their vote from the spring to win the third largest share of the votes. As in the general election, however, the landslide was not quite what it appeared, the electoral system producing a misleading impression of the voting pattern. Despite their achievements, the two liberal parties still polled well below 50 per cent of the votes cast nationwide, while in Budapest, where the liberals gained most, the vote for the Democratic Forum fell by only 1 per cent on the spring result. This is explained by the fact that the government parties lost most in the countryside, but not only to the liberals; whereas the liberals gained most in Budapest – in this case not only from the government parties.

In smaller communities of under 10,000 inhabitants, however, almost two-thirds of votes were cast for independent candidates, with over 70 per cent of elected councillors and over 80 per cent of mayors being independents, many themselves former council leaders under the old regime. Perhaps most significant of all, while turnout in the first round was generally above 50 per cent in the smaller communities where the independents did best, the poll was down to 30 per cent or less in Budapest and the large towns where the parties dominated the scene, and in some working-class districts it was even below 20 per cent. In the second round turnout was even lower. The clear lesson of the local elections was not only that the government had lost popularity, but that enthusiasm for the opposition parties was also on the wane – that none of the parties had established any firm implantation either in the working-class districts of the cities or at local level in the countryside. The voters were clearly saying 'a curse on all your parties'.

This was finally brought home towards the end of October 1990, when a sudden rise in petrol prices sparked off a spontaneous blockade of Budapest and most other cities by taxi and lorry drivers that turned within 24 hours into a popular nationwide protest against the arrogance and incompetence of the government. Neither the government nor the opposition parties proved capable of handling the situation and working towards a compromise settlement. Instead, the bargaining was carried out live in front of the television cameras by representatives of the interest groups themselves, leaders of trade unions and workers' councils, small businessmen and employers, who hammered out an agreement that was finally accepted by the government. While none of the political parties came out of the blockade well, it did show the potential for self-organization and interest-representation inherent within society itself.

The blockade demonstrated the fundamental weakness in Hungary's new party system: the immense gap separating all parties from society itself. The parties are, almost without exception, elite groups of intellectuals, often long-standing personal friends; more like political clubs than representative institutions. They do not represent social interests or constituencies; nor are they held together by any common ideas, programmes or ideologies. As the Free Democrat Gáspár Miklós Tamás has put it, they are 'more like tribes than parties', held together by friendship ties and often a common past in Budapest's intellectual sub-culture, rather than by common beliefs and principles. The political identities and cleavages they represent are based not on social interests, political programmes, or structured belief systems, but on the cultural, emotional or even spiritual identifications through which their members have come to belong to socio-cultural communities with shared life-styles and attitudes which, in turn, provide a basis for common political styles and patterns of behaviour.

Some commentators have described these parties as 'spiritual communities' or 'intellectual milieux parties' (Markus 1994). Their self-identifications are based on such abstract concepts as nation, race or religion, anti-communism, Europe or simply the West. Even such ideologies as liberalism or democracy take on a similarly emotionally charged and Manichaean form. Such political styles are very good at identifying enemies and scapegoats; they are of less use when it comes to bargaining and reaching compromises. They may serve to mobilize social masses at times of major social change or revolutionary trans-formations, or to mobilize voters in elections when some very general cause is at stake. They do not, however, serve to mobilize citizens for active participation in politics through the development of political associations and democratic institutions, nor in elections when the choice is between specific policies and alternatives. Moreover, these political styles also render the parties both incompetent and impotent when faced with the tasks of coping with serious economic problems and managing social crises – as was so clearly demonstrated by the blockade of October 1990.

Another consequence of the nature of the present parties is that they are likely to be around for some time yet. It is far too early to predict, as the English historian Timothy Garton Ash (1991) has, that they will 'disappear within a few years'. By the very nature of the loyalties binding them together, they are unlikely either to split or to fuse. Although on strictly rational grounds the Smallholders and Christian Democrats might be expected to fuse with the Democratic Forum to form a united party of the centre-right, this is unlikely to happen for that reason. Even less likely, however much sense it might make, is a *rapprochement* between the Free Democrats and the Socialists, while the Young Democrats will fight to the last to defend their separate identity from that of the Free Democrats. And while almost all the parties are riven by bitter internal divisions, final splits are unlikely, as to join another party would be a form of heresy. Even less probable is the emergence of any new party to represent the 'social democratic constituency' or fill the 'national democratic centre' as some pundits predict (Bihári 1991: 38–9; Szelényi and Szelényi 1991).

It would thus be mistaken to expect a development in the direction of a two-party system along a Western left–right axis, or a polarization between christian democratic and social democratic coalitions, or even the emergence of a three-party system of national conservatives, liberals and social democrats. The Hungarian political spectrum is divided by many axes – but rather than separating the parties from one another, they cut across each other equally. The Hungarian six-party system is thus likely to persist for a good time yet (Kéri 1991: 87–92, 103–12). The real question at issue concerns not the number of parties but the (qualitative) nature of the party system; whether it will develop along authoritarian lines into a new form of corporate state in which 'the one-party dictatorship would be replaced by a multi-party one', as the Hungarian political sociologist Lászlo Kéri has suggested, or whether it can grow into a modern, pluralist and participatory democracy.

There have already been indications, which have increased since it has been losing popularity, that the Democratic Forum might strive to establish a new party-state in which it would play the role of the new dominant or hegemonic state party. In a speech to the parliament in September 1990, Foreign Minister Géza Jeszenszky declared that the Democratic Forum was the 'one and only' true representative of the Hungarian nation and of the ideals of Christianity and European civilization, and that if any members of the opposition parties shared these ideals they should join the Forum. In September 1991, a leaked document prepared by the Forum's parliamentary caucus leader, Imre Kónya, called on the government to extend its controls over the media, and academic and cultural life. Even more right-wing Forum members like István Csurka openly call for a thoroughgoing purge of all former functionaries of the old regime and their replacement by cadres loyal to the new government. The lack of respect for tolerance and differences of opinion inherent in this political style will, at best, prove continuing obstacles to the consolidation of a viable democracy; at worst, it will provide the soil in which a new authoritarianism could take root.

Alienation from the parties has already grown to the point that, by the end of 1991, opinion polls were showing the number of those not predisposed to vote 'if an election were held tomorrow' to have risen above 60 per cent, suggesting the new party system was already in a state of some crisis. Participation by the people, argues Hungarian political scientist Attila Agh (1991: 119), 'is now much more important here than in the consolidated democracies'. In the final analysis, the prospects for democracy revolve around the modernization of the political parties which are, in many ways, still institutions of a pre-modern age or, as some would put it, 'pre-parties' (Kéri 1991: 87; Kiss and Kovács 1991: 17). Their modernization, and hence democratization, depend on the capacity to come to represent and articulate both interests and values, to play the role of mediator and communicator between society and government. They cannot, however, do this in a vacuum. Modern democratic politics cannot exist in the absence of an independent civil society, and the development of one is the condition for the development of the other.

CZECHOSLOVAKIA

In contrast to Hungary, in 1990 Czechoslovakia found itself in a situation that was to prove less favourable for viable party development than might initially have been expected. Despite the rapid establishment of a multi-party 'Government of National Understanding' on 10 December 1989, less than a month after the November 1989 'velvet revolution' challenged the power monopoly of the communist party, the transition to a stable multi-party system in Czechoslovakia was a much slower process than might have been expected. Indeed, the basic features of a potentially durable party system only began to take shape about a year after the collapse of communist rule and almost six months after elections were held, on 8 and 9 June 1990, to the country's three parliaments: the bicameral Federal Assembly and the National Councils in each of the constituent Czech and Slovak Republics.

In some ways this was surprising, since what might have formed the core of a pluralist party structure already existed at the time of the communist collapse. Four satellite parties – in the Czech Republic, the Czechoslovak Socialist Party and Czechoslovak People's Party; in Slovakia, the Freedom Party and the Party of Slovak Revival (under a new name, the Democratic Party) – moved quickly after the November events to establish their independence from the communists. All four, like the communists, had the advantages of an existing organization and a far from negligible membership base, and the first two of those parties, moreover, had roots dating back to the pre-war First Republic, and in the case of the Socialist Party to the last decades of the Austrian Empire. The two Slovak parties, by contrast, had a much shorter history and were founded only in the 1940s. The Party of Slovak Revival's claims to its new name were somewhat questionable since it had in fact been formed with communist encouragement after the 1948 coup as a breakaway from the original Democratic Party whose 62 per cent share of the Slovak vote had made it the most popular of those standing in the 1946 elections.

The six weeks between the 'velvet revolution' and the end of 1989 also witnessed the re-establishment of the Czechoslovak Social Democratic Party, which had been swallowed up by the communists in July 1948, but which had been a major force in Czech politics since the last quarter of the nineteenth century. At the same time, a number of new parties surfaced, often based on the 'independent initiatives' that had been active in the last few years of communist rule ('Czechoslovakia: heat in January' 1989: 177–8; Precan 1989: 6–16). These included a Christian Democratic Movement in Slovakia, a Christian Democratic Party in the Czech Lands, a Green Party throughout Czechoslovakia, and the Czechoslovak Democratic Initiative which had the distinction of having applied for registration as a political party almost a week before the 'velvet revolution'.

These were also forces which the leaders of the two new political movements, Civic Forum and the Public Against Violence, appeared initially to expect to play a role in the new pluralist polity. Members of the Socialist Party and People's Party were included in the new Government of National Understanding, alongside representatives of Civic Forum, the Public Against Violence and the Communist Party. Their nominees, along with representatives of the Social Democrats, the Greens, the two Slovak former satellite parties, the Czechoslovak Democratic Initiative, the Christian Democratic Party and the Hungarian Independent Initiative, were included among new deputies coopted to the Federal Assembly in the first months of 1990 to replace discredited members of that parliament who were persuaded to give up their seats (*Rudé Právo*, 21 February 1990). The Slovak Christian Democratic Movement did not form part of the group, but its adherents may have been among deputies nominated by the Public Against Violence and officially recorded as non-party, as were those nominated by Civic Forum.

New political parties proliferated well before the elections of June 1990, and as many as 66 were reported to have been registered with the authorities by 1 March 1990 (*Fórum*, 6 June 1990). However, the stipulation in the new Electoral Law of 27 February 1990 that only parties, political movements or coalitions with a membership of 10,000, or able to present a petition with sufficient signatures to make up any shortfall, could stand in the elections, and the requirement that contenders would have to get at least 5 per cent of the vote in one of the two republics to qualify for seats in each chamber of the Federal Assembly and in the Czech National Council, encouraged the more astute among them to form coalitions or shelter under the umbrella of Civic Forum and the Public Against Violence. Civic Forum, for example, included in its lists of candidates members of the Czechoslovak

Democratic Initiative, the Club of Social Democrats, the *Obroda* Club (founded in early 1989 by reform communists who had been expelled from that party after the Prague Spring), and new parties such as the Civic Democratic Alliance. The Public Against Violence also included *Obroda* on its lists as well as Slovak-based parties like the Hungarian Independent Initiative. In all, 22 contenders – parties, movements and coalitions of parties – sought the favour of the electorate in June 1990, 11 throughout Czechoslovakia, a further 5 only in the Czech Republic and another 6 just in Slovakia (Wightman 1990a: 319–26; 1990b: 18–23; 1991a: 94–113; 1991b: 70–1; Batt 1991: 123–6).

Only eight of those 22 contenders, however, won seats in the federal parliament. For Civic Forum, the elections were an unequivocal success when it won half the Czech votes (53.1 and 50 per cent for the two chambers of the Federal Assembly, the House of the People and the House of the Nations; 49.5 per cent for the Czech National Council). The Public Against Violence did less well, but emerged as the largest Slovak party with 32.5 and 37.5 per cent of the Slovak vote for the two houses of the Federal Assembly and 29.5 per cent for the Slovak National Council. Of the six other groups that won seats in the federal parliament, only one – the Communist Party – was successful in both republics with around 13.6 per cent of the vote throughout the country. A second 'federal' party, Coexistence, which stood jointly with the Hungarian Christian Democratic Movement, won seats only in Slovakia where it attracted the support of a large proportion of the half-million Hungarian minority in that republic, and around 8.6 per cent of the Slovak vote.

The remaining successful contenders were parties which had faced the electorate in only one of the two republics. In the Czech Lands, the Christian and Democratic Union (a coalition comprising the People's Party and the Christian Democratic Party) won around 8.5 per cent of the vote; the Movement for Self-Governing Democracy – the Society for Moravia and Silesia, a contender advocating autonomy for two provinces in the eastern half of the Czech Republic, around 9 per cent. In Slovakia, the Christian Democratic Movement came second, after the Public Against Violence, with 19 per cent for the House of the People, 16.7 per cent for the House of the Nations and 19.2 per cent for the Slovak National Council. In fourth place in the elections to the Federal Assembly in that republic, behind the communists, came the separatist Slovak National Party which, despite having been formed only in March, won 11 per cent of the vote for both houses of that parliament and beat the communists into third place in the Slovak National Council with the support of 14 per cent of Slovak voters.

A striking feature of the elections was the failure of all the former satellite parties, except the People's Party, to win sufficient public support in the June elections to cross the 5 per cent threshold. Only the lower, 3 per cent, threshold set for the Slovak National Council enabled the Democratic Party (along with the Greens) to scrape into that parliament. Overall, early expectations as regards the traditional parties were confounded. Even the Social Democrats, discredited by internal squabbles over their new leader, Jirí Horák, a political exile since 1948, and by the loss of some prominent members (who had been active in dissent but preferred to compete in the elections within Civic Forum), failed to reach the 5 per cent barrier. The success of Civic Forum and the Public Against Violence in elections in which 96 per cent of the electorate took part led Czech observers to conclude that voters had seen the elections as a plebiscite for democracy rather than the opportunity to choose between competing parties (Hájek 1990; Juna 1990).

That was a view shared by President Havel who, writing in the summer of 1991 a little over a year later, observed that:

> our last elections were not yet elections in the true and traditional sense of the word. They were rather a popular referendum in which the idea of democracy prevailed all down the line, but which did not yet constitute a real democracy. They could not reveal the real political stratification of society, because this stratification was only then being born and because at that time there did not, and could not, yet exist in our country a spectrum of political parties that was at least a little differentiated, comprehensible and stable.
>
> (Havel 1991: 11–12)

This concept of a plebiscite was almost certainly apposite in so far as the popularity of Civic Forum and the Public Against Violence reflected a desire on the part of a significant proportion of the Czech and Slovak electorate to vote for the two movements which unequivocally represented democracy, pluralism and the shift to a market economy. Commentators at the time, however, also saw the failure of parties like the Socialists and Social Democrats to the left of centre and the Free Bloc coalition to the right to win any seats, as an indication of a kind of political backwardness in relation to their perceptions of a need to establish something closer to an ideal Western pluralist system with well-defined parties spanning the political spectrum.

But the elections provided evidence of a somewhat greater political differentiation than Czech observers allowed. The relatively even vote for the Communist Party throughout Czecoslovakia was one example –

however unwelcome. Moreover, the two Christian Democrat contenders, which might well be regarded as parties of a Western type, had
done reasonably well. In the Czech case, support for the Christian and
Democratic Union emerged most strongly in areas where its main
constituent, the People's Party, had been most popular during the pre-
war republic (Jehlicka and Sykora 1991: 81–95). Of greater concern to
those who believed that the creation of a democratic, pluralist polity
depended on the overall emergence of a spectrum of left, centre and
right-wing parties was the degree of support accorded regional and
nationalist parties (Vávra and Stern 1990). That was evident not only
in the vote for the Slovak Nationalist Party but also in the support
accorded the Movement for Self-Governing Democracy–the Society for
Moravia and Silesia, which had not been expected to cross the 5 per
cent barrier, let alone win over 20 per cent of the vote in the two
constituencies of North and South Moravia where it had presented a full
list of candidates.

Slovak society, moreover, appeared more clearly differentiated than
did that of the Czech Republic, albeit not in left–right terms. Political
allegiance among non-communist voters there was divided among a
civil libertarian movement (the Public Against Violence), a clerical
party (the Christian Democratic Movement), and a proponent of
extreme nationalism – the Slovak National Party. Although support had
fluctuated over time between those forces (Bútora, Bútorova and
Rosová 1991), it seemed likely that they would remain features of a
political scene that appeared in that respect more settled than in the
Czech Republic.

Local elections in November 1990 brought little overall change in the
political map. In the Czech Republic, Civic Forum's support fell to just
over 35 per cent on a 73.5 per cent poll (compared with 96 per cent in
June) and in Slovakia the Public Against Violence (which won 20.4 per
cent of the seats) ceded first place to the Christian Democratic Movement
(with 27.4 per cent). Both the Movement for Self-Governing Democracy–
the Society for Moravia and Silesia and the Slovak National Party saw
a dramatic fall in their support to around 3 per cent (in the latter case, a
temporary phenomenon that was to be partially recouped later) but there
was little evidence of growing support for parties that had been
unsuccessful in the parliamentary elections (*Lidové noviny* and *Rudé
Pravó*, 26 and 28 November 1990).

However popular Civic Forum remained with Czech voters, it proved
too disparate a movement to survive growing differences, both among
its leaders and activists, over its viability and the policies it should
pursue. By the end of 1990, it was clear that it was seriously split. On

the one side were advocates of its transformation into a right-of-centre political party based on individual membership and excluding the various clubs and small parties which had sheltered under its umbrella. They also believed that the radical economic reform proposed by Václav Klaus, the leading proponent of Civic Forum's transformation, was the key political strategy. On the other side were those who believed that the broad movement created by the 'velvet revolution' should be retained until the next elections due to be held in June 1992 and who were less than comfortable with Klaus's wholesale rejection of supporters of a 'third way' in politics and economics. Klaus had been elected Civic Forum's first chairman on 13 October 1990 and made his views clear two months later at a meeting of the movement's officials in Olomouc on 8–9 December (Klaus 1990).

Only the absence of any provision in the 1990 Law on political parties for Civic Forum's transformation from a movement into a political party prevented that change being made following a Republic Assembly of the movement in January 1991, at which Klaus's supporters were in the ascendancy. Nevertheless, a breach was by then inevitable and the next few months saw the emergence of two new political forces, the right-of-centre Civic Democratic Party, headed by Klaus, and a centrist Civic Movement led by Foreign Minister Jiří Dienstbier, which remained committed to the idea of a broadly based organization. The collapse of Civic Forum also strengthened some existing parties. The Civic Democratic Alliance, which had stood in the elections as part of Civic Forum, attracted a number of prominent figures, like Economics Minister Vladimír Dlouhy, for whom membership in the Civic Democratic Party was unappealing, at least in part because of its rank-and-file's hostility towards former communists. The Social Democrats gained the parliamentary representation they had failed to obtain at the elections when six deputies transferred their allegiance to that party.

All in all, at the end of 1991 the Czech political scene appeared much more fragmented than it had after the June 1990 elections. Within parliament, Civic Forum had been replaced by five parliamentary groups, with those on the right divided by conflicts of personality more than differences over policy. In the latter respect, there appeared to be few differences between the Liberal Democratic Party (the former Czechoslovak Democratic Initiative), the Civic Democratic Alliance and the Civic Democratic Party, and it was the combination of Klaus's personality, stronger grass-roots activity and a clear commitment to radical reform that helped establish the last-named as the major force in that part of the political spectrum. The support of around 20 per cent of Czech voters in opinion polls suggested it would emerge from the 1992 elections not only as the most popular right-of-centre party, but also as the largest Czech party in the new legislatures (*Lidové noviny*, 20 November 1991). To that extent, party formation on the centre-right had advanced dramatically, marred only by the inability of the various parties, up to that point in time, to reach agreement either for merger or an electoral coalition with other forces in the same part of the political spectrum, as a way of forming a grouping potentially even stronger.

By that time it was clear that, in contrast to the Civic Democratic Party, the Civic Movement had failed to make much headway with the electorate despite the presence in its ranks of leading figures from the years of dissent. In November 1991 it could only register the support of 4 per cent of the Czech electorate in the opinion poll, a result which suggested that, unless it arrived at an electoral agreement with other parties that would broaden its appeal, it would fail to win any parliamentary representation in 1992.

At the same time, the other parties of the political spectrum remained as fragmented as the right. The November 1991 opinion poll suggested that only the communists and the Social Democrats to the left of centre (both then with 9 per cent support) and the People's Party on the centre-right (with its traditional base among Christian voters) were assured of sufficient votes to win seats, given the 5 per cent threshold for parliamentary representation. Of the unsuccessful parties in 1990 (apart from the Social Democrats), only the extremist right-wing Association for the Republic – the Republican Party of Czechoslovakia, with 5 per cent, was attracting a level of support that would bring them parliamentary seats in 1992.

In Slovakia too the party structure that had emerged from the 1990 elections had undergone dramatic changes. The Public Against Violence split in two in the spring of 1991, shortly after the demise of Civic Forum. In this instance the break occurred, not as in Civic Forum with the emergence of a right-of-centre grass-roots movement anxious to push ahead with radical economic reform, but as the result of a shift within its ranks towards a more left-of-centre and nationalist stance, identified with Vladimír Meciar, the Slovak prime minister between June 1990 and April 1991. The breakaway organization he founded in June 1991, the Movement for a Democratic Slovakia, immediately established its primacy in opinion polls and remained the most popular party in that republic at the end of the year, with the support of just under a quarter of Slovak voters. Its success may be attributed in part to Meciar's record as head of government in Slovakia, where his

promotion of greater devolution of power to the republics had established him in Slovak eyes as a firm defender of their interests. His
advocacy of greater protection for the Slovak economy against the
impact of privatization and marketization was yet another source of
widespread support and indicated that Slovak public opinion was out
of step with political trends evident in the Czech Republic, where voters
were more enthusiastic about radical economic reform and hostile to
what they feared might be too much devolution of power.

As the 1992 elections approached, it was clear that the Public Against
Violence, which was transformed into a political party in October 1991
and assumed a new name, the Civic Democratic Union, the following
March, would be eclipsed by the Movement for a Democratic Slovakia's
dominance of the political scene in that republic. Even the Christian
Democratic Movement, which supported maintenance of a federal
system until Slovakia could join the European Community with its 'own
little star' and its own seat at the European negotiating table at some
future date, witnessed a drop in its popularity.

The second post-communist parliamentary elections in June 1992
confirmed these divergent trends in the two republics (Wightman 1992,
1993). In those for the Czech National Council, the Civic Democratic
Party, which stood in an electoral coalition with the small Christian
Democratic Party, attracted 29.7 per cent. With the support of the
People's Party (standing in the elections as the Christian Democratic
Union – Czechoslovak People's Party) and the Civic Democratic
Alliance which had each won 6 per cent, right-of-centre parties had 105
of the 200 seats in that parliament. The remaining places were taken by
five other contenders. The Left Bloc (a coalition in which the Communist Party of Bohemia and Moravia was the dominant partner)
formed the second largest parliamentary group, with 14 per cent of the
vote, a slight improvement on its 1990 performance. The Social
Democrats attracted 6.5 per cent, the extremist Association for the
Republic – Republican Party of Czechoslovakia, the regional Movement for Self-Governing Democracy – Society for Moravia and Silesia,
and the Liberal Social Union, a movement formed by the cooperative-
farm based Agricultural Party, the middle-of-the-road Czechoslovak
Socialist Party and the Greens – each won 6 per cent.

In the Slovak parliament, the Movement for a Democratic Slovakia,
with 37.3 per cent, gained 74 of the 150 seats, only two short of an
overall majority. Meciar's subsequent inclusion in his new government
of the chairman of the separatist Slovak Nationalist Party, whose 8 per
cent share of the vote had given it 15 seats in parliament, ensured it of
a parliamentary majority and reinforced the nationalist tenor of his

administration. The second largest party in the Slovak National Council, however, was the post-communist Party of the Democratic Left, which had won almost 15 per cent of the vote. It was joined on the opposition benches by the Christian Democratic Movement, which had attracted 9 per cent, and the coalition representing the Hungarian minority, involving the Hungarian Christian Democratic Movement and Coexistence, which had retained the support of just over 7 per cent of the electorate.

It was not only the creation of parliaments in the republics with majorities committed to divergent programmes, however, that proved fatal for Czechoslovakia. A broadly similar pattern was evident in the elections to the Federal Assembly. It was clear within a week of the poll that no coalition government capable of maintaining a simple majority, let alone obtaining the qualified majorities required for constitutional bills, could be formed at federal level other than as a caretaker administration to oversee the break-up of the state.

That decision was in part justified by the size of the vote for the two largest parties in each republic (and especially that for the Movement for a Democratic Slovakia for the Slovak National Council) and the majority support each of those parties could obtain in the National Councils for their respective programmes. Meciar's insistence in negotiations with Klaus immediately after the elections that the federation should be replaced by what Klaus saw as no more than 'an economic and defence community' proved unacceptable to the latter, whose party had, during its campaign, made clear that the only alternative it would accept to a federal system was the break-up of Czechoslovakia.

The subsequent 'velvet divorce' on 31 December 1992 thus came about as the result of the political impasse created by the parliamentary elections. If the populations in both republics accepted the inevitability of Czechoslovakia's dissolution, neither intentionally intended that outcome. The decline in the share of the vote by the Slovak National Party (six points lower than the 14 per cent it had attracted in 1990) was the clearest indication that Slovaks rejected separatism. The combined vote for the Movement for a Democratic Slovakia and the Party of the Democratic Left (which advocated 'a federation with confederative elements') showed, however, that a narrow majority among the Slovak population appeared to favour greater autonomy than had so far been agreed with the Czechs, but within what they believed would still be a common Czech and Slovak state. The Czechs, on the other hand, had chosen parties which believed that anything weaker than a federal system was neither practicable nor desirable. Even confederation represented, in their eyes, a first step towards two independent states – and, moreover, moves in that direction, they believed, would undermine progress towards a privatized market economy. Faced by Meciar's intransigence, the Czech victors in the elections preferred their second option: Czechoslovakia's dissolution.

The elections also demonstrated that support for parties in the former parliaments which remained wholeheartedly committed to the maintenance of a Czechoslovak state was, not necessarily for that reason, surprisingly weak. In the Czech Republic the Civic Movement, which had been more amenable to finding a compromise with the Slovaks on the constitutional issue, failed to reach the 5 per cent threshold. In Slovakia, the contenders most strongly committed to a federal system – the Civic Democratic Union and the Democratic Party, which had contested the elections in coalition with Slovak branches of Klaus's Civic Democratic Party – were also defeated. Even the Christian Democratic Movement which had adopted a clearer pro-federal position following the departure of its more nationalist members three months before the elections, saw its share of the vote halved.

The 1992 elections thus sealed the fate of Czechoslovakia. Since the two republic parliaments subsequently became the legislatures in the successor states on 1 January 1993, they also determined the initial character of the party systems in the independent Czech and Slovak Republics. In the Czech case, some elements of a durable system appeared to be more firmly in place. The success of the Social Democrats in 1992 suggested they would become part of a more permanent political spectrum embracing the communists on the left, the Civic Democratic Party, the Civic Democratic Alliance and the People's Party on the right.

The future was less certain for other parties. Its appeal to the discontented and to the anti-Romany vote may ensure the survival of the Association for the Republic–the Republican Party of Czechoslovakia. The small Christian Democratic Party, however, had won seats only thanks to its alliance with Klaus's Civic Democratic Party, and its continued presence would seem to depend on maintaining that relationship. A resolution of the Moravian question would probably deprive the Movement for Self-Governing Democracy of the issue on which its success has been based in the past, while the Liberal Social Union seemed too much of a hybrid to avoid disintegration.

In Slovakia, the party system appeared much narrower than in the Czech Republic, given the defeat of parties on the right of the political spectrum, and also much less stable. While the Party of the Democratic Left and the Christian Democratic Movement had solid enough bases of support (albeit weaker in the latter case than in 1990), the future of the Slovak National Party and the Movement for a Democratic Slovakia was less certain. The attainment of Slovak independence deprived the Nationalists of their main purpose and put them in need of a new identity. How long Meciar's movement, a loose association encompassing people of diverse and scarcely reconcilable views (including, for example ex-communists and anti-communists, proponents and opponents of marketization), would survive the pressures of office, remained to be seen.

Three years after the 'velvet revolution', the political scene in both Czech and Slovak Republics was very different from what might have been anticipated. Most striking was the disappearance of the original 'revolutionary' political movements, Civic Forum and the Public Against Violence. The defeat in the 1992 elections of the Civic Movement in the Czech Lands had, moreover, removed from the political stage most of the leading figures from dissent during the last two decades of communist rule who had initially led that movement.

Nevertheless, in the Czech Republic a multi-party system had emerged which formed a good basis for its continued transition to democracy. In Slovakia, authoritarian inclinations among some of its politicians, uncertainty about the durability of the governing movement, and the more difficult economic circumstances it faced as an independent state made its path towards that goal appear much more difficult.

POLAND

Among the countries of East-Central Europe the process of party development was weakest in Poland. This could be attributed to the factors outlined in the Introduction, some of which emerged in Poland with particular force. The important part played by Solidarity as a collectivist, non-pluralist force was important in this respect, as was the role of personality and the influence within Polish political life of a number of key individuals – and the personal conflicts that developed between them. The question of timing was also critical. Poland was the first country to divest itself of communist rule, but by no means completed the process at the outset and remained for some time in an uneasy situation of regime transition. In the early stages, then, Poland was in the vanguard of political change and pluralist development in East-Central Europe but soon fell back in relative terms as free elections were held and party systems rapidly established in neighbouring countries. Thus amongst the already diverse experiences of East-Central European democratization some of the greatest contrasts could be seen in Poland, the scene of the first and most influential movement to emerge in Eastern Europe and also the first example of a negotiated political settlement between opposition representatives and the communist establishment. The outcome of these complex negotiations was a qualified, if potentially explosive solution: the arranged elections held on 4 June 1989 in Poland, which were the trigger for the whole process of decommunization and system change in Sovietized Europe.

This was the first of a series of four elections from which insights may be derived on the emergence of a multi-party system in Poland, although only in the fourth – the parliamentary election of October 1991 – did the likely shape of an eventual party system finally emerge. The participation of political parties was, as noted earlier, explicitly discouraged in the aftermath of the round-table agreement concluded in April 1989. The process of change that followed the agreement was, firstly, one that involved political forces established before the political flux of the late 1980s which had few associations with ideas of pluralism in the search for a practical political accommodation; and, secondly, one that as yet carried little idea of the possibility of the collapse of communist rule and the onset of liberal democracy in Eastern Europe. There was at that stage little hope of establishing a parliamentary system in which independent, electorally competitive parties might play a significant role.

The agreement reached in April 1989 thus permitted groups outside the establishment to propose candidates only for 35 per cent of the 460 seats in elections to the Polish parliament (*Sejm*), the remainder being reserved for candidates of the Polish United Workers' (communist) Party, two allied political parties and several official Catholic organizations. During the first round of elections in June 1989 Solidarity-proposed candidates won 160 of the 161 seats available to them in the *Sejm* and 92 of the 100 Senate seats. A devastatingly low level of support for the ruling coalition was thus evident. When run-off elections for the unfilled seats were held, Solidarity-sponsored candidates won all 161 (35 per cent) of the *Sejm* seats open to them and 99 of the seats in the Senate. Solidarity also had an influence on the election of some of the official candidates who successfully contested the other unfilled seats (Lewis 1990). The opening of the electoral system to the opposition thus paved the way for the creation of a *de facto* competitive party system in which, however, the challenging force showed no desire to present itself as a political party, and had entered the election with the intention of acting as a stabilizing presence endowed with the capacity of exercising political influence rather than that of mounting a direct challenge to the communist power structure.

Neither were there many signs pointing to the development of a party system in the following months. The advantages of a popular, mass movement sustaining the authority of a government which felt itself constrained to take economic measures with a high potentiality for public unpopularity were self-evident and proved their value for a lengthy period, lasting well into the period during which Minister of Finance Leszek Balcerowicz implemented his tightly structured programme of economic stabilization and recovery. The political climate remained remarkably mild during the months which followed the implementation of the Balcerowicz programme from January 1990 with its severe consequences for Polish industry and the living standards of much of the population. There were certainly few major signs of the development of alternative political forces, new parties or the institutionalization of a political opposition. Local elections were held in May 1990 and, although more than a hundred organizations and political groupings were reported to have taken part in the campaign, final results tended to confirm the existing constellation of political forces.

Candidates proposed by Solidarity and its civic committees took 43 per cent of the 51,987 seats (48 per cent if the now autonomous Rural Solidarity was included), and a further 38 per cent were occupied by candidates who were independent or not affiliated to any particular party. In practice, therefore, it seemed to be the form of the social movement that continued to appeal to the Polish public rather than that of the formally constituted political party. Only the Polish Peasant Party took as many as 6.3 per cent of the seats in the local elections, and all other parties a far smaller proportion. Social Democracy, the reformed rump of the Communist Party (PUWP) gained 0.2 per cent, right-wing groups 0.1 and the Confederation of Independent Poland also 0.1 per cent of the available seats. But there were also signs during the spring and early summer of 1990 of growing dissatisfaction with the Solidarity-sponsored government and its economic policies. At the same time, relations within the Solidarity elite worsened and Lech Walesa, leader of the politically marginalized trade union and occupying no seat in either parliament or the government, launched a campaign to accelerate the pace of political and economic change.

Thus began the 'war at the top' which fragmented the Solidarity movement, hastened processes of political division and put the idea of party formation firmly on the political agenda. While political groupings and specialized parties proliferated, few had much of a following and there was little sign of popular enthusiasm for the formation of political parties or the breakup of the existing Solidarity movement. It was, indeed, not initially with the development of parties and their parliamentary representation that the conflicts within the elite were concerned. Other areas of the political system were at issue. By early 1990 the political situation in East-Central Europe looked quite different from that in the summer of 1989, when Tadeusz Mazowiecki's Solidarity-led government had emerged slowly and cautiously and careful attention had been paid to the satisfaction of what were seen as continuing Soviet interests. By 1990 Poland was just one among several post-communist countries, the PUWP was no longer in existence, and what was left of the communist establishment had only a minimal organizational presence in Polish political life.

In concrete terms, the occupation of the presidential office by General Wojciech Jaruzelski – not just a relic of the communist establishment but also a stark reminder of martial law and the military underpinnings of communist rule in Poland – already appeared highly anachronistic. When Walesa's role became increasingly marginal, both as leader of the Solidarity union during a period of Solidarity government and as head of only one of a number of union organizations (the old regime-sponsored Confederation of Unions, OPZZ, had twice as many members as Solidarity at the end of 1989), it was hardly surprising that his attention was drawn to the question of the presidency. Significantly, though, it soon became evident that this interest met with little sympathy from the Warsaw intellectuals who had increasingly dominated Poland's political establishment since the installation of the Mazowiecki government and the melting away of communist power (Zubek 1991). For Walesa, very much the worker rather than intellectual and at home not in Warsaw but in Gdánsk in more ways than one, this response only impressed on him more firmly the conviction that the process of political change needed to be not just faster but also more thoroughgoing. The tensions between the former Solidarity leaders that led to this outcome came to a head, it appears, some time during the spring of 1990 (Geremek 1991).

Influences from the long-standing divisions of Polish society and significant personal antagonisms both played a part in the decomposition of the Solidarity movement and the acceleration of existing processes of party formation. They help to explain the bitterness of the conflict surrounding the subsequent presidential elections and the prominent role played by personality in the development of Poland's party system (neither attribute, of course, in any way missing from Western political life). These features became more prominent with Walesa's recall of the respected Solidarity parliamentary club chairman, Henryk Wujec, from his post on June 1. Support was also withdrawn from Adam Michnik as editor of the daily *Election Gazette*, established in 1989 to inform and mobilize support for Solidarity candidates. The growing tensions took on more organized form with the establishment of a 'Centre Coalition' in Gdánsk by Senator Jaroslaw Kaczynski, a close associate of Walesa.

In Cracow a 'Citizens' Accord' was formed during June to provide an infrastructure to channel public support for the government. In July, a Citizens' Movement for Democratic Action was founded (ROAD, following its Polish initials) with a view to encouraging the holding of new elections as soon as possible and mobilizing support for them. It denied any left- or right-wing affiliation but took a stand against Walesa's pronouncements and expressed broad support for the Mazo-wiecki government. Divisions grew within the Citizens' Parliamentary Club, leading to the dissolution of its Presidium in October (although the final split in the group did not occur until January 1991). The movement for a more decisive confrontation between the different political currents was clearly growing stronger, the occasion finally arriving with Jaruzelski's decision to resign the presidency. The conflict between Walesa and Mazowiecki and their respective supporters under-standably emerged as the immediate focus of the presidential campaign, but in the first electoral round Mazowiecki (with 18 per cent of the votes) was defeated both by Walesa (40 per cent) and a somewhat mysterious Polish émigré, Stanislaw Tyminski (23 per cent), who appeared to have some support from security forces and former communists.

Turnout for the first round of the election was 60 per cent, higher than that for the local elections (43 per cent) and slightly below the turnout in June 1989 (62 per cent). These figures showed a markedly lower turnout than in Czechoslovakia but were not greatly different from those recorded in Hungary (63 per cent in the first round of the general election of March 1990 and 40 per cent in local elections held the following September). In the light of such experience it should not be surprising that relatively high levels of anomie (around 70 per cent of the Polish population were reportedly affected) were reported to have been found in Poland and that levels were rising in the wake of the recent social changes. Tyminski voters were found to show the highest level of anomie amongst the electorate of all six candidates and levels higher than those of Poles who had decided not to vote (Korzeniowski 1991: 125, 135). In December 1990, though, Lech Walesa was elected to the presidency by a decisive majority, gaining 74 per cent of votes cast to Tyminski's 26 per cent.

The relatively low levels of turnout in successive elections, apparent instability of electoral behaviour and evidence of the electorate's confusion and psychological disorientation all suggested that the emergence of a stable multi-party system in Poland would be an

arduous process. While Mazowiecki had resigned after his poor performance in the presidential election, Solidarity forces remained strong
in parliament and the influence of the Mazowiecki government persisted
in relatively undiluted form. Walesa's election to the presidency thus
changed little in terms of government policy and the focus of political
conflict was transferred to the question of the timing of the coming
parliamentary elections and the nature of the electoral law adopted as
the basis for them. The president's hope that they would be held within
a matter of months was not fulfilled and they were planned for the end
of October, disagreement continuing over the electoral framework
within which they would be held.

An initial proposal for a simple majority system from the Solidarity
camp had been rejected by the *Sejm* as far back as June 1990, largely
because of fear on the part of representatives of the former establishment (who still, of course, held 65 per cent of parliamentary seats)
that a single political force might sweep all before it – and that, more
practically, the former communists might be deprived of all representation and influence. Nor were all within Solidarity convinced that
the achievement of stable, party-based government should be a prime
objective of the electoral system – resistance to the idea of party
persisted and significant numbers felt that the idea of the political party
itself belonged to the past (*Polityka*, 15 June 1991). The outcome of a
proportional or mixed majority–proportional system became virtually
inevitable. Further conflict and disagreements within the parliament as
well as between it and the president meant that the decision on this was
a protracted one, and many felt dissatisfied with the final result and
complicated nature of the voting system decided on.

Political groupings and associations had, of course, begun surfacing
and often pursued a reasonably autonomous public existence even
before the demise of the communist system. By April 1989 over 1,200
associations of a general character had been registered in Warsaw, and
around 2,000 (many of them not registered) were estimated to be
operating at a national level. New legislation which permitted the
formal registration of political parties only took effect in August 1990,
though, and under its guidelines 42 organizations had been registered
by the end of January 1991 (Dehnel-Szyc and Stachura 1991: 15). By
the time preparations for the October elections were complete, voting
lists to the *Sejm* were presented by 112 different organizations –
although representatives of the different groupings did not stand in each
of the 37 constituencies (*Życie Warszawy*, 26–7 October 1991). In
Warsaw, for example, 35 lists were presented, each containing from
three to as many as 17 candidates, leaving the voter to opt for any one

of the lists (although a preference could also be expressed for any one of the candidates, which would have the effect of moving him up the list and offering a stronger personal chance of election).

By no means all could be called parties in the conventional sense of the word. The national students' union presented candidates, as did a policemen's law-and-order grouping and several offshoots of Solidarity which offered candidates for election as union representatives. With a low turnout of 43 per cent, it appeared that the anomic condition of the Polish electorate identified the previous year had taken firmer hold – exacerbated by the complicated voting mechanism, the extended wrangle that had attended its production, increasing disillusionment with the course and tenor of national political life and (by no means least) the continuing burdens of everyday life in post-communist Poland. The low turnout favoured parties with firmer support and stronger organization – and helped explain the success of the ex-communist Democratic Left Alliance (*Sojusz Lewicy Demokratycznej*), which gained 60 parliamentary seats, only two behind the Democratic Union (*Unia Demokratyczna*), which included Mazowiecki and former members of his government. Five other groups, Catholic Election Action (*Wyborcza Akcja Katolicka*), the post-communist Peasant Party (*PSL 'Sojusz Programowy'*), the nationalist Confederation for Independent Poland (*Konfederacja Polski Niepodlegeej*), Centre Accord (*Porozumienie Obywatelskie Centrum*) and the Congress of Liberal Democrats (*Kongres Liberalno-Demokratyczny*), each obtained 37 or more seats in the 460-place parliament.

The proportional emphasis in the electoral system finally adopted had indeed borne out predictions of a fragmented parliament – but this also reflected the nature of an increasingly diverse society and its fragmented political culture. An artificially contrived majority might have made the process of government formation easier, but it would also have reduced the *Sejm's* capacity to establish its legitimacy as a representative body and created further problems in the sphere of government capacity and its authority in terms of policy implementation. As many as ten groups gained significant parliamentary representation (12 seats or more, a further 19 parties or associations receiving lower levels of representation) and accounted for 79.16 per cent of total votes cast. It was not clear how a single-party majority or one constructed by a small number of parties could have been realistically achieved, however (at any rate, through a single ballot), as it took five parties to reach a near-plurality in electoral terms of 49.19 per cent of the vote and, on that basis, to win 265 seats in the *Sejm*.

This, further, would have included such diverse forces as the

Democratic Union, Union of the Democratic Left, the post-communist Peasant Party, Catholic Action and the Centre Citizen's Accord – an association which offered no hope of a government coalition. Apart from the difference in post-communist electoral systems within East-Central Europe, then, it was by no means clear that a reasonably clear-cut parliamentary majority could have been achieved in Poland in any case. Six parties took 375 (97.2 per cent) of the 386 seats in the Hungarian parliament, while in Czechoslovakia the political movements Civic Forum and the Public Against Violence together had a clear-cut majority in both chambers of the Federal Assembly: 87 of the 150 seats in the House of the People and 83 in the House of Nations (Wightman 1991a: 108). It was difficult to see how such forms of representation and majorities were available in Poland without doing considerable violence to the principle of democratic representation and leaving large parts of Polish society without any sentiments of democratic efficacy. It was becoming clear that the emergence of multi-party systems in East-Central Europe would be determined not just by political agreement and the nature of electoral systems but also, to a significant degree, by social conditions and the sequence of post-communist developments.

The indecisive outcome of the election and the wide distribution of parliamentary seats made the process of government formation a difficult and complex one. Matters were not helped by the fact that the largest parties in the new parliament were precisely those with which others were reluctant to enter into coalition. The Democratic Union was based on groups and individuals associated with the Mazowiecki government of 1989–90 and remained committed to the principles of the rigorous economic policy it had followed during that period. This, however, was precisely what the bulk of the electorate was rejecting or voting against. The persistence of this commitment, in combination with the social-democratic aura and tendency to favour a well-defined separation of Church and state of many of its leaders, was sufficient to leave it in relative isolation. The Democratic Left Alliance, with the second largest number of seats, as a direct descendant of the former Communist Party had even fewer sympathizers and was quite unacceptable as a partner to virtually all those groups spawned by the Solidarity movement – which meant most political forces of any significance. This did not include the Confederation of Independent Poland, the dark horse of the October election, but its brand of nationalism hardly disposed it to seek partners in that quarter.

After several weeks a group of five, with 205 seats in the parliament, emerged with the proposal of Jan Olszewski of the Centre Alliance as prime minister. The president, whose role it was to nominate the premier, had decided views of his own, however, and promoted the candidacy of the incumbent prime minister, Jan Bielecki, whose determined pursuit of economic liberalism he continued to favour. Bielecki, whose Liberal Congress held only 37 seats, declined for want of broader support and President Walesa eventually acquiesced in the proposal of the 'five'. But the uncertainties were far from over. The Congress of Liberal Democrats departed from the group as the contours of its likely economic policy became clear and, as the likely apportionment of cabinet seats was made known, the support of the Confederation of Independent Poland (which did not receive the offer of any post) was also withdrawn. Of the three groups that remained – the Centre Accord, Christian National Union (the political core of the Catholic Action group) and the Peasant Accord – the latter had already split by the end of the year while the other two were also riven by considerable conflict, mostly concerning relations between the leadership and rank and file or provincial organizations.

Nevertheless, by 23 December 1991, Olszewski had succeeded in assembling a cabinet and received the *Sejm's* endorsement of it (with, however, 60 voting against and 139 abstaining). Following the first free parliamentary elections since the war (and, indeed, since those of 1928), the new Polish government entered 1992 in a state of considerable uncertainty. That its parliament now held a plurality of political groupings and associations was uncontestable; whether they should be regarded as parties or having entered into a system of relations with one another such as to prove capable of sustaining democratic government was quite another matter.

Such problems were apparent throughout the first half of 1992 as the Olszewski team struggled to establish its authority and establish a viable basis for multi-party government. In June 1992 it finally collapsed amidst mutual charges of treachery and political disloyalty. After various false starts a new prime minister, Hanna Suchocka, was identified from the largest parliamentary group (the UD) to head a broad coalition whose constituents showed little sign of obvious political compatibility. Her government's capacity to survive for the rest of 1992 and the ability to secure the passage of its budget in early 1993 nevertheless testified to a significant degree of political resilience and the achievement of a certain level of post-communist political stability.

CONCLUSIONS

Now, some several years into the period of democratic transition, all the countries of East-Central Europe have held free elections for parliaments, installed new presidents and changed the composition of local councils. As the newly adopted principles of liberal democracy have been put into practice, legislators have been elected and councillors installed to develop processes of self-government. Political parties have, to varying degrees, played a part in these events, helping to aggregate and articulate political views and interests, sustain leaders and organize their support, and generally structure the political landscape. The idea of a stable party system, capable of representing social groups and their changing interests, providing the basis in parliament for effective government, and guiding the processes of leadership change at appropriate times, has become increasingly attractive in these countries – but it is one which has proved to be difficult to grasp in practical terms or to put into practice under the testing conditions of post-communist development.

Even during this short time-span, recognition of the important role played by parties during democratic transition and efforts to bring them into existence came rather late to many groups. Social movements like Solidarity and Civic Forum were initially often seen as a substitute for parties: not just a force that was instrumental in bringing about the end of communist rule but also one that could transcend the petty divisions and self-interested competitiveness of Western democracies. It soon became obvious, though, that while these broad movements were effective in counterposing the force of public opinion to the bureaucratic rule and geriatric structures of late communism, they were hardly able to cope with the differentiation and internal complexity needed if a diversity of opinions on future strategies and tactics was to emerge, imaginative policy options defined and a variety of organized groups formed to confront the diverse demands of a post-communist, pluralist society. It was probably inevitable that this recognition was also accompanied by a certain degree of disillusionment and personal acrimony as perceptions of the changing situation diverged and contrasting solutions were promoted.

In this context, it is hardly surprising that the emergence of parties has not always been welcomed, the political activities surrounding their growth sometimes turbulent and the parties' performance erratic. It is understandable in view of the dramatic shift from authoritarian communist rule to democratic transition and the introduction of a far-reaching programme of economic change that has accompanied it. Equivalent political turbulence, far-reaching fragmentation of the party system and considerable economic dislocation were also not lacking from earlier cases of democratic transition, like those in Southern Europe – but the relative success of the outcome, in combination with the passage of time, has tended to mask their problems and uncertainties. In comparison, too, with other countries of the former communist Eastern Europe, conditions for the emergence of viable party systems and the reasonably steady progress of democratization in the three countries of East-Central Europe are by no means unfavourable. By comparison, some of the questions that have emerged about the very statehood of territories in Yugoslavia and the former Soviet Union suggest the existence of a very shaky basis for any political process.

Thus the emergence of a stable party constellation in Hungary, even if marked by elements of authoritarian corporatism, and signs of the growing fragmentation of the organized political framework in Poland and Czechoslovakia should by no means be judged a mark of failure, particularly at this early state of democratic transition. A major requirement of the emerging liberal democracy is the achievement of balance between a party system that reflects the divisions and conflicts in post-communist society (one, moreover, which is particularly complex and fluid) and the formation of governments with effective powers derived from and sustained by a reasonably representative parliament.

It is hardly surprising if incipient democracies place greater emphasis in their operation on one *desideratum* than the other: thus Hungary, having established a relatively stable party system, has yet to develop a modern political culture and an independent civil society capable of sustaining effective pluralism and has shown signs of some vulnerability to elements of the authoritarian temptation. Czechoslovakia and Poland on the other hand, having experienced the break-up of major social movements, appear at the present time to be facing the institutional consequences of this decomposition in terms of party organization. At this early stage, though, such developments are by no means indicative of serious distortions in the process of regime change or major hiatus in the transition to democracy.

BIBLIOGRAPHY

Agh, A. (1991) 'Transition to democracy in East-Central Europe: a comparative view', in G. Szoboszlai (ed.) *Democracy and Political Transformation*, Budapest: Hungarian Political Science Association.

Arató, A. (1990) 'Revolution, civil society and democracy: paradoxes of the decent transition in Eastern Europe', in *Working Papers on Transitions from State Socialism*, Cornell Project on Comparative Institutional Analysis, Center for International Studies, Cornell University, Ithaca, New York.

Ash, T. G. (1991) 'A mai pártok néhány éven belül eltünnek' (Today's parties will disappear within a few years), *Heti Világgazdasság*, 22 June: 30–1.

Barany, Z. D., and Vinton, L. (1990) 'Breakthrough to democracy: elections in

Poland and Hungary', *Studies in Comparative Communism* 23: 191–212.
Batt, J. (1991) *East-Central Europe from Reform to Transformation*, London: Royal Institute of International Affairs.
Bihári, M. (1991) 'Rendszerváltás és hatalomváltás Mayarországon (1989–1990)' (Change of regime and power in Hungary), in S. Kurtan, P. Sandor and L. Vass (eds) *Magyarország Politikai Évkönyve 1991*, Budapest: Okonómia Alipitvány-Economix RT.
Bozóki, A. (ed.) (1992) *Tiszta Lappal: A Fidesz a magyar politikában: 1988–1991* (With a Clean Sheet: Fidesz in Hungarian Politics; 1988–1991), Budapest: Fidesz.
Bruszt, L. (1990) '1989: the negotiated revolution in Hungary', *Social Research* 57: 365–88.
Bútora, M., Bútorová, Z., and Rosová, T. (1991) 'The hard birth of democracy in Slovakia: the eighteen months following the "tender" revolution', *Journal of Communist Studies* 7: 435–59.
'Czechoslovakia: heat in January 1989' (1989) *Acta* 3 (Special issue 9/12): 177–8.
Dahl, R. A. (1989) *Democracy and Its Critics*, New Haven: Yale University Press.
Dehnel-Szyc, M., and Stachura, J. (1991) *Gry polityczne: orientacje na dzis*, Warsaw: Volumen.
Fórum (1990), Prague.
Geremek, B. (1991) 'Geremek sie nie zniecheca', *Gazeta Wyborcza*, 24 October.
Glenny, M. (1990) *The Rebirth of History*, Harmondsworth: Penguin.
Hájek, M. (1990) 'Co pozitrí?', *Lidové noviny*, 18 June.
Havel, V. (1988) 'Anti-political politics', in J. Keane (ed.) *Civil Society and the State*, London: Verso.
—— (1991) *Letní premítání* (Summer Reflections), Prague: Odeon.
Huntington, S. P. (1984) 'Will more countries become democratic?', *Political Science Quarterly* 99: 193–218.
Jehlícka, P., and Sykora, L. (1991) 'Stabilita regionální podpory tradicních politickych stran v ceskych zemích (1920–1990)' (The stability of regional support for traditional parties in the Czech Lands, 1920–1990), *Sborník Ceské geografické spolecnosti* 96, 2: 81–95.
Juna, J. (1990) 'Jak budu volit', *Lidové noviny*, 3 May.
Kéri, L. (1991) *Összeomlás után* (After the collapse), Budapest: Kossuth.
Kiss, J., and Kovács, E. (1991) *Többpártrendszer Magyarországón 1985–1991* (Multi-Party System in Hungary 1985–91), Budapest: Jelenkutató Alapitvány.
Klaus, V. (1990) 'Kde jsou mantinely?' (Where are the boundaries?), *Forum*, no. 47.
Konrad, G. (1984) *Antipolitics*, London: Quartet Books.
Körösényi, A. (1990) 'Pártok és szavazók: parlamenti választások 1990-ben' (Parties and voters: parliamentary elections in 1990), *Mozgó Világ* (Budapest) 16, 8 (August): 39–51.
Korzeniowski, K. (1991) 'Anomia polityczna a preferencje wyborcze w pierwszej turze wyborów', in *Polski wyborca '90, tom 1*, Warsaw: Instytut Psychologii PAN.
Kurtán, S., Sándor, S., and Vass, L. (eds) (1991) *Magyarország Politikai*

Évkönyve 1991 (Hungarian Political Yearbook), Budapest: Okonómia Alapit-
vány-Economix RT.
Lengyel, L. (1991) *Micsoda Év !* (What a year), Budapest: Szépirodalmi.
Lewis, P. G. (1990) 'Non-competitive elections and regime change', *Parlia-
mentary Affairs* 43: 90–107.
Lidové noviny (1990–1), Prague.
Lijphart, A. (1968) 'Typologies of democratic systems', *Comparative Political
Studies* 1: 3–44.
Lomax, B. (1991) 'Hungary – from Kádárism to democracy: the successful
failure of reform communism', in D. W. Spring (ed.) *The Impact of
Gorbachev*, London: Pinter.
Markus, G. G. (1994) 'Parties, camps and cleavages in postcommunist
Hungary', in M. Waller, B. Coppieters and K. Deschouwer (eds) *New
Directions for Social Democracy in Eastern Europe*, London: Frank Cass.
Mezník, J. (1992) 'Stíny disridentsví' (Shades of the dissident movement),
Lidové noviny, 18 February.
Moldován, T. (ed.) (1990) *Szabadon Választott: Parlamenti Almanach 1990*
(Freely Elected: Parliamentary Almanac 1990), Budapest: Idegenforgalmi
Propaganda és Kiadó Vállalat.
Polityka (1991), Warsaw.
Powell, G. B. (1982) *Contemporary Democracies: Participation, Stability and
Violence*, Cambridge, Mass.: Harvard University Press.
Precan, V. (1989) 'Democratic Revolution', in 'Czechoslovakia: heat in
January 1989', *Acta* 3 (Special issue 9/12): 6–16.
Pridham, G. (1990) 'Southern European democracies on the road to con-
solidation: a comparative assessment of the role of political parties', in G.
Pridham (ed.) *Securing Democracy: Political Parties and Democratic
Consolidation in Southern Europe*, London: Routledge.
Rudé Právo (1990), Prague.
Schapiro, L. (1972) *Totalitarianism*, London: Macmillan.
Staniszkis, J. (1989) 'The obsolescence of Solidarity', *Telos* 80: 37–50.
Szelényi, I., and Szelényi, S. (1991) 'The vacuum in Hungarian politics: classes
and parties', *New Left Review*, No. 187 (May–June): 121–37.
Szoboszlai, G. (ed.) (1990) *Parlamenti Választások 1990* (Parliamentary
Elections 1990), Budapest: MTA Társadalomtudományi Intézet.
—— (ed.) (1991) *Democracy and Political Transformation: Theories and East-
Central European Realities*, Budapest: Hungarian Political Science
Association.
Vávra, J., and Stern, J. (1990) 'Kdo vyhrál?' (Who won?), *Forum*, No. 20.
Weiner, M., and LaPalombara, J. (1966) 'The impact of parties on political
development', in J. LaPalombara and M. Weiner (eds) *Political Parties and
Political Development*, Princeton: Princeton University Press.
Wightman, G. (1990a) 'Czechoslovakia', *Electoral Studies* 9: 319–26.
—— (1990b) 'The June 1990 elections in Czechoslovakia: a plebiscite for
democracy', *Representation* 29: 18–23.
—— (1991a) 'The collapse of communist rule in Czechoslovakia and the June
1990 parliamentary elections', *Parliamentary Affairs* 44: 94–113.
—— (1991b) 'Czechoslovakia', in B. Szajkowski (ed.) *New Political Parties
of Eastern Europe and the Soviet Union*, London: Longman.
—— (1992) 'The 1992 Parliamentary Elections in Czechoslovakia', *The
Journal of Communist Studies* 8, No. 4.

—— (1993) 'The Czechoslovak Parliamentary Elections of 1992', *Electoral Studies* 12, No. 1.
Zubek, V. (1991) 'Walesa's leadership and Poland's transition', *Problems of Communism* 40: 69–83.
Zycie Warszawy (1991), Warsaw.

Part III

The external dimension

7 The Soviet Union and Eastern Europe, 1988–9

Interactions between domestic change and foreign policy

Tomas Niklasson

INTRODUCTION

Most of the literature analysing the democratization process (or redemocratization as the process is often referred to) of Italy and the Federal Republic of Germany in the 1940s, Spain, Portugal and Greece in the 1970s and a number of countries in Latin America in the 1970s and the 1980s, gives expression to the belief, or to the conclusion, that external actors played no more than a marginal role in these countries' transitions towards democracy. Based on that, a defensible presumption would be that the democratization processes within East and Central European countries are merely domestic processes, in which international actors and structures did not, and cannot, play any significant role. It would therefore be beside the point to focus on the role of external actors or structures in order to gain knowledge of the development in Central Europe. That conclusion is, however, premature, since these cases may well differ from earlier cases, in some significant respects.

In this chapter, I will therefore focus on the relationship between changes in the Soviet Union under Gorbachev and the development in Eastern and Central Europe during 1988 and 1989. I will first discuss some characteristics of earlier cases of democratization and how the transition processes in Eastern Europe differ from those cases. From there, I will proceed to what the literature has to say about the impact of external actors, and see whether the characteristics of these cases make it plausible (which I will argue) that external actors had and can have more influence here. Finally, I will discuss various ways of looking at the relationship between changes in the Soviet Union and changes in Eastern Europe since 1988. In other words, I would like to make it more clear what people have in mind when they talk about 'Gorbachev's role' or the 'Gorbachev effect' on the democratization of Eastern Europe.

CHARACTERISTICS OF THE PROCESSES OF DEMOCRATIZATION

If our ambition is to generalize about democratization processes, a good start would be to distinguish between (1) common traits among all kinds of democratization processes, (2) unique or common traits of the processes already studied elsewhere, and (3) unique or common characteristics of the processes that are now taking place in Eastern Europe. Concerning the first kind of traits, I believe that there are some general similarities among all cases of democratization. Nevertheless, there are also important non-trivial differences among the cases, and it may indeed be difficult to distinguish between traits common to every democratization process and traits that are not necessary but which have been characteristic for every democratization process in history. I will now try to find some characteristics of earlier cases and compare them with Eastern Europe.

Characteristics of earlier cases

Laurence Whitehead, in an article on international aspects of democratization (Whitehead 1986: 4), lists some of the common characteristics of the cases studied in the Wilson Center's project on 'Transitions from Authoritarian Rule'. These characteristics are:

1 peacetime transitions;
2 transitions from 'rightist' regimes;
3 countries with a liberal, European tradition (what Whitehead calls 'children of the French Revolution');
4 developing or newly industrializing countries;
5 a geopolitical position within, or close to, the Western bloc.

Whitehead says that these factors taken together may be an important restriction on the role of foreign actors, and by excluding other cases, the 'project narrowed its frame of reference to those recent experiences of attempted redemocratization in which local political forces operated with an untypically high degree of autonomy' (Whitehead 1986: 4). It should also be clearly stated that this project limited its study of international influence to the influence of actors – governmental or non-governmental. As we can see, one of these traits refers to the character of the regime (2); two, or possibly three, refer to characteristics of the state (3, 4, 5); and two or three refer to the international system as such, or the position of the state within that system (1, 4, 5). A comparison with Eastern Europe shows that it differs from these cases mainly on the character of the regime (2), and in one of the characteristics of the state, i.e., the economic situation (4). What the democratization processes of Eastern Europe have in common with the cases studied is that they occurred in peacetime, that the countries had a liberal tradition to some degree, and possibly that they were close to, and beginning to integrate into the Western bloc. I believe that a distinction between characteristics of the regime, the state and the international situation is a good starting-point, when we proceed to speculate about the role of external[1] influence on our cases.[2]

Characteristics of current cases

Using this distinction between characteristics of the regime, the state and the international situation, we can focus on the preconditions for a democratization process in Eastern Europe. Our main hypothesis here is that international actors have played and can play a more important role in the development of this region than has been the case in other regions, based on the general tendency in international relations, often referred to as *interdependence* (when discussing international politics or economics) or as *internationalization* (when discussing domestic politics) as well as on three 'case specific' traits.[3]

The first case-specific trait refers to the character of the former regimes, i.e., that these regimes were 'leftist' as compared to the 'rightest' or military regimes of Southern Europe and Latin America. The other two case-specific traits refer to the international situation. The first of these traits, somewhat linked to the former, is 'the Soviet connection', i.e., the special circumstantial fact that the democratization processes taking place are at the same time processes of domestic liberation and of national liberation from Soviet influence. It is impossible to discuss the development in Eastern and Central Europe without taking the impact of *glasnost, perestroika*, and *demokratizatsiya* in the Soviet Union into consideration. The processes are very complex. Just consider the fact that the development in the former Soviet Union was a precondition for the national democratization processes in Eastern Europe, at the same time as it opened the way for democratization in the relations between the Eastern European states and the Soviet Union. It was, in other words, a complex mixture of a national and an international democratization process. The former 'special relationship' to the Soviet Union made the democratization process both easier, since the actors could get support or ideas from the earlier leader of the bloc, and more difficult, since two extremely complex processes took place at the same time.

The third case-specific trait is the fact that there are a number of somewhat similar democratization processes taking place at the same time in a number of states. This gives a new character to the processes, since political parties and other organizations or movements can make contacts, cooperate, borrow ideas or strategies and even coordinate their actions. The issue of dissident contacts between Eastern European states would be an extremely interesting field of study. This trait may favour comparisons with the democratization processes in Southern Europe in the early 1970s.

Having discussed some characteristics of earlier as well as of recent cases of democratization, I will now proceed to see what efforts external actors have previously made to influence democratization processes, discuss the impact of such efforts, and by observing the characteristics of these cases, speculate about the potential forms of efforts and their impact on Eastern Europe today.

Efforts at influencing by external actors

Whitehead elaborates on the position of some potentially important international actors, e.g., the US government, governments of Western Europe and the Socialist International in promoting democracy in foreign states. There are a number of methods available for supporting a democratization process. The four methods Whitehead examines are: international treaties, the scope for diplomacy in interpreting and modifying the terms of treaty provisions, economic incentive, and activities of NGOs (Whitehead 1986: 19). As we can see, Whitehead blurs the concept by mixing actors, strategies, and resource bases into one concept – methods. He stresses the important point that 'many of these methods are of uncertain effect, some may be mutually inconsistent, and all are difficult to apply in a sustained manner over the long term' (Whitehead 1986: 19). It also goes without saying that some of these methods, when applied jointly, may have synergetic effects, thus reinforcing the impact of the actors. Whitehead's distinction also points out that it is of fundamental significance at what point an actor intervenes. He distinguishes between three types of 'promotion of democracy' which can be linked to the timing of the 'intervention' (1) 'pressure on undemocratic governments to democratize themselves', (2) 'support for fledgling democracies that are attempting to consolidate' and (3) 'maintenance of a firm stance against antidemocratic forces that threaten or overthrow established democracies' (Whitehead 1986: 44).

Whitehead's distinctions may be used as a starting point to structure the various concepts in a democratization process. When discussing external influence we should ask ourselves:

1 what kind of actor acts? – e.g., government, NGO, political party, labour union.
2 when? in the *disintegration of the authoritarian regime* or in the process of *emergence of democratic institutions.*
3 Using what kind of strategy/means?
4 Based on what resource base? – material or immaterial, e.g., laws, ideas or strategies.
5 For what purpose?/in what role?
6 Against what target group/partner?

In order to draw conclusions about the impact of external actors, we can finally proceed to make comparisons between (a) characteristics of the processes, (b) characteristics of the external influence and (c) the impact. The impact in this model is seen as being dependent on both the characteristics of the processes and on the actions of external actors.

Effects of efforts at influencing

What are the effects of these efforts to influence the democratization process? Most authors claim that external actors are not important actors in that process. But few authors deny the potential impact of external actors.[4] Robert M. Fishman (1990: 425) puts it in this way: 'This is not to argue that class forces or the international context are irrelevant; rather, the point is that these forces are not the *sole* determinants of political developments and actions.'

Whitehead emphasizes that it matters who intervenes, since democracy is such a contested concept:

> European definitions of 'democracy' seem to give more stress to social and economic participation, whereas the Americans give almost exclusive emphasis to the electoral aspect. The political spectrum in most West European countries is reasonably congruent with that likely to emerge in Southern Europe and Latin American nations as they redemocratize . . . whereas the U.S. spectrum may only correspond to that ranging from the Center to the far Right, leaving emergent left-wing currents with no *interlocuteurs* in the American political process.
>
> (Whitehead 1986: 17–18)

Concerning the impact of historical trends/the international context, one author makes the conclusion, based on a comparative study of transitions from authoritarian rule in Latin America, that 'not only has redemocratization rarely occurred in isolation from broader Latin American political trends, but historical timing also appears to have affected possibilities for the consolidation of competitive political institutions' (Remmer 1985: 259. For a discussion on these periods, see also Huntington 1984: 195–8). Karen L. Remmer's emphasis on the international trend is confirmed by Larry Diamond writing on democratization in Asia. 'International influence, such as it may exist, is more prodemocratic when the regional or global trend is toward democracy, and when the powerful external actors make the promotion of democracy a more explicit foreign policy goal' (Diamond 1989: 42).

If we proceed to an evaluation of specific cases, the picture diverges. According to Whitehead (1986: 20), the examples of Spain and Nicaragua confirm 'the view that in peacetime external factors can play only a secondary role in redemocratization', whereas Samuel P. Huntington comments on Spain, among other cases, in the following way:

> Regional external influence can also have a significant effect on political development within a society. The governments and political parties of the European Community (EC) helped to encourage the emergence of democratic institutions in Spain and Portugal, and the desire of those two countries plus Greece to join the community provided an additional incentive for them to become democratic.
>
> (Huntington 1984: 206–7)

Clearly, then, how we interpret the influence of external actors is based both on our expectations about that influence and on empirical observations. I tend to sympathize with Huntington's more modest expectations, from which we cannot expect the impact of external actors to be necessarily the decisive factor in the process. I thus agree that a democratization or redemocratization process is essentially a domestic process, and so if our interest were to find the main causes of democratization we had better concentrate on the domestic aspects. However, studying the role of external actors, regardless of whether or not their influence was of fundamental importance in the democratization process itself, contributes to our general knowledge of transnational cooperation. I therefore focus on behaviour as well as on effects.

Characteristics of the Eastern European cases – implications for the effects of external influence

What implications do the above-mentioned differences have when we discuss the importance of external influence? The fact that the world is more interdependent today than ever, would give support to the assumption that external factors are more important in these processes than earlier ones. The extensive transnational contacts and communications open up a market for goods and services, but also for ideas. The countries of the Soviet bloc, including its Central European member states, have been relatively insulated from the world markets of goods, services and ideas. Today, when these markets are opening up, there is a rising demand not only for Coca Cola and VCRs, but also for constitutional arrangements and voting systems. This opens up a possibility for external actors trying to influence the democratization process. At the same time, the more abstract ideas about democracy have been part of the knowledge of dissidents, and perhaps even part of the knowledge of the whole population. What external actors can contribute, in this latter phase of the democratization process, is probably more in the realm of strategies, organizational skills and relatively concrete ideas, rather than lofty interpretations of democracy.

What are the implications of the first case-specific trait: that the regimes of earlier cases were 'rightist' or military regimes whereas the regimes of Eastern Europe have referred to themselves as socialist or communist? Regardless of whether they were 'truly socialist' or not, these regimes have been characterized by other traits than those of the regimes of Latin America or Southern Europe. This is a truly new element, and the effect of these differences could have an impact on the effect of external influence. The cold warriors tended to portray the 'Eastern bloc' and its communist regimes as the enemy. Therefore, they should now be more interested in assisting the rebuilding of democracy. Since the processes have taken place at the same time as, and partly as a consequence of, the decline of Soviet power, that could well increase the role of external actors in the process. At the same time, however, we should not ignore the fact that the communists of East and Central Europe were the main obstacle to democratization. Especially if we study the first part of the democratization process (i.e., the disintegration of the authoritarian regime), the fact that we are dealing with leftist regimes is rather an argument against the importance of external, non-leftist, actors.

If we for the time being limit our focus a little, and concentrate on the effectiveness of *governmental* support in a democratization process, our answer concerning the potential impact must be even more cautious. There are two general trends in Western Europe, on the one hand integration, i.e., the EC process, and, on the other, fragmentation or a diminished role for the state and more emphasis on (trans-border) regions. The power of the state and its capacity to put pressure on, or influence, another actor is thus diminishing. To summarize this part of the discussion, a certain number of external actors can play a more important role in the process of today but the influence of governments in this process, as compared to that of other actors, has probably decreased.

Furthermore, since democratization contains two main processes – one of internal, political liberation/democratization, and one of external liberation, or democratization from the pressure of the Soviet Union and from the narrowly defined role of the states within the SEV (COMECON) and the Warsaw Treaty Organization – the processes themselves have an international dimension. A simple theory of power would lead to the assumption that where one superpower withdraws and leaves a power vacuum, other powers will try to fill up the vacant space.

Finally, the fact that there are a number of democratizing countries in the same region (which was also the case in Southern Europe) may open up the possibility for a diffusion (for the discussion of policy diffusion, see Karvonen 1981a and 1981b) of ideas and strategies between the states concerned (Fülöp and Póti 1990: 3–4). In this context it may well be of some importance to discuss the mythological Central European heritage including a tradition of trans-border and transnational contacts (as well as pogroms), as an ideal for many people in Central Europe today (for a discussion on 'Central Europe', see for example Jahn 1988 and 1990; and a number of the essays in Schöpflin and Wood 1989). The speed of the processes, however, may diminish the impact of external actors in the beginning of the process, i.e., before and immediately after the authoritarian regime has disintegrated.

Whether these four characteristics together increase or decrease the space of manoeuvre for external actors is an open question. To give a definite answer we must first try to answer the question about the characteristics of the actor and the way he acts.

In starting to answer the question of when the external actors intervene, a distinction must be made between the Soviet Union and its Communist Party, on the one hand, and other actors, on the other. The Soviet Union played an important role in the first phase of the democratization processes, i.e., what Przeworski called the disintegration of authoritarian rule. Thereafter, in the emergence of democratic institutions, Soviet influence has been marginal, and here we had better focus on actors from Western or neutral countries. Nevertheless, it may also be true that Western influence played a more important role in the disintegration process than we have so far grasped.

CHANGES IN THE SOVIET UNION AND DEVELOPMENTS
WITHIN EASTERN EUROPE

To many observers trying to analyse why a flood of democratizations
swept over Eastern Europe in the autumn of 1989, the main reason
seems to be 'the Gorbachev factor'. Indeed, from reading these
commentators, it seems as if Mikhail Gorbachev was the explanation
for the development in Eastern Europe that year. However, this cannot
by any means be assumed and is somewhat misleading; and in any case
we need to discuss this argument in more detail. I am aware of the fact
that it might be premature to make definitive statements concerning the
role of President Gorbachev, the Soviet Union or the KGB for the
changes in Eastern Europe, since there is as much confusion as there is
a lack of reliable sources. Nevertheless, a discussion concerning the
possible influences of the Soviet Union is of some relevance.

If we believe that Mikhail Gorbachev was important for the development in Eastern Europe, we must specify what we mean by this.
Do we imply that Gorbachev himself was important or do we mean that
the changes in the Soviet Union since 1985 were important? A question
somewhat related to this is whether the changes in the Soviet Union
were caused by some structural factors which made reforms acute, or
whether the Soviet leader had much freedom of action.

To start with the second question, there were fundamental structural
causes within Soviet society, in the world surrounding the Soviet
Union, and in the relations between the Soviet Union and the external
world that made reform necessary.

> Most of the questions asked in the west, and many of the answers
> given seem to me to have missed the point. They have tended to focus
> upon the person of Mikhail Gorbachev: his intentions, his prospects
> of survival, whether we should help him and if so how. . . . Changes
> are occurring, and have for long been going on, in Soviet society –
> developments of which Gorbachev is as much the symptom as he is
> the catalyst.
>
> (Howard 1990: 99–100)

It is therefore important not to exaggerate the importance of Mikhail
Gorbachev. He was merely 'the holder of the dam lock' as Norman
Davis eloquently put it in a lecture in Gothenburg in early 1991. True
this role is important too, and for a deeper understanding of the changes
going on, structural determinants are not enough. 'The structural
determinants of reform . . . are the long-term causal factors of change.
However important they may be, they are not sufficient factors of

change, but have to interplay with conditional factors of change at the level of actors, and the level of cognition. A comprehensive explanatory model of reform in the Soviet-type systems would have to include the latter' (Skak 1990: 13).

The first question is harder to answer at the present moment. Under Gorbachev's leadership it became more obvious that various pressure groups exist within the Soviet political system. Whether Gorbachev was the initiator of reforms, reacted to reformist circles, or more likely, a mixture of both, is not easy to say. From this perspective, it becomes important to acquire a deeper knowledge of Gorbachev's belief system, which may have changed significantly during the last six years. For heuristic reasons, it is helpful to distinguish two main Gorbachev (or 'Gorby' as he is often called) models. *Gorby Model One* is that he is a convinced liberal democrat who is doing the maximum possible to reform his country and to integrate it into the world community under tremendous resistance from the conservative forces. *Gorby Model Two* is that he himself has grown up in this communist *nomenklatura* environment, that he 'shares all the prejudices and all the restrictions of this closed society and that he has already reached the limits of his democratic potential. I don't think that either model is true. The truth is a mixture of both' (Piontkowsky 1990: 187).

Soviet domestic reforms as model or reforms in foreign policy as precondition?

An important demarcation line should be drawn between changes in the domestic policy of the Soviet Union (often summarized in the three words *glasnost, perestroika* and *demokratizatsiya*) and changes in its external policy, referred to as *novoe myshlenie* or new thinking (for a further discussion of the concept of *novoe myshlenie*, see Holloway 1989; Legvold 1989). In other words we can imagine that the reforms carried out in the domestic political and economic system of the USSR inspired reform-minded communists or, in some cases, leftist opposition groups, to follow Big Brother once again.

Domestic changes in the Soviet Union

The impact of the domestic reforms is rather difficult to assess. 'Clearly, the Soviet debate on democratization had a major direct and indirect influence on the events in Eastern Europe. Soviet pronouncements were followed by communist and noncommunist circles in these countries, with reform leaders able to introduce the same ideas into the public

debate in allied capitals without fear of censure from Moscow' (Dawisha
1990: 210). Poland and Hungary had already reached the limits of
reform within the system. What the opposition in those countries
demanded instead was a change of system. Within the ruling parties of
those countries and among opposition groups in Czechoslovakia,
Bulgaria and Romania the prospect of reform looked much brighter.
However, to most leading communists in Romania and Chechoslovakia
reform was not an accepted solution. 'The winds of change blow from
the Soviet Union to Eastern Europe and not the other way around – and
most East European regimes, making use of their newly granted if still
limited autonomy, are disassociating themselves from Mikhail Gorbachev's policies of reform. Most are, in fact, united against almost
everything he stands for, and they are unwilling to follow his example'
(Gati 1989: 101). These leaders had every reason to be negatively
oriented towards reform. This is clearly seen from the historical context
in which they came to power. 'Unlike Gorbachev, Eastern European
leaders do not have a "previous administration" upon which to blame
all their troubles. In fact, Gorbachev's attacks on the Brezhnev era
generally come uncomfortably close, from the East European perspective, to involving them in guilt by association' (Cynkin 1988: 312).
If they were unwilling, 'paradoxically, the very nature of *glasnost*
inhibits Moscow's ability to proselytize it throughout the Eastern Bloc.
Public promotion of "democratization", respect for local conditions,
and espoused toleration of national flexibility in implementation of
reforms mitigate the Soviet Union's control of events within the Bloc'
(Cynkin 1988: 312). The GDR was a special case because of the national
question. The extent to which diffusion or imitation was possible
therefore varied to a significant degree between the various countries of
Eastern and Central Europe, and in some cases the situation was rather
paradoxical in that the Communist Party tried not to follow Moscow
while parts of the opposition looked East for help.

But the reforms within the Soviet Union also affected the politics of
Eastern Europe in another way. The reforms changed the image of the
Soviet Union as a state and caused a modification of the expected
behaviour of the USSR. 'The democratization of the country [the Soviet
Union] delivered a powerful blow to the image of a closed, menacing
society – the main source of the "Soviet threat"' (Karaganov 1990:
122). Even among some of the hard-liners 'the process of transformation
was clearly affected by the international demonstration process as well.
The fact that the Soviet Union was no longer a force for the *status quo*
but in the vanguard of reform was significant in making it more difficult
to keep change off the agenda' (Schöpflin 1990: 9).

Many analysts agree that 'the reforms in Eastern Europe owe their beginnings to the process of *perestroika* initiated in the Soviet Union after 1985' (de Nevers 1990: 27). It took some time, however, before the reaction came: 'it was not until 1988 that political initiatives comparable to *perestroika* and *glasnost* emerged in Eastern Europe' (de Nevers 1990: 27).

Changes in Soviet foreign policy

More important than the domestic reforms were the changes in Soviet foreign policy, although this is not meant to imply that there is not a relation between the changes in domestic and foreign policy. Renée de Nevers (1990) talks about 'the catalytic role played by Gorbachev's new thinking'. Researchers do not agree, however, on when these changes were initiated, or did start, to use a less voluntaristic expression. They also take different stands on the question of Gorbachev's foresight.

None of the literature has noticed any substantial changes in the foreign policy towards Eastern Europe before the 27th Party Congress in 1986. After that, however, some authors see changes, and increasingly so from 1988 (Dawisha 1990: 199). According to Karen Dawisha (1990) 'Gorbachev realized that the Europeanization of the Soviet Union could not proceed without the de-Sovietization of eastern Europe. . . . Beginning in 1987 and 1988, Gorbachev began to assemble a group of experts who shared his radical vision of the East European future.'

In his main address of 2 November 1987 in commemoration of the 70th anniversary of the Bolshevik Revolution, Gorbachev stresses the independence of all the communist parties. To counter scepticism emanating from the fact that already Khrushchev had said so, he continued: 'We talked about this as far back as the 20th Congress. True, we did not free ourselves of old habits at once. However, now this is an immutable reality' (quoted in Cynkin 1988: 311). Also in the declarations of Prague (April 1987), Belgrade (March 1988) and Warsaw (July 1988), Gorbachev stressed the right of every party to be '"sovereign" in the solution of "questions pertaining to the development" of the country governed by it. At the same time, Gorbachev expected the allied parties to accept a joint responsibility for the fate of socialism' (Oldenburg *et al.* 1990: 242).

In the beginning and middle of 1988 leading Soviet specialists started to discuss the role of the Soviet Union in Eastern Europe since the war. They blamed '"the hegemonic aspirations of the Soviet leadership" for "the deep political crisis" in Hungary 1956, in Czechoslovakia in 1968, and in Poland in 1956, 1970 and 1980–1'.[5] These comments, however, did not come from Gorbachev personally. Commenting on the events of 1956 and 1968 to the *Washington Post* in May the same year he said: 'When you speak about interference, I understand what you have in mind. I have in mind that before what you are talking about happened, another kind of interference had occurred' (Gati 1989: 104). It seems as if it were easier to change position than to accept guilt for earlier mistakes. Already in 1987 Gorbachev wrote 'that "the independence of each [Communist] Party, its sovereign right to decide the issues facing its country and its responsibility to its nation are unquestionable principles"' (Gati 1989).

In the spring of 1988 there were also organizational and personnel changes in the administration dealing with Eastern Europe. The CPSU abolished the old Department for Liaison with the Communist and Workers' Parties of Socialist Countries. At the same time, the Politburo created a Commission on International Policy and appointed Aleksandr N. Yakovlev, one of Gorbachev's closest advisers, as its chairman. The purpose of the newly created commission was to coordinate Soviet foreign policy in Eastern Europe and around the world. The organizational change had the effect of lessening the importance of the region, signalling that it would no longer be treated as a special case. Moscow's East European policy was henceforth to be made in the context of global and geopolitical rather than ideological considerations (Gati 1990: 164–5. See also Oldenburg 1990: 242). Further changes were carried out in September 1988 (Dawisha 1990: 199).

Robert Legvold has observed important changes in the policy of the Soviet Union towards Eastern Europe in the beginning of 1989. He stresses the new concepts used when discussing Eastern Europe as one of four changes in the use of basic concepts, including the fact that important Soviet politicians did not any longer believe in the fundamental harmony in the relations between Eastern Europe and the Soviet Union (Legvold 1989: 86). Still, however, many observers were unsure how to interpret the new signals from Moscow (see e.g., Holloway 1989). From 1989 Gorbachev became more active 'in advocating reforms in the East European states' (de Nevers 1990: 4). The means by which he tried to cause changes will be discussed below. That the Soviet view of the past had changed by 1990 is obvious from the following statement by Eduard Shevardnadze: 'Surely the Czechoslovak Spring couldn't be regarded as imperialist intrigue' (Eduard Shevardnadze at the February 1990 plenum of the CPSU Central Committee, quoted in Dawisha 1990: 197).

204 The external dimension

Why did the foreign policy change?

It is of course interesting to speculate about the causes of the changes in Soviet foreign policy under Gorbachev. What we consider to be a satisfactory explanation and which of these we regard as probable depends on the perspective we have on the Soviet Union and Eastern Europe, and also on what we really want to explain. Is it the fact that things changed at all? Or is it rather that things developed the way they did when they did? In other words, what kind of explanations we look for depends to a great extent on how we perceive Gorbachev and his role in history.

Most researchers see Gorbachev's change in foreign policy more as *reactions* to various forms of pressure than as *actions*. 'Moscow's policy toward Eastern Europe does not seem to have been driven by a master plan; rather, it appears to have been improvised, largely in response to developments in the region itself' (de Nevers 1990: 4). Writing in early 1989, Valerie Bunce interprets Gorbachev's choice in the following way: 'Gorbachev has no easy answers to the crisis in Eastern Europe. What Gorbachev does know is that something needs to be done – and fast – about the bloc. While the bloc is not integrated enough to achieve a rational division of labor, its political and economic integration is sufficient to make Eastern European problems Soviet problems as well' (Bunce 1989: 237). This also implies that Gorbachev's views, policies and reasoning have undergone changes during the last years. He may well have started the changes in foreign policy in order to promote reform, not revolution, and only eventually understood the consequences of his actions (Gati 1989: 102).

But even if Gorbachev could not foresee the consequences of his decisions there must have been some driving forces behind them. Some authors point to a change in how the concept of security is understood, and this change is reflected in *novoe myshlenie*. 'It was a new conception of the Soviet Union's western border security, a conception which has plainly been accepted in Moscow' (Piontkowsky 1990: 167–8). An important reason behind this change may well be the experience of Afghanistan. 'The experience of the Afghanistan war was crucial in stimulating this rethinking. Afghanistan showed the limitations of military power very clearly and convincingly. . . . It was not so much thinkers in the corridors of the Kremlin as the *mujahadin* in the hills of Afghanistan who were the real liberators of Eastern Europe' (Piontkowsky 1990: 168–9).

Charles Gati also mentions Gorbachev's domestic problems and his wish to diminish military spending. He also points to the importance of Gorbachev's intervention with Eastern Europe itself and mentions

Gorbachev's personal frustration with the 'gang of four' and their resistance to his own perestroika and glasnost. . . . Whether Gorbachev fully anticipated the consequences of his decisions remains uncertain as well. It is quite possible that he misjudged East European popular sentiments by assuming that his version of reformist communism would take root in the region.

(Gati 1990: 163)

A problematic question is how people in the Soviet Union responded to the loss of the Empire. Karen Dawisha (1990: 215) believes that 'the failure to improve the Soviet economic situation only increased the conviction among a large section of the Soviet elite that Eastern Europe should be allowed to go its own way'. Michael Howard (1990: 101) agrees, writing that 'not only did the Soviet government asquiesce in this, but the Soviet people remained apparently indifferent', whereas Mette Skak (1990: 21) takes another position, claiming that 'the discussion in the Soviet media confirms that the East European revolutions and the ensuing uncertainty concerning the Soviet role there and in European affairs in general is hard to digest for the Soviet public'.

Passive or active Soviet support for the changes in Eastern Europe?

Yet another differentiation could be made over a dimension ranging from passivity to activity, in other words between active support and passive tolerance or between intervention and non-intervention. Intervention is a contested concept, and this distinction is not easy to uphold. How should we judge withdrawal of support for example? Is it to be considered as an active move or rather as a return to passivity or as non-intervention? Again, our conclusions depend on what we consider as normal or as the existing situation. If we look at Eastern Europe in a very short historical perspective we accept the Soviet dominance as a given fact and then withdrawal of support is clearly seen as intervention. On the other hand, if we remember what happened in Eastern Europe after the Second World War withdrawal of support to existing regimes is better seen as return to a normal situation, a normalization process. Most authors stress the importance of what Moscow did not do or stopped doing. Whether we consider these measures or non-measures as active or passive depends on our perspective. Schöpflin mentions the effect on the GDR when 'in October 1989, in connection with the 40th anniversary celebrations of the communist state, the Soviet Union withdrew its moral support' (Schöpflin 1990: 10). Janus

Ziolkowski (1990: 44–5) makes the same point: 'Perhaps even more important for Europe is what Gorbachev has *refrained* from doing. . . . The vital point is that last November there were not scenes reminiscent of Tienanmen Square in the streets of Eastern Europe, and that Soviet policy was fundamental to that happy fact.' Mette Skak (1990: 1) talks about the Soviets 'pulling the carpet under orthodox communists in an attempt to pave the way for radical reform communism in Eastern Europe', while commenting on Gorbachev's speech to the 27th CPSU Congress, Karen Dawisha (1990: 207) says: 'The impression of a historic shift was supported as much by what Gorbachev did not say as by what he did say about Eastern Europe and the socialist commonwealth.'

The dynamics between Soviet and East European politics

When scepticism is expressed about the importance of the changes in the Soviet Union as the key factor behind the changes in Eastern and Central Europe in 1989, we have in mind the domestic development within each of the six countries affected. In all of these states there was an internal dynamic which led to a situation ripe for radical change. In a way the changes in the Soviet Union made the explosion come earlier but an explosion would have come even without Gorbachev. It is therefore most fruitful to look at the events as an outcome of a dynamic relation between domestic and external factors. George Schöpflin for instance points out very clearly that there were major crises within each of the East or Central European states before 1989: 'For all practical purposes, by the end of the 1980s Soviet-type systems were no longer capable of self-reproduction' (Schöpflin 1990: 5). He also makes an extremely interesting point concerning the legitimacy of the communist regimes. There has been much discussion about the concept of legitimacy in relation to those regimes. One popular explanation to the speed by which those governments were toppled, once the process started, is that they lacked legitimacy or popular support. Others, however, have argued that this argument is not very convincing since they had lacked legitimacy for a long time already, if they ever were legitimate in the eyes of their own peoples. Schöpflin, however, points to the importance of self-legitimation. 'An authoritarian elite sustains itself in power not just through force and the threat of force but, more importantly, because it has some vision of the future by which it can justify itself to itself' (Schöpflin 1990: 6).

As already stated, the regimes and the opposition in the various countries reacted in different ways to the new signals from Moscow.

One very important signal was Gorbachev's speech at the UN in December 1988, mentioning troop withdrawals from Eastern Europe. 'While Gorbachev's decision to withdraw some Soviet forces has no bearing on Moscow's military capacity to handle East European crises of any type, it is going to heighten the East European regimes' already existing doubts about Soviet intent' (Gati 1989: 111). Or, also in the words of Gati,

> The Soviet military decision to retrench contained a critical political message to the region's communist leaders: the Soviet Union would no longer protect unpopular East European regimes from their own peoples. Once that message was conveyed and absorbed, reformers and diehards alike were left with the choice of either making the best deal they could with their own populations or using force to break the people's will.
>
> (Gati 1990: 161–2)

> Hence the strange reason why this region is becoming more unstable now is that the East European regimes are in effect deprived of the tools of both governing and ruling. They lack sufficient resources – carrots that are sweet enough and sticks that are stout enough – to either reward or repress their people.
>
> (Gati 1989: 111)

Gorbachev – sufficient or necessary actor?

A rather philosophical question is whether Gorbachev was sufficient, necessary or neither sufficient nor necessary for the changes that have taken place in Eastern Europe, and in the relations between Eastern Europe and the Soviet Union. George Schöpflin (1990: 16) says that 'without the weakening of the Soviet Union the transformation would not obviously have begun'. In the last chapter of *We the People*, discussing more generally the causes of 1989, Timothy Garton Ash stresses the importance of changes in Soviet foreign policy.

> That Moscow permitted the former 'satellite' countries to determine how they want to govern themselves was clearly a *sine qua non*. But the nature and direction of the processes of domestic political self-determination cannot be understood by studying Soviet policy. The causes lie elsewhere, in the history of individual countries, in their interaction with their East European neighbours and with the more free and prosperous Europe that lies to the west, north and south of them.
>
> (Ash 1990: 133)

Both Schöpflin and Ash see the changes in the Soviet Union as
necessary, but Ash, at least, does not consider them to be sufficient as
an explanation of this development.

> To the outside world, the sequence of revolution in 1989 looked like
> a powdertrail fired spontaneously by the sparks from the pickaxes
> biting into the top of the Berlin Wall. From the inside, it didn't look
> like that because in each country there was a long and particular
> preparation. The image of clocks is less explosive but more apt. The
> various East European clocks ran at different speeds, and the
> internal mechanisms of each brought them to chime in 1989. This
> is not to deny a demonstration effect, and certainly not to deny the
> vital harmonising role of Gorbachev and of Soviet military *non-
> intervention*; only to propose the virtue of proper context to secure
> understanding.
>
> (Prins 1990: XIII)

But once again our answer depends on the perspective we have, and
again reference is made to Professor Davies's metaphor 'the holder of
the dam lock'. Therefore the changes in the Soviet Union were neither
necessary nor sufficient conditions for what happened in Eastern
Europe. Without the pressure within the East European states themselves due to a lack of legitimacy for the existing authoritarian regimes,
basing their power on support from Moscow, changes would not have
followed automatically from changes in the Soviet Union, and vice
versa that pressure itself would eventually have toppled the old regimes.

> The factor 'Gorbachev' alone does not suffice to explain why these
> ruling élites did not more vigorously deploy their own, still for-
> midable police and security forces in a last-ditch defence of their own
> power and privilege. Is it too fanciful to suggest that the constant,
> persistent harping of the west on certain international norms of
> domestic conduct, the East European leaders' yearning for inter-
> national respectability, and the sensed linkage between this and the
> hard currency credits they so badly needed, in short, the factor
> 'Helsinki', played at least some part in staying the hands of those
> who might otherwise have given the order to shoot?
>
> (Ash 1990: 141)

The 'Eastern Europeanization' of the Soviet Union

Once things started to happen in Eastern Europe we can also observe
how that development affected reality in the Soviet Union itself. As

Seweryn Bialer (1990: 112) stated in the spring of 1990: 'There is a process of "Eastern Europeanization" in the present Soviet development.' This link is also stressed by a Soviet commentator, rather optimistic about the outcome. 'The changes in the German Democratic Republic, Czechoslovakia and Romania have provided a potent push for *perestroika*. . . . They have strengthened its irreversibility, and showed that there is no reasonable alternative to the democratization of the political system and the marketization of the economy' (Karaganov 1990: 122). 'Yet the popular movement for national and social self-determination did not stop neatly at the western frontier of the Soviet Union. What happened in Eastern Europe directly encouraged the Baltic States, not to mention the Romanians of Soviet Moldavia (Ash 1990: 150). But this is clearly a mechanism working in many directions, or in many stages. Some authors, for instance, mention the influence of the various opposition movements in Eastern Europe on the opposition groups within the Soviet Union:

> In the early stages of *perestroika*, many of us in the Soviet Union dreamt that there might come about some movement in Eastern Europe like Solidarnosc had been briefly in Poland in 1980 or like the Prague Spring in 1968. We felt that if such developments occurred, it would greatly influence our own chances. This, we thought, would push the USSR very strongly towards a democratic solution and that might precipitate things. . . . Plainly, the current Russian Revolution . . . is related to the events of 1989 in Eastern Europe. It was related in two ways: as *cause* and as *effect*.
>
> (Piontkowsky 1990: 164–5)

The same author points to a great paradox, namely that 'the same Gorbachevian Government simultaneously lifted the threat of armed intervention from Eastern Europe, thus permitting spring to flower in the winter of 1989, yet refused to accept the logic and moral imperative of liberalisation at home' (Piontkowsky 1990: 166–7).

A most important question for all parties in Eastern Europe, and for Western Europe as well, is what the relations between the former Soviet Union (the Commonwealth of Independent States) and Eastern Europe will look like in the future. A development in which the peoples of Eastern Europe reject in anger everything connected to Russia is just as conceivable as it is dangerous. The Commonwealth of Independent States and the states of Central and Eastern Europe are likely to be forced to cooperate over the coming years, for economic reasons at least.

This is the reason why we use our contacts from the past with the

Soviet dissidents to try to get as much information as possible from there, and to get as much information about our experiences from them. . . . The other part of our tactic is to strive not for the extinguishing, but for the normalisation of economic relations with the USSR. . . . I think we all in Eastern Europe are realist enough to understand that at the very least for economic reasons, it is unwise to get rid of such a good and huge market as the USSR for our goods, which are still of low quality by world standards. Who else would buy them?

(Urban 1990: 130–1)

Based on that assumption Elemér Hankiss is wrong in his analysis: 'Let Gorbachev survive until the last Russian troops leave Hungary. After that I think that we will not really be affected by anything that may happen in the future in the Soviet Union' (Hankiss 1990: 36). Eastern Europe can be still very much affected by what happens on the territory east of it, whatever it is called. One example of this is Eastern Europe's dependency on imported oil. Already in 1990 the Soviet Union had reduced its export of oil, and raised prices (Glenny 1990: 33).

THE SOVIET INFLUENCE ON THE VARIOUS COUNTRIES

Even during the dramatic months of 1989, Moscow seems to have played an important role in the change of governments in at least some of the six countries. Since the situation in the various countries was so different it goes without saying that Moscow played different roles in different countries. We need therefore to examine these cases in turn and comparatively.

Hungary and Poland

The reform processes started in Hungary and Poland, although in Hungary it was more one of reform activities within the ruling party (the HSWP) than in Poland, where Solidarity led the opposition. The demands for change were much more radical in these two countries, probably at least partly based on their experience of economic reform. 'Unlike other East Europeans who eagerly await reforms, many Poles and Hungarians have reached the conclusion that their system cannot be reformed' (Gati 1989: 101).

What was important for these two countries was not the idea of reform coming from the Soviet Union but rather the signals that Moscow accepted, or even supported, reform. Charles Gati refers to a private conversation with Károly Grósz in October 1988 who told him that 'it was no longer either necessary or customary to ask for Moscow's "permission" before undertaking a new initiative. He said that recently, before making a particularly difficult decision, the substance of which he did not mention, he had called Gorbachev and asked for his "opinion". The answer was that Grósz should be "guided by his conscience"' (Gati 1989: 106). Beside the effects in Hungary itself, the Hungarian goverment also very much influenced the democratization process in the GDR by letting German refugees leave for West Germany. 'Moscow simply did not order the Hungarians any longer to keep their barbed wire intact. Nor could they have insisted upon it if they had and the Hungarians had refused' (Reich 1990: 89). It also seems as if the Hungarians consulted the Russians before allowing the Germans to leave (Skak 1990: 1).

In Poland, too, there were demands for reforms even before Gorbachev but these demands mostly came from Solidarity. In this case it seems as if Moscow acted as a moderator between the Polish government and the illegal trade union. Even within the Polish party, however, there were reformists as seen in the support given to Gorbachev's reforms announced at the 27th CPSU Congress (de Nevers 1990: 34–5). Gorbachev's visit to Poland in July 1987 'demonstrated that he continued to back Jaruzelski, and that he accepted Jaruzelski's increasingly unorthodox methods for trying to solve the country's internal problems' (de Nevers 1990: 34–5). After the semi-free parliamentary elections in the summer of 1989 it took quite a long time before a government could be formed. During the process Gorbachev changed his policy from demanding communist control into pressing the Polish Party leader, in a phone-call on 22 August, to participate in a non-communist led government (de Nevers 1990: 34–5; see also Gati 1990: 168; Skak 1990: 1). Already in July, speaking to the Council of Europe in Strasbourg, Gorbachev went further than ever before to emphasize 'new thinking' in Soviet policy towards Eastern Europe: 'Social and political orders in one or another country changed in the past and may change in the future. But this change is the exclusive affair of the people of that country and is their choice. Any interference in domestic affairs and any attempts to restrict the sovereignty of states, both friends and allies or any others, is inadmissible' (Gati 1990: 169).

'The gang of four'

In the other four countries, the GDR, Czechoslovakia, Bulgaria and Romania, the situations were different. The ruling parties of these

212 The external dimension

states, later on known as 'the gang of four' were all, with the possible exception of Bulgaria, stubbornly opposing reform. 'The East German government was one of the first in Eastern Europe to make clear that it did not intend to follow the Soviet example and restructure its economy or political system. The first signs of this appeared in 1986, when Honecker refused to accept that the GDR needed to change. This attitude persisted well into 1989' (de Nevers 1990: 39). When discussing the reform processes or revolutions among these countries, de Nevers says: 'The impact of the reform process in the Soviet Union, Hungary and Poland generated widespread domestic pressures for political reforms. . . . The fundamental change in Moscow's attitude toward reform in Eastern Europe convinced the leadership in these countries that change was inevitable' (de Nevers 1990: 27). When discussing the collapse of the East German regime and why it fell so fast, one of the factors Timothy Garton Ash mentions is precisely what he calls 'the Gorbachev effect'. He quotes the East German Constitution and claims that 'the "Gorbachev effect" was strongest in East Germany because it was more strongly oriented towards – and ultimately dependent on – the Soviet Union than any other East European state'. Gorbachev is quoted as saying, on the 40th anniversary of the East German Republic on 7 October 1989, that 'life itself punishes those who delay' (Ash 1990: 65; see also Gati 1990: 176). As Reich points out (see also Ash 1990: 141):

> Mr Gorbachev seems to have realized that matters for the Party in the GDR were lurching into disaster and he obviously gave up on the Honecker leadership. During his visit on the occasion of the fortieth anniversary of the creation of the GDR . . . he ordered his car to be stopped in the streets and he addressed young people who were waving at him. . . . 'If you really want democracy, then take it, and you will get it'. News of statements of this kind spread like wildfire on the grapevine.
>
> (Reich 1990: 85)

Jens Reich discusses why the demonstrations in East Germany did not cause the military to use violence, in a similar way as the military in China did less than six months earlier. 'One of the factors is said to have been the refusal of the highest command of the Warsaw Pact – Gorbachev in other words – to leave GDR Volksarmee troops in the towns' (Reich 1990: 88. See also Skak 1990: 1; Piontkowsky 1990: 169–70; Gati 1990: 164). According to Krenz 'Gorbachev was consulted on the decision to open the Berlin Wall' (de Nevers 1990: 43–4).

Bulgaria differs from the other three states within the 'gang of four' in the sense that here reforms started within the party, even though they started late. During Zhivkov's rule 'Habitual allegiance to the Soviet policy line, and the country's chronic economic shortfalls, led Zhivkov to fall more in step with Gorbachev's policies. The need for change was publicly accepted in January 1987, and in July 1987 a series of reforms was announced. . . . Whether Zhivkov ever actually intended to implement them was, however, unclear' (de Nevers 1990: 49). Just as in many other countries the development of new media techniques came to influence the development in Bulgaria.

> One of the most important developments in Bulgarian politics in early 1987 was Sofia's agreement to boost Soviet television signals so that 90 per cent of Bulgarians were able to view the programmes. The impact on public opinion was considerable. From that time on Bulgarians realized that the changes going on in the Soviet Union were fundamental. Six months later, in January 1988, Bulgaria's first structured dissident organization, the Independent Society for Human Rights, came into being.
>
> (Glenny 1990: 170–1)

In November 1989 Mladenov took over from Todor Zhivkov. 'Mladenov decided to act by mobilizing anti-Zhivkov sentiment in the party. He was very careful to include the Soviet leadership in his plans. On his return from a visit to China in November 1989 he stopped off in Moscow for a final briefing on the forthcoming dénouement of the Bulgarian leadership crisis. He appears to have been given the final go-ahead, and Zhivkov's fate was sealed' (Glenny 1990: 172; see also de Nevers 1990: 51). The development in Bulgaria has been described as 'essentially a Soviet-inspired "palace revolution"' (Gati 1990: 182).

The Czechoslovakian situation was similar to the German one in the sense that the distance between the party and the people was considerable. 'The Czechoslovak leadership, however, which took its legitimacy from the Brezhnevite occupation, became increasingly isolated and derided, not least for its attempts to talk about *Prestavba* – our *Perestroika*. It answered in the only way it knew – with increased repression' (Urban 1990: 113). Because of the extensive purges from the party in the wake of 1968, there were not many reform-minded communists left to whom Gorbachev could turn for support. Instead, it was the opposition, concentrated around Charter 77, who looked to Moscow for new signals. Despite the virtual non-existence of reform communists in Czechoslovakia, Gorbachev tried to support their standpoints, by referring to the Prague Spring in more friendly words. In a speech in Prague on 10 April 1987, he said:

No one has the right to claim a special position in the socialist world. The independence of each Party, its responsibility to its own people, the right to resolve questions of the country's development in a sovereign way –for us, these are indisputable principles. At the same time, we are profoundly convinced that the successes of the socialist commonwealth are impossible without concern on the part of each Party and country not only for its own interests but for the general interests, without a respectful attitude towards friends and allies and the mandatory consideration of their interests.

(Quoted in Cynkin 1988: 311)

'Gorbachev also emphasized the importance of change, saying that "minor repairs will not be enough. Overhauling is in order"' (de Nevers 1990: 45). On the same visit, Gennadi Gerasimov, spokesman for the Soviet Ministry of Foreign Affairs, explained the difference between the Prague Spring and *perestroika* and *glasnost*, in just two words: 'Nineteen years'. But Gorbachev himself shied away from openly criticizing Brezhnev's protégés in Prague. At that time, he was guided by the belief that extending his process of renewal to Czechoslovakia might destabilize that country (Gati 1990: 178).

In the summer and early autumn of 1989 a number of articles in *Izvestia* and broadcasts on Soviet television showed that the Soviet leadership was preparing a reassessment of the Prague Spring (Gati 1990: 178). 'By the end of September, it was clear both to leaders of the opposition and to party officials as well that the country's old guard did not have Moscow's support' (Gati 1990: 180). Later on in October the Soviet Union helped the revolution along by a nicely timed retrospective condemnation of the 1968 Warsaw Pact invasion (Ash 1990: 141). Misha Glenny comments on the events in Czechoslovakia in the following words:

By the time Czech security forces lit the spark of revolution on 17 November 1989 by brutally dispersing a huge demonstration on National Street in Prague, the fate of Czechoslovakia had already been determined by two events. The first was the fall of Honecker in East Germany, the greatest ally of the Czechoslovak communist leadership. The second was the decision made by the leadership of the Soviet Communist Party to denounce as a grave political error the invasion of Czechoslovakia in 1968.

(Glenny 1990: 22–3)

In November demonstrations started in Czechoslovakia. The Soviet Union may have been involved in the most important one on 17

November. A report of the new government commission investigating the activities of the StB

> suggests that the course of events on 17th November was carefully planned and orchestrated jointly by General Lorenz, Head of StB, in collaboration with the KGB. . . . The primary purpose was to cause the overthrow of the Jakes and Husak regimes as a result of popular fury and to open the way for the installation of a moderate reformist communist, Zdenek Mlynar, as president in place of Husak. If this was the intention, it certainly bears a marked similarity to the substitution of Krenz for Honecker in the GDR.
>
> (Urban 1990: 117)

Even if the KGB was not involved in this plot, even if it was not a plot, Gorbachev still may have played a role by his 'public adaptation of the most famous catchwords of the Prague Spring, "socialism with a human face", a week after demonstrations spread across Czechoslovakia' (de Nevers 1990: 48).

Jonathan Eyal tries to explain why Romania was a deviant case, in the sense that the power-shift there involved much more violence than in the other countries.

> Romania was only important as long as Europe remained a chessboard between East and West. . . . Mikhail Gorbachev's policies changed the situation in three different ways. The Soviet Union's interest in disarmament and a relaxation of tensions automatically reduced Romania's importance for the West. Secondly, the Soviet leader's tolerance of diversity in Eastern Europe transformed Ceausescu's objections to Soviet hegemony from an act of defiance into a historical irrelevance. . . . Finally, the political and economic reforms which the Soviet Union instituted threatened the control of Communist parties throughout the region.
>
> (Eyal 1990: 153–4)

Ceausescu made his opinion of Gorbachev's domestic reforms known shortly after the 27th CPSU Congress in 1986. While he praised the Soviet Union's foreign policy line, pointedly reiterating Gorbachev's statements regarding relations between independent states, Ceausescu declared that Romania itself had no need for internal reforms. More visible signs of Romania's rejection of the new Soviet model appeared during Gorbachev's visit to Romania in May 1987. In contrast to his cautious tone in the GDR a year earlier, Gorbachev bluntly championed reform, and insisted that the Romanian model had grave problems. This criticism was met with

silence from his hosts, who responded with praise for the Romanian
model of socialism.

(de Nevers 1990: 52)

In 1989 Ceausescu talked about reforms as 'capitulation to capitalism'
(Gati 1990: 99–100). Because of the relative autonomy of Ceausescu
before 1989 it seems as if Moscow had more limited possibilities of
causing change in Romania than in the other reform-opposing countries
(de Nevers 1990: 55). 'It was . . . unclear . . . whether the Soviet Union
had communicated with and had encouraged these officials who so
promptly formed a provisional government under the auspices of the
newly established Council of National Salvation. One tentative answer
was that in 1989 Romania had simultaneously experienced both a
popular revolution, there for all to see, and a "palace revolution" that
had taken place behind closed doors' (Gati 1990: 185).

CONCLUSIONS

I have argued in this chapter that a closer look at external factors is
fruitful for a more complete understanding of the recent and current
development in Eastern and Central Europe. The democratization
processes in the countries in this region differ in many respects from
other earlier cases of democratization. The picture is difficult to grasp,
but I tend to believe that most of these differences suggest that external
actors have played, and can play, a more prominent role in this
development than earlier research suggested. Therefore, it would be
interesting to follow the development in Eastern Europe, and look at it
from within this theoretical framework.

A second conclusion is that the so-called Gorbachev effect is
composed of a number of different linkages between changes in the
Soviet Union and the development in Eastern Europe. There were
fundamental structural causes within Soviet society, in the world
surrounding the Soviet Union, and in the relations between the Soviet
Union and the external world that made reform necessary. Therefore,
the importance of Mikhail Gorbachev himself should not be exagger-
ated. The reforms carried out in the domestic political and economic
system of the USSR inspired reform-minded communists or, in some
cases, leftist opposition groups. But the reforms within the Soviet
Union also affected the politics of Eastern Europe in another way by
changing the image of the Soviet Union as a state and by causing a
modification of the expected behaviour of the USSR. Even more
important than the domestic reforms were the changes in Soviet foreign

policy. In various speeches during 1987 and 1988 Gorbachev stressed the independence of all communist parties and their sovereignty. In 1988, he also changed the structure and personnel of the administration dealing with Eastern Europe. In this context, the new interpretation of national security, possibly due to the tragic experience of the war in Afghanistan, should also be mentioned.

If we look at the actions of the Soviet Union in relation to Eastern Europe, a distinction can be made between active support and passive tolerance. Most authors seem to agree that what the Soviet Union did not do or say was probably more important than what it did do or say. But regardless of the actions of the Soviet Union or Mikhail Gorbachev, there was an internal dynamic in all of the six Eastern and Central European states which led to a situation ripe for radical change. In a way, the changes in the Soviet Union made the explosion come earlier, but an explosion would have come even without Gorbachev. In order to grasp the whole picture, we must therefore study the dynamics between internal and external factors.

To answer briefly the question whether Gorbachev was sufficient, necessary or neither sufficient nor necessary for the changes that have taken place in Eastern Europe, the changes in the Soviet Union are not considered either as necessary or as sufficient conditions for what happened in Eastern Europe. Without the pressure within the East European states themselves due to a lack of legitimacy for the existing authoritarian regimes, basing their power on support from Moscow, changes would not have followed automatically from changes in the Soviet Union, and, vice versa, that pressure itself would eventually have toppled the old regimes.

Thirdly, as events of 1991 have shown, the linkages between the Soviet Union and Eastern and Central Europe were not one-way linkages. What happened in Eastern Europe affected reality in the Soviet Union itself. Indeed, we can say that the dissolution of the Soviet Union was partly a consequence of the democratization of Eastern Europe. What happened in Eastern Europe directly encouraged the Baltic States and other peoples of the former Soviet Union in their struggle for political democracy, economic reform and national rights. We can only hope that these linkages will change rather than be completely broken. It is important for all of Europe that the contacts between Eastern and Central Europe and what comes after the Soviet Union are kept open.

Finally, as already emphasized, the situation in the various countries varied to such an extent that we must treat each of them as a separate case. Due to the revolutions of 1989 the approach of this Chapter, of

218   *The external dimension*

studying 'Eastern Europe' as a bloc, has become rather obsolete. And after the dissolution of the Soviet Union and Gorbachev's resignation as president in 1991, it has now become impossible to study their respective impact on the development in Eastern Europe.

NOTES

1 For a discussion on the border between the national system and the environment, or, in other words, between 'internal' and 'external', see Deutsch 1966.
2 Robert M. Fishman (1990) looks on the transition processes in Southern Europe and tries to account for the differences by examining whether the sources of contradiction leading to the democratization lay within the state or within the regime itself.
3 That the world has become more interdependent is true, also when discussing the former 'Soviet bloc' (see Polack 1986).
4 See e.g. Huntington 1984: 205: 'External influences may be of decisive importance in influencing whether a society moves in a democratic or nondemocratic direction.'
5 Gati 1989: 103, quoting a paper by the Institute of Economics of the World Socialist System of the Soviet Academy of Sciences, later published in *Problems of Communism*, May–August 1988: 60–7. See also Gati 1990: 161–5.

BIBLIOGRAPHY

Ash, T. G. (1990) *We the People – the Revolution of 89 witnessed in Warsaw, Budapest, Berlin and Prague*, Cambridge: Granta Books.
Bialer, S. (1990) 'The passing of the Soviet order?', *Survival* 32: 107–20.
Bunce, V. (1989) 'Eastern Europe – Is the party over?' *PS: Political Science and Politics* 22: 233–41.
Cynkin, T. M. (1988) 'Glasnost, perestroika and Eastern Europe', *Survey*, July/August.
Dawisha, K. (1990) *Eastern Europe, Gorbachev and Reform – The Great Challenge* (2nd edn), Cambridge: Cambridge University Press.
Deutsch, K. W. (1966) 'External influences on the internal behavior of states', in R. Barry Farrell (ed.) *Approaches to Comparative and International Politics*, Evanston Ill.: Northwestern University Press.
Diamond, L. (1989) 'Introduction: persistence, erosion, breakdown, and renewal', in L. Diamond, J. J. Linz and S. M. Lipset (eds) *Democracy in Developing Countries. Asia*, Boulder, Colo.: Lynne Rienner Publishers.
Eyal, J. (1990) 'Why Romania could not avoid bloodshed', in G. Prins (ed.) *Spring in Winter*, Manchester: Manchester University Press.
Fishman, R. M. (1990) 'Rethinking state and regime: Southern Europe's transition to democracy', *World Politics* 42: 422–40.
Fülöp, M., and Póti, L. (1990) *An East European Party Census*, Hungarian Institute of International Affairs, Policy Paper Series No. 2, Budapest.
Gati, C. (1989) 'Eastern Europe on its own', *Foreign Affairs* 68: 99–119.

Tomas Niklasson 219

—— (1990) *The Bloc that Failed – Soviet–East European Relations in Transition*, London: I.B. Tauris.

Glenny, M. (1990) *The Rebirth of History – Eastern Europe in the Age of Democracy*, London: Penguin.

Hankiss, E. (1990) 'What the Hungarians saw first', in G. Prins (ed.) *Spring in Winter*, Manchester: Manchester University Press.

Holloway, D. (1989) 'Gorbachev's new thinking', *Foreign Affairs* 68: 66–81.

Howard, M. (1990) 'The remaking of Europe', *Survival* 32: 99–100.

Huntington, S. P. (1984) 'Will more countries become democratic?', *Political Science Quarterly* 99: 193–218.

Jahn, E. (1988) 'Europa, Osteuropa og Mellemeuropa', in Jens-Jyrgen Jensen (ed.) *Europa i opbrud*, Esbjerg: Sydjysk Universitetsforlag.

—— (1990) 'Wo befindet sich Osteuropa?' *Osteuropa* 4: 5/Mai.

Karaganov, S. A. (1990) 'The year of Europe: a Soviet view', *Survival* 32: 121–8.

Karvonen, L. (1981a) 'Semi-domestic politics: policy diffusion from Sweden to Finland', *Cooperation and Conflict* 16: 91–107.

—— (1981b) *Med vårt västra grannland som förebild*, Åbo: The Research Institute of the Åbo Akademi Foundation.

Legvold, R. (1989) 'The revolution in Soviet foreign policy', *Foreign Affairs* 68: 82–98.

de Nevers, R. (1990) 'The Soviet Union and Eastern Europe: the end of an era', *Adelphi Papers*, 249, March.

Oldenburg, F. *et al.* (1990) 'Soviet policy toward Eastern Europe', in The Federal Institute for Soviet and International Studies, Cologne (ed.) *The Soviet Union 1987–1989 – Perestroika in Crisis?*, London: Longman.

Piontkowsky, A. A. (1990) 'The Russian sphinx: hope and despair', in G. Prins (ed.) *Spring in Winter*, Manchester: Manchester University Press.

Polack, J. (1986) *Dependence Patterns in the Soviet Bloc – the Case of Romania and East Germany*, Lund: Studentlitteratur.

Prins, G. (1990) 'Introduction', in G. Prins (ed.) *Spring in Winter*, Manchester: Manchester University Press.

Reich, J. (1990) 'Reflections on becoming an East German dissident', in G. Prins (ed.) *Spring in Winter*, Manchester: Manchester University Press.

Remmer, K. L. (1985) 'Redemocratization and the impact of authoritarian rule in Latin America', *Comparative Politics* 17: 253–75.

Schöpflin, G. (1990) 'The end of communism in Eastern Europe', *International Affairs* 66: 3–16.

—— and Wood, N. (eds) (1989) *In Search of Central Europe*, Cambridge: Polity Press.

Skak, M. (1990) 'The changing Soviet–East European relationship', Paper for the IV World Congress for Soviet and East European Studies, Harrogate, 21–6 July.

Urban, J. (1990) 'Czechoslovakia: the power and politics of humiliation', in G. Prins (ed.) *Spring in Winter*, Manchester: Manchester University Press.

Whitehead, L. (1986) 'International aspects of democratization', in G. O'Donnell, P. C. Schmitter and L. Whitehead (eds) *Transitions from Authoritarian Rule – Comparative Perspectives*, Part III, Baltimore: The Johns Hopkins University Press.

Ziolkowski, J. (1990) 'The roots, branches and blossoms of Solidarnosc', in G. Prins (ed.) *Spring in Winter*, Manchester: Manchester University Press.

8 Democratization in Eastern Europe

The external dimension

Adrian G. V. Hyde-Price

> It was the best of times, it was the worst of times, it was the age of wisdom, it was the age of foolishness, it was the epoch of belief, it was the epoch of incredulity, it was the season of light, it was the season of darkness, it was the spring of hope, it was the winter of despair . . .
>
> (Charles Dickens, *A Tale of Two Cities*)

Charles Dickens's opening words from his epic novel aptly sums up the contradictory and ambiguous mood prevalent today in much of Eastern Europe. On the one hand, the collapse of communist rule created a 'spring of hope', which promised to the peoples of this much-abused region a new era of democracy, prosperity and national independence. On the other, it has led to growing worries about the future, as the pains of market-oriented economic reform and resurgent nationalism have generated fears about the emergence of various forms of authoritarian nationalism in at least some of these post-communist countries. Without doubt, the mood of optimism and hope which characterized the heady days of the autumn of 1989 have been replaced by a more sober realization of the difficulties involved in making the transition to political democracy and a social market economy. As Dominique Moisi (1991: 7) has noted, 'The euphoria of 1989, with its rejoicing over European unity, seems light-years away. Today in the West, Euro-pessimism is back in fashion where Eastern Europe is concerned.'

Since the heady days of late 1989, the prospects for a relatively rapid and painless transition to democracy in Eastern Europe have appeared bleaker, given two major developments in the wider international environment. Firstly, the Gulf War: this had a serious economic impact upon a number of the countries in the region, given the rise in oil prices and the costs arising from the imposition of economic sanctions against Iraq. Hungary was the first country in the region to face the political consequences of this, when, in October 1990, taxi and lorry drivers staged a crippling strike to protest at the increased price of petrol (see Reich 1990). Moreover, the Gulf crisis has meant that the eyes of foreign policy-makers in the West were diverted from Eastern Europe to the pressing problems of the Gulf and the wider Middle East. The East Europeans have since had to compete for investment and aid with the countries of this troubled region.

Secondly, the disintegration of the Soviet Union. Escalating political turbulence in the former USSR was a major source of worry to the East European states, caught as they were in the shadow of the one-time superpower to their east. Trade between the East Europeans and the former Soviet Union has largely collapsed, and there is considerable unease at the prospect of a wave of emigrants flooding westwards from Russia, the Ukraine and the former USSR's other successor states. The emergence of an independent Ukraine, with weak democratic structures and a planned army of possibly 400,000 or more, adds to the uncertainty facing the East Europeans. For these reasons, many East Europeans are concerned about the chill winds that have been blowing from the east over recent years.

These two sets of developments – in the Gulf and the former Soviet Union – highlight the vulnerability of the fragile democratic structures in Eastern Europe to events in the broader international system which are largely beyond their control. The purpose of this chapter is to consider how, and to what extent, the process of democratization in Eastern Europe can be supported and encouraged by external factors. In the opening section, I will briefly summarize the prerequisites for democratization; the main threats to the democratization process; and the way in which the external environment and foreign actors can influence the course of political and economic reform in the region. In the main section, I will examine more closely the policies of three key international organizations – namely, the European Community (EC), the Conference on Security and Cooperation in Europe (CSCE), and the Council of Europe – towards the region, in order to assess their impact on the transition to democracy in Eastern Europe. These three multilateral organizations will undoubtedly play a significant external role in strengthening and encouraging the process of political democratization in the former communist states of Eastern Europe, although in very different ways.

DEMOCRACY: ITS NATURE AND PREREQUISITES

Before attempting to assess the impact of external factors on the process of democratization in Eastern Europe, the term 'democratization' itself needs to be more precisely defined. We also need to identify the main problems facing the East Europeans as they embark on the difficult task of effecting their transition to democracy.

Defining 'democracy' is notoriously difficult, because it is both a normative and an analytical concept. The word 'democracy' comes from the Greek words *demos*, 'the people', and *kratos*, meaning 'power'. Literally, therefore, it means 'people power' – or in the famous words of Abraham Lincoln, 'government of the people, by the people, and for the people'. A definition such as this, which is so sweeping in scope, does not provide a useful analytical tool for assessing the process of democratization in Eastern Europe. In his recent study, however, Vanhanen has provided a working definition of the term as follows:

> a political system in which ideologically and socially different groups are legally entitled to compete for political power and in which institutional power holders are elected by the people and are responsible to the people.
>
> (Vanhanen 1990)

On the basis of this definition of democracy, Vanhanen in his study uses public contestation and the right to participate as the two key variables in assessing progress towards democratic government. Taking Vanhanen's definition as a conceptual reference point, we can see that democracy depends on both formal, constitutional structures, and a broader structure of pluralist power relations in society. In formal terms, a democratic system of government consists of institutionalized mechanisms for interest articulation and integration, based on broadly agreed constitutional and political structures. These structures must include limited government founded on the rule of law; free, secret and competitive elections; a system of checks and balances between different branches of government; and guaranteed civil and human rights.

A flourishing democracy, however, must be grounded on much more than formal constitutional and political structures. Such structures can only provide a mechanism for democratic government if they are based on a pluralist distribution of economic and social power in society, and on a democratic political culture – in short, on a healthy and well-developed 'civil society'.[1] East European democrats have attached considerable importance to the notion of 'civil society', by which they understand the existence of a network of formal and informal groups, representing different social, political, professional and economic groups, and organized autonomously from the state (for a discussion of the meaning of 'civil society', see Keane 1988a, and especially

Z. A. Pelczynski's essay in Keane 1988b). Such a civil society can only flourish with the support of a free press, high levels of political participation and a lively public discussion of political issues. At the same time, a consensus has developed throughout Europe that planned economies based on wide-scale state ownership are inimitable to the development of viable democracies. Only when the rights to private property and private enterprise are guaranteed, it is suggested, can a degree of economic independence of citizens from the state be achieved. However, the transition to market economies is likely to lead to the emergence of extreme inequalities of wealth and income, and this is not necessarily conducive to the development of a stable democracy.[2] There is, therefore, a certain tension between the goals of political democratization and market-oriented economic reform.

THREATS TO THE DEMOCRATIZATION PROCESS IN EASTERN EUROPE

The creation of stable and durable systems of democratic government in Eastern Europe will not be an easy task. There is no easy way to transform authoritarian political systems based on centrally planned economies into liberal and pluralist societies. Transforming values and ways of thinking is perhaps the most difficult task of all, and some suggest that this will take a generation or more in Eastern and Central Europe.[3] But in the short to medium term, there are number of specific problems faced by the reforming governments of post-communist Eastern Europe.

Firstly, economic dislocation. The transition to the market cannot but be painful in Eastern Europe. It will mean growing unemployment, widening social and economic inequalities, falling living standards and a deepening mood of insecurity.[4] This will in turn generate social unrest and simmering political unrest, which could erupt at any moment. Recent developments in Poland, Hungary, Romania and Bulgaria provide sobering evidence of such political volatility. The problem for the governments of Eastern Europe is that they do not yet possess the formal institutional and political mechanisms for channelling, absorbing and responding to these popular upsurges. Given the weakness of their political structures, there is a very real danger of the emergence of what Samuel Huntington has called 'praetorian politics' in the region. In a praetorian system, he argues,

> social forces confront each other nakedly; no political institutions, no corps of professional political leaders are recognised or accepted

as the legitimate intermediaries to moderate group conflict. Equally important, no agreement exists among the groups as to the legitimate and authoritative methods for resolving conflict. . . . Each group employs means which reflect its peculiar nature and capabilities. The wealthy bribe; students riot; mobs demonstrate; and the military coup.

(Huntington 1968: 196)

Secondly, national and ethnic tensions. The collapse of the illusion of 'proletarian internationalism' in Eastern Europe has been accompanied by a rising tide of nationalism and ethnic-based conflicts. Signs of growing nationalist, religious and political intolerance have become increasingly evident over the past few years, including new manifestations of that old poison, anti-semitism (see Deak 1990). At a conference of East-Central Europeans in Bratislava in April 1990, Adam Michnik and Gyorgy Konrad both warned that national bigotry and intercommunal violence represented the biggest threat to the peaceful and democratic evolution of these countries. Indeed, Michnik has argued that the central political cleavage in Eastern Europe is not between left and right but between those – primarily urban-based, secular, liberal-progressive groups – who speak of a 'European potential' and who favour an outward-looking and liberal approach, and proponents of an inward-looking and parochial obscurantism who emphasize the need for a revival of pre-communist, national traditions and cultures (often linked to the more conservative trends in Catholicism) (Michnik 1990: 7). The latter may well lead to xenophobism and chauvinism, and has already been painfully evident from the increase in anti-gypsy and anti-semitic prejudice in Poland and Hungary. It certainly does not bode well for the process of democratization in these countries.

Thirdly, the combination of economic dislocation, fragile political institutions and rising nationalism could lead to the emergence of forms of 'authoritarian populism' in the region. Given the weakness of indigenous traditions of political compromise, cooperation and consensus in many of these countries, there is a very real risk that the pre-war patterns of nationalist authoritarianism could reassert themselves.

Finally, there is the fear of inter-state conflict in Eastern Europe and the Balkans. The collapse of the 'Pax Sovietica' in Eastern Europe has produced what is frequently described as a 'security vacuum' in the region. Fanned by the flames of economic dislocation, political turbulence and rising nationalism, some fear that the disputed borders and national minorities in the region could provide the spark for inter-state conflict. In the light of the experience of Greco-Turkish relations over recent decades, this does not seem as fanciful as it once did. Such inter-state conflict – even if it did not lead to full-scale military hostilities – would poison the political atmosphere in Eastern Europe, which would create an unfavourable environment for democratic traditions of compromise and consensus-building to develop.[5]

THE IMPACT OF EXTERNAL FACTORS ON THE DEMOCRATIZATION PROCESS

Having considered the difficulties involved in the transition to democracy in Eastern Europe, it is now time to specify how external factors can facilitate this process of domestic political reform. The extent to which domestic politics are affected by the external environment (and conversely, the degree to which a state's foreign policy is determined by domestic political concerns) is one of the most contentious and vigorously disputed issues in international relations theory. That there is a relationship between the two, few would deny. But specifying precisely how, and to what extent, international factors influence the course of domestic political developments is a much more difficult task.

In the case of Eastern Europe, there is substantial evidence to suggest that the domestic political forces in the region – especially in East-Central Europe – have been greatly influenced by their proximity to Western Europe. Western Europe has exerted a powerful and pervasive influence on Eastern Europe by virtue of its political, economic and cultural characteristics. Western Europe has presented an attractive political model characterized by limited government, the rule of law, competitive elections and traditions of political liberalism and tolerance. Economically, it is seen as a area of prosperity, dynamic technological innovation and consumerism, based on a social market economy. Its vibrant culture – from its avante-garde artists and writers, to its pop music and even its television soaps – has also been much admired. As Timothy Garton Ash has argued, if the revolutions of 1989 were inspired by anything, it was by the 'ideology' of liberal-democracy, and by the 'model' of Western Europe (Ash 1990; 1989: 3–10). This is apparent from the call by the post-communist elites of Eastern Europe for a 'return to Europe'. That this should be the strategic aim of the political leaderships of the region reflects the enduring attractiveness of Western Europe as a model for their newly liberated neighbours.

Western influence on political developments in Eastern Europe was enhanced by the revolution in information technology that occurred in the 1970s and 1980s. Television and radio in particular have had a profound impact on the popular consciousness of East Europeans over past decades. As Ernest Kux has pointed out,

By penetrating the Iron Curtain, whose main purpose was to block 'imperialistic propaganda', television played an important role in the revolution of 1989. When Eastern Europe could no longer be barred from Western television, the information monopoly of the party was broken and its propaganda unmasked as a lie. Moreover, Western television broadcasts of the demonstrations spread the uncensored slogans of the protests, had a mobilizing effect on other citizens, and in all probability inhibited the authorities from using force and so contributed to the peaceful course of events. The 1989 revolution was the first television revolution in history.

(Kux 1991: 8)

As the countries of Eastern Europe begin the process of political democratization and market-oriented economic reform, there are two ways in which Western countries and multilateral organizations can buttress and support these reforms. Firstly, they can offer political support and advice. This can take a number of forms: (1) Western agencies can offer advice on electoral systems, constitutional arrange-ments, and party organization;[6] (2) They can develop international links at the level of 'civil society', including, for example, political parties, churches, trade unions, peace and ecology movements and civil rights organizations; (3) The West can also help foster commonly agreed standards of human rights, democratic practices and free elections: in this respect, the CSCE and the Council of Europe are particularly important; and (4) By involving the East European political and other elites in the work of international organizations, the West can help provide them with the experience of multilateral negotiation and consultation. The processes of political bargaining, compromise and consensus-building that this involves will be relevant to the strengthen-ing of a domestic democratic political culture.

Secondly, they can provide economic aid and cooperation. This includes food aid, debt rescheduling and direct financial aid; technology transfers; joint ventures and foreign private investment; as well as trade agreements, lowering tariff barriers and providing 'most favoured nation' status. A thickening of the economic relationship between Western and Eastern Europe can help the process of democratization in two distinct but complementary ways: (1) By alleviating some of the strains of the transition to a market economy: Western economic aid and financial support can help mitigate the social costs of unemployment, regional inequalities, low wages and falling living standards; (2) On a more constructive note, targeted economic support and private invest-ment can help restructure socio-economic relationships in ways that are more conducive to the development of pluralist politics. This can include economic aid and advice which facilitates privatization; the development of the financial infrastructure of a market; the wider diffusion of private ownership; and the emergence of an entrepreneurial class.[7]

The East European desire for Western economic aid and support offers the West a powerful set of policy tools for shaping political developments in the region. Closer economic links between East and West can be made contingent on steady progress towards democratization and respect for human rights. In this way, Western economic aid and support can provide a positive inducement for democratic change in countries of post-communist Europe.[8]

It should also be noted that the international conditions for a successful transition to democracy in Eastern Europe are much more favourable in the 1990s than they were in the interwar years. In the 1920s and 1930s, the countries of the region faced an international economic system in severe recession; they had only recently experienced world war, revolution and the collapse of three great multinational empires; and they were surrounded by powerful and threatening totalitarian countries – Nazi Germany and Stalinist Russia. Moreover, fascism and communism were on the march throughout Europe, and the Western democracies were wracked by economic crisis and political uncertainty (Janos 1970; an excellent political history is Rothschild 1974; on Hungary see Janos 1982). Today the situation looks radically different: Western Europe presents an attractive and broadly successful model of liberal democracy and welfare capitalism; the Continent has been transformed by a deepening network of interdependencies; and the CSCE embodies a pan-European commitment to democracy and human rights.

Finally, the transition from right-wing authoritarianism in Southern Europe in the 1970s – Greece, Spain and Portugal – provides valuable lessons for the East Europeans in the 1990s. The Spanish experience is particularly attractive to the East-Central Europeans. Although there are many substantial differences between these Southern European countries and Eastern Europe today (not least in terms of their very different social and economic structures), it has been suggested that the democratization process in Southern Europe was considerably encouraged and supported by a favourable external climate – to which the European Community as well as the Council of Europe greatly contributed.

DEMOCRATIZATION: THE ROLE OF EXTERNAL ACTORS

Having considered some of the difficulties involved in the democratization process in Eastern Europe, let us now go on to assess the influence of the key external actors on the political reform process in the region. There are a whole variety of international actors who currently play a role in political and economic developments in Eastern Europe. These include multilateral economic organizations, such as the OECD, the IMF, the World Bank, GATT, COCOM and the Paris Club; countless non-governmental organizations; and non-European countries such as the USA,[9] Japan, China and some of the 'four little Dragons' (notably South Korea). However, in this section, I want to concentrate on three main organizations: the European Community, the CSCE and the Council of Europe. These three bodies are the three most closely involved in the political and economic reform process in Eastern Europe, and are therefore most likely to be able to affect the democratization process in the region. Let us look at all three in turn, beginning with the EC.

The European Community: from 'cooperation' to 'association' and beyond

The EC has emerged as the central body of post-Cold War Europe. It not only operates as a forum for institutionalized cooperation and supranational integration between its twelve members, it is also becoming the focus for the wider integration process in Europe. Moreover, as new security problems such as ethno-national conflict and migration occur, the EC is emerging as a crucial pillar of the post-Cold War security system in the Continent (see Hyde-Price 1991). Above all, as the Irish Foreign Minister Gerry Collins has said, 'The European Community is a depository of the norms on which the countries of Central and Eastern Europe can draw in their efforts to transform themselves' (quoted in Sobell 1990: 48). It is for these reasons amongst others that the East Europeans – especially Poland, Hungary and Czechoslovakia – have set their sights on becoming full members of the Community, if possible by the end of the century.

Relations between the Community and East European states are, however, a relatively recent development. In 1974, the Community offered to conclude bilateral agreements with East European countries, but – given Soviet hostility toward the EEC at this time – only Romania accepted.[10] It was only on 25 June 1988 that a Joint Declaration was signed in Luxemburg establishing official relations between the EEC and the CMEA. This paved the way for the establishment of diplomatic relations between the Community and individual Central and East European countries. This in turn led to the signing of a series of commercial and economic cooperation agreements. The Hungarians led the way here, signing a 10-year trade and commercial and economic cooperation agreement with the EC on 26 September 1988. This was followed by a 4-year agreement (limited to trade in industrial products) between the EC and Czechoslovakia, signed on 19 December 1988; a 5-year Trade and Cooperation Agreement between Poland and the EC, signed on 19 September 1989; and a 10-year Trade and Economic and Commerical agreement (including EURATOM) between the EC and the USSR, signed on 18 December 1989 (for details, see *EC–Eastern European Relations 1990*).

A qualitative change in the nature of EC relations with the East European countries occurred in July 1989. At the Paris Summit of the Arch in July 1989, the Heads of State and Government of the Group of Seven (G7) and the Commission reached two key decisions. Firstly, that any East European country embarking on the path of democratic and market-oriented reform would receive Western aid; and secondly, that this aid would be coordinated by the European Commission.

The G7 and the Commission were joined by other leading developed countries in the OECD Group of 24, who agreed to contribute to a substantial aid programme for reforming East European countries – which in mid-1989 meant Poland and Hungary. Thus was born the PHARE ('Poland/Hungary: Aid for Restructuring of Economies') operation, which the Commission has been coordinating. Western aid to Eastern Europe needed to be coordinated because of the large number of governments and agencies involved.[11] There were a number of potential candidates for this crucial task of coordinating Western aid, including the OECD Secretariat, the World Bank and the European Bank for Reconstruction and Development (EBRD), but it was the Commission which was seen as the most suitable body. The reasons for this are threefold: the EC was already by far the Soviet bloc's largest trading partner; the Community was geographically close to the region, and already exercised a considerable influence on developments there; and because the Community was both neutral in security terms (unlike NATO, for example), and not regarded as an American-dominated organization (as were, for example, the IMF or World Bank). This last point was particularly important in terms of the political sensibilities of the Soviet leadership, given that the West was now playing a growing economic and political role in what had until recently been part of the 'Soviet bloc'.

As a result of the historic decisions reached at the July 1989 Paris Summit, therefore, the European Community became the leading Western organization involved in the unfolding reform process in Eastern Europe. With the revolutionary upheavals of November and

230 The external dimension

December 1989, the Community found itself facing a rapidly changing East–West relationship in Europe, which would profoundly affect the whole course and direction of the integration process in Europe. When the European Council met in Strasbourg in December 1989, it was clear that the Community would now have to respond to the rising expectations and new demands from the post-communist regimes to its east.[12] As the countries of Eastern Europe embarked on the road of political democratization and market-oriented economic reform, they were looking to the Community for economic and political support. Indeed, for nearly all of them, the Community became a central focus of their post-communist foreign policies, with the goal of achieving full membership high on the agenda of the East-Central Europeans. In this situation, the Council concluded its Strasbourg meeting by stating that the EC would 'continue its review of appropriate forms of association with those countries which are on the road to economic and political reform' (Andriessen 1990: 5).

Following the Strasbourg summit, the debate on EC–East European relations now switched to the issue of negotiating 'Association Agreements' (now to be called 'European Agreements') with individual East European countries, which would replace the more limited series of trade and economic cooperation agreements mentioned above. These would be based on Article 238 of the Treaty of Rome, and would include institutionalized political dialogue and regular consultations as well as more substantial forms of economic, industrial and commerical cooperation. Their main objective was to be the comprehensive liberalization of trade, which was to be followed later by measures facilitating the free movement of people, services and capital. However, these would not automatically lead to full Community membership.

One significant feature of the Community's evolving relationship with the countries of Eastern Europe was that it was made explicit from early on that the granting of associate status to East European countries would be conditional not only on market-oriented economic reform but also on progress towards political democratization. At the EC Foreign Ministers, meeting in February 1990, for example, five principles were agreed as preconditions for the signing of 'Association Agreements'. These were the establishment of the rule of law; respect for human rights; the introduction of multi-party democracy; the holding of free and fair competitive elections; and the development of market-oriented economies. In March 1990, the Commission sent fact-finding missions to several of the East European countries in order to examine progress in these five areas.

As a result of the Commission's reports, the G-24 ministerial meeting formally decided to extend its coordinated assistance programme to Bulgaria, Czechoslovakia, the GDR and Yugoslavia. Subsequently, on 17 September 1990, the EC Council also decided to extend the PHARE programme to the other East European countries (including the GDR until German unification on 3 October 1990), with the notable exception of Romania. This again highlights the political criteria which have governed the Community's dealings with the East Europeans. Following the overthrow of Ceausescu's form of 'socialism in one family', diplomatic relations with the EC were re-established at the end of March 1990. The Council authorized the Commission on 7 May 1990 to negotiate a trade and cooperation agreement between Romania and the EC (including EURATOM), and one was initialled on 8 June. However, because of the deteriorating human rights situation in the country, it was not formally signed. Romania was also excluded from the PHARE scheme because of these human rights abuses.[13] This was only changed in January 1991 when the EC decided that the human rights situation in Romania had substantially improved, and that the country could now be added to the list of beneficiaries of the PHARE scheme.

In July 1992 the EC Commission, following an initiative taken by the European Parliament, launched a pilot project called the PHARE Democracy Programme. With an initial budget of ECU 5m, it provided support for 52 projects (out of a total of 350 submitted). They were divided into six broad categories: parliamentary practice, promoting and monitoring human rights, independent media, development of NGOs and representative structures, local democracy and participation, and education and analysis. The countries involved included the four Visegrad states, the three Baltic republics, Bulgaria, Romania, Albania and Slovenia. All projects were to involve a partnership between East and West European non-profit-making organizations (two or more in different EC member states) or a transnational body based in the EC, and at least one partner in one or more Central and East European countries. Projects were also expected to be non-partisan, cross-party initiatives. Following the success of the initial success of the PHARE Democracy Programme, its budget was increased to ECU 10m in 1993 (details in Strasbourg Conference on Parliamentary Democracy 1993: 4).

Thus in a remarkably brief period of time, the historic changes in Eastern Europe have led to a major redefinition of Community relations with the countries of the former Soviet bloc. As the East Europeans seek to effect their 'return to Europe', they are looking above all to the European Community to provide both economic and political support.

Given its magnetic attraction as a focus of European integration, the Community can exercise a considerable influence on the democratization process in the East – above all, by providing a positive economic incentive for a strengthening of the rule of law and respect for human rights.[14] At the same time, the EC's changing relationship with the East European countries has intensified the debate on the integration process within the Community itself – and beyond that, on the future institutional structure of a Europe 'whole and free'. The prospect of a 'widening' of the EC to include new members from both the former CMEA and EFTA (and perhaps Turkey too, and the other 'Mediterranean orphans') has given a further twist to the debate on 'deepening' the Community's integration (see for example Featherstone and Hiden 1991). The Maastrict summit of Community Heads of State in December 1991 – which agreed a comprehensive programme of steps towards an 'ever closer union'– marked a key moment in the history of the Community, but since then growing doubts have been expressed across Europe about the pace and scope of the integration process. Eastern Europe's relations with the European Community are therefore evolving at a time when the EC itself is in a process of remarkable change, and when the architectural contours of a Europe beyond the Cold War are still uncertain and ill-defined.

In the debate on 'widening' versus 'deepening', the two processes are frequently presented as opposites. Margaret Thatcher, for example, has advocated the widening of the Community in order to slow-down progress towards closer integration. On the other hand, 'Euro-federalists' such as Jacques Delors and President Mitterrand have emphasized the importance of a substantial 'deepening' of the EC's supranational integration, and have consequently tended to resist calls for an early accession of new members. In practice, however, a further 'deepening' of the Community's integration (in other words, more effective mechanisms for collective decision-making and policy-implementation, including a greater use of qualified majority voting) is an inevitable prerequisite for subsequent widening. Without such a deepening, a future Community of perhaps twenty or more members would face institutional paralysis. Deeper EC integration – including the development of a common foreign and security policy – would also make possible a coordinated EC Ostpolitik towards the emerging democracies in the East. This would correspond to the post-Cold War requirements of closer European integration, and would prevent a 'go-it-alone' policy by the German government in Eastern Europe, thus helping to reduce the dangers of a perceived German hegemony in the region (Pinder 1991: 108).

The much-trumpeted Association Agreements – also known more grandly as 'European Agreements' – were finally initialled with Czechoslovakia,[15] Hungary and Poland on 16 December 1991 (after months of often bad-tempered negotiations). Similar agreements were initialled with Romania in autumn 1992 and with Bulgaria in December 1992. Their aim was threefold: to improve the opportunities for access by the East-Central Europeans to EC markets; to prepare the associated countries for eventual Community membership; and to then create a preferential system of trade with developing countries. The Agreements also established a framework for regular political dialogue, consultation and joint decision-making between the EC and the associated countries. These agreements did not promise full membership, nor did they rule it out: rather, they left this crucial question open and shrouded in ambiguity. They also left in place substantial limits on the access of agricultural goods, steel and textiles to EC markets, after fierce protectionist pressures from a number of individual member states.[16] The agreements therefore disappointed the expectations of the Central Europeans for a rapid movement to free market access and early full membership. In particular, they provided only a partial opening up of EC markets in the areas of agricultural products, textiles and steel – all of which are crucial to the economic prospects of the East Europeans. Despite this, the agreements will have a significant impact on the economic sovereignty of the associated countries: Jacques Delors, for example, has estimated that, by 1995 as a result of these agreements, 50 per cent of economic decisions concerning Poland will be made in Brussels.

The Visegrad states have continued to pressurize the Community for an explicit list of conditions for membership, as well as a timetable for negotiations leading to union. On 11 September 1992 they presented a Memorandum to this effect to the Community. In response to such persistent requests, the European Council meeting in Edinburgh in December 1992 issued a document entitled *Towards a Closer Association with the Countries of Central and Eastern Europe*. Unfortunately, this failed to specify any such conditions for membership, nor did it clearly affirm the prospect of future membership. It was only at the Copenhagen summit on 19 June 1993 that the European Council issued a clear statement that the Visegrad four, along with Bulgaria and Romania, could become members once they met certain conditions. The EC also announced further limited trade concessions at Copenhagen. The conditions laid down by the Community for future membership were as follows: a willingness to accept membership obligations (the *acquis communautaire*); guarantees of stable democratic institutions;

234 The external dimension

observance of human rights and respect for minorities; a market economy; endorsement of the European Union; and the capacity to cope with competitive pressures within the union. As is apparent, these conditions are very general, and no timetable for negotiations and eventual membership has been specified. None the less, it does represent a broadly propitious response to the constant, concerted pressure on the Community by the countries of Central and Eastern Europe.

The East-Central Europeans quite rightly resented the Community's failure to substantially liberalize trade in the three sectors crucial to their economies. They argued that they had largely eliminated trade barriers against Western goods, but were not only being denied free access to the markets they could best compete in, but were also being asked to open their service and financial sectors to competition from stronger Western firms (Brada 1991: 31). The short- to medium-term economic benefits of the Association Agreements may therefore be disappointing from the East-Central European point of view. This is serious matter of concern to the governments of Poland, Czechoslovakia and Hungary: the macroeconomic policies of these three countries are designed to combat inflation by a combination of restrictive monetary policies and tight fiscal policies. Given the associated need to reduce the government deficit, any reduction of unemployment and improvement in economic growth cannot be achieved by domestic reflation, but only by the expansion of foreign trade. Hence export-led growth may be the only way to prevent long-term structural unemployment and continued domestic recession. If the economic situation in the region remains bleak, the prospects for a strengthening of democratic institutions and political practices in Eastern Europe will be greatly reduced. As the experience of Europe in the interwar years demonstrates, in conditions of deep-seated recession and acute social tensions, support for authoritarian and demagogic political leaders may well grow to alarming proportions.

The European Community therefore faces a real test of commitment: is it prepared to support the reform process in Eastern Europe with more than rhetoric and statements of good intention? If so, it must practice what it preaches – i.e., free trade and market liberalization – and open its markets to Eastern Europe. However, trade liberalization is not enough: there is also a need for substantial resource transfers if the reform process in the former communist East is to stand any chance of success. Financial assistance must consequently be greatly increased.[17] At the same time, EC aid should draw upon the experience of the Marshall Plan: Community assistance should be designed to encourage joint economic decision-making and cross-border cooperation in Eastern

Europe. For example, the Community could provide a hard-currency reserve for an East European Payments Union, which would facilitate intra-regional trade in the wake of the collapse of COMECON. Such forms of multilateral cooperation in Eastern Europe might contribute to resolution of common transnational problems (such as pollution, poor transport links and weak infrastructures). The experience of such practical cooperation could also help ameliorate the national tensions and rivalries which bedevil this region.

Whilst greater access to West European markets and political partnership with the European Community is of vital importance for the reform programmes of the new democracies, their central demand remains full membership of the EC, along with other Western institutions such as NATO, the WEU and the Council of Europe. They place considerable emphasis upon this because of the security concerns generated by the institutional vacuum which resulted from the dismantling of the Warsaw Pact and COMECON. As the Hungarian foreign minister, Geza Jeszensky, has argued,

> Full membership in institutions that provide political, economic and military security – organizations like the Council of Europe, the European Community and NATO – is essential for consolidating Central and Eastern Europe, although it cannot be brought about automatically.
>
> (*International Herald Tribune*, 22 October 1992)

Such institutional *Einbindung* is regarded as vital to the success of democratization in post-communist Europe. Many Central European academics and policy-analysts stress in particular the importance of acquiring full membership of the European Community. This, they believe, will provide an institutional guarantee against political recidivism, and will help accustom the new elites of Central and Eastern Europe in the political culture of compromise and consensus, which are so vital to the success of modern liberal democracies. This idea has been clearly articulated by the Hungarian political scientist, Attila Agh;

> it is above all out of political necessity that we need the EC association. . . . The political future of the country is still open and a positive political coercion is in any case necessary for us. . . . Europe is not merely means and goals, but a protection against proponents of parochialism, who are not weak but gaining strength day by day. . . . Evidently, the democratic consolidation can only be finished and economic consolidation take place inside the EC.[18]
>
> (Agh 1993)

Thus if the European Community is to fulfil its potential and to match up to the demands placed upon it by the dramatic events on its borders, it must overcome its own short-sighted sectional interests, and begin to develop the vision necessary for bold and innovative schemes in pan-European cooperation and integration.

The CSCE and political reform in Eastern Europe

Democratic government and human rights have a dual nature: legal and political. This duality is inescapable. Democratic government not based on the rule of law and a firm legal framework is inconceivable. But at the same time, democracy implies more than a set of legal principles. As we have already seen, it implies a tolerant political culture, a pluralist distribution of power and a well-developed civil society.

These two aspects of democracy and human rights – legal and political – have been addressed in different ways by two important multilateral European organizations, the Council of Europe and the Conference on Security and Cooperation in Europe (CSCE). The work of the Council of Europe relates primarily to legal questions, whereas the CSCE has played a major role in elaborating commonly agreed criteria for democratic government and human rights. Together, these two bodies play a complementary role in reinforcing the process of political democratization in Eastern Europe. Let us begin by considering the nature and function of the CSCE.

The CSCE stands out as one of the great unexpected success stories of modern European diplomacy. Since the signing of the Helsinki Final Act on 1 August 1975, the CSCE has developed into an ongoing 'process' of follow-up meetings and specialist forums which has provided a framework for deepening East–West cooperation and consultation. The Helsinki Final Act consisted of three main 'baskets', which covered security issues, economic cooperation and human rights. Basket III has been particularly important as a means of strengthening respect for human rights throughout the Continent. It created a political framework which allowed both for Western governments to raise human rights cases with communist regimes in the East and for East European dissidents to challenge arbitrary and authoritarian acts of their governments.

A significant step forward in this aspect of the CSCE's work was the Third Follow-Up Meeting which began in Vienna on 4 November 1986. The Vienna meeting took place at a time of extraordinary change in East–West relations, inspired primarily by the comprehensive reform programme of Mikhail Gorbachev. Given the democratic and emancipatory impulses implicit in *perestroika* and *glasnost*, it was possible for the CSCE to make great strides forward in the sensitive area of human rights – formally one of the most contentious issues in East–West relations. The Vienna Concluding Document – adopted by consensus on 19 January 1989 – removed many of the previous ambiguities regarding individual civil liberties, and agreed on a joint position which reflected the West's concern with protecting the rights of individual citizens against any infringement by the state.[19] It also established new procedures for the continuous monitoring of human rights in all CSCE participating states. This meant that the concern voiced by one state (or group of states) with alleged human rights violations in another CSCE state could no longer be dismissed as unwarranted interference in a country's internal affairs.[20]

With the disintegration of 'developed socialism' in Eastern Europe in late 1989, the political context in which the CSCE operated has drastically changed – for the better. Whereas the CSCE had previously been seen as a forum for developing further cooperation between the two blocs in Europe, it was subsequently to begin to map out the political principles and cultural values for a Europe 'whole and free'. A landmark here was the Conference on the Human Rights Dimension of the CSCE which met in Copenhagen from 5–29 June 1990. It enumerated a series of commonly agreed features of competitive elections and respect for individual and minority rights. These principles were formally incorporated into the historic Paris Charter, which was adopted at the CSCE Summit of the 34 Heads of State and Government held between 19–21 November 1990. In the context of this chapter, it is also interesting to note that the Copenhagen Conference acknowledged the 'important contribution of international instruments in the field of human rights to the rule of law at the national level'. They also agreed to consider acceding to the regional or global conventions concerning the protection of human rights, such as the European Convention on Human Rights or the first Optional Protocol to the International Covenant on Civil Political Rights, which provide for procedures of individual recourse to international bodies.[21]

There are good reasons for suggesting that the CSCE, which since the Paris summit has acquired a more permanent institutional structure, will emerge as a significant focus of pan-European cooperation. Firstly, because of the constructive part played by the CSCE in European politics in the 1970s and 1980s. Secondly, because of the enormous reserve of political legitimacy it has won for itself in Central and Eastern Europe, as well as in the USSR. The provisions of the Helsinki Final Act afforded considerable political sustenance to dissident groups like Charter 77 and Solidarity, many of whose activists are now in leadership positions in Eastern Europe. Thirdly, because the CSCE provides the institutional expression of the wider Europe, embracing as it does all major European states (even Albania, which finally joined the CSCE at the CSCE Council of Ministers meeting in Berlin, 19–20 June 1991), along with the United States and Canada.

The CSCE can help reinforce the process of democratization in Eastern Europe in a number of ways. To begin with, by codifying a common agreed set of democratic principles, it can provide a strong external stimulus for continued political reform in former communist states. This has already had a significant impact on political developments in Romania and Bulgaria. Albania's desire to join the CSCE also created a powerful external impetus for domestic political reform from late 1990 onwards. Moreover, as a result of the Paris Summit, the CSCE has acquired a number of new institutional structures, one of which is an Office of Free Elections (based in Warsaw). Furthermore, in early 1991 the CSCE discussed the possibility of establishing a mechanism for the peaceful resolution of conflicts. This was further discussed in Valletta in January 1991, and was seen as having a particular relevance to Eastern Europe, given the national and ethnic conflicts which have bedevilled the politics of Eastern and South-eastern Europe for centuries (see Buzan *et al*. 1990: 157–9). Later in the year, at the Berlin CSCE Council of Ministers meeting (19–20 June 1991), a decision was taken to establish an 'Emergency Mechanism' procedure. This laid down clear steps for the convening of emergency meetings of the CSCE Committee of Senior Officials in the event of a major crisis emerging. This Emergency Mechanism was subsequently used four times between June and December 1991 to discuss the deepening crisis in Yugoslavia.

Faced with an escalating number of increasingly severe ethno-national conflicts throughout the post-communist world, the CSCE in the course of 1992 sought to develop new mechanisms and institutional structures. By this stage, most European governments had arrived at more sober evaluations of the prospects facing the Continent after the end of the East-West divide. This was reflected in the work and documents of the CSCE. The hyperbole about democracy, peace and freedom was replaced by attempts to address the very real security problems facing contemporary Europe. For the CSCE, this meant a new emphasis on the importance of conflict prevention and crisis management. In January 1992, the Council of Foreign Ministers meeting in Prague adopted the 'consensus minus one' principle for most decisions. In July 1992, the CSCE Heads of State and Government agreed an important document, 'The Challenge of Change'. This defined the CSCE task as 'managing change', and resulted in a major restructuring of the CSCE's institutional structures and decision-making mechanisms (for details, see Ghebali 1992). Of particular importance from the perspective of strengthening the trend towards democratization was the creation of the office of High Commissioner of National Minorities. The former Dutch foreign minister, Max van der Stoel, was subsequently appointed to this post, and his role is to provide an early-warning service to the CSCE about areas of nationalist tension and discrimination. Finally, the CSCE in October 1992 in Geneva agreed two new procedures for the peaceful settlement of disputes, building on the existing Valletta mechanism: the first of these was 'directed conciliation'; the second was the creation of a 'court of conciliation' to be based on a legally-binding convention.

Although the CSCE has not yet notched up any major successes in terms of conflict management and crisis resolution, its importance lies in the area of preventive diplomacy and normative 'standard-setting'. In this way, the CSCE may be able help prevent conflicts escalating into serious conflicts by building a political consensus around common norms of democratic behaviour and respect for human rights. At the same time, the CSCE will continue to play a unique role in the new international relations in Europe because it is the only viable pan-European body in which all aspects of peaceful relations between states – both to each other and to their citizens – are dealt with. It has thereby helped generate a broader understanding of the nature of 'security' on the Continent, and it has developed an all-European consensus on the highly sensitive issue of human rights and democratic freedoms. However, it would be wrong to suggest that the CSCE's new structures and mechanisms alone can prevent the outbreak of conflicts which threaten the consolidation of liberal democracy in the former communist world. The CSCE can help strengthen a Euro-Atlantic consensus around the importance of democratic institutions and human rights. It does not, however, yet possess the decision-making mechanisms or the capability for implementing effective sanctions which could prevent national governments from violating these democratic norms if they believe it is in their national interest to do so. As Frederick Sherman Dunn noted way back in 1937,

> The widespread notion that by the mere calling of conferences, the establishment of international commissions of inquiry or the devising of new techniques of negotiation it will be possible to find acceptable solutions for all demands for change is largely a product of wishful

thinking. It is useless to pile up additional institutions unless they take full account of existing values and attitudes which determine national politics.

(Dunn 1937, quoted in Long 1993: 23)

None the less, the CSCE has entered a new phase in its development. From being an organization designed to ameliorate the worst aspects of the East–West conflict between what were then two distinct and antagonistic blocs, the CSCE has now become a forum for preventive diplomacy and the development of pan-European cooperation. A central task of the CSCE today is to build, consolidate and strengthen democracy as the only system of government of the participating states. This was clearly spelt out in the Charter of Paris, and has been reflected in the themes of specialist meetings agreed upon at the CSCE Summit in Paris: the Protection of National Minorities (Geneva, July 1991) and the Promotion of Democratic Institutions (Oslo, November 1991). The Third Meeting of the Conference on the Human Dimension in Moscow (10 September–4 October 1991) also explicitly reaffirmed that the effective exercise of human rights is the legitimate concern of the wider international community. The CSCE has thus emerged as one of the key international organizations concerned with the promotion of democratic institutions and civil liberties in Europe, and its activities will hopefully strengthen the resolve of East Europeans to build and consolidate stable liberal democracies.

The Council of Europe

Despite its undoubted virtues and its considerable potential, the CSCE has nevertheless a number of weaknesses. The CSCE has developed as a forum for political negotiation and consultation. Its various documents have the character of declarations of political intent, in which a certain standard is agreed upon and a frame of reference established. These declarations of intent thus do not carry the full weight of international law. Although the CSCE has now acquired a more institutionalized structure, with a permanent secretariat and a number of agencies, it is hamstrung by two factors: first, all decisions of the CSCE have to be agreed unanimously; and second, the CSCE does not possess any mechanism for enforcing its decisions.

It is for this reason that the Council of Europe has an important role to play in encouraging the democratization process in Eastern Europe. In particular, the Council of Europe can address some of the *legal* aspects of democratic government which are beyond the remit of the

CSCE. Moreover, as Catherine Lalumiere, the organization's Secretary-General, has argued, the Council of Europe enjoys the advantage of already possessing 'a solid structure for multilateral governmental and parliamentary co-operation in the field of human rights and has the experience and potential to expand its activities in this field' (*The Secretary General's Contribution to the Informal Ministerial Conference on Human Rights* 1990). The Council consists of a small secretariat; a Parliamentary Assembly; three legal instruments (the European Convention on Human Rights [1950], the European Social Charter [1965] and the European Convention for the Prevention of Torture and Inhuman and Degrading Treatment or Punishment [1989]); and a court of appeal – the European Court of Human Rights at Strasbourg. It thus operates with legally binding agreements, and has a mechanism for supervision and control. The jurisdiction of the European Court of Human Rights, for example, supersedes that of national courts, and is therefore a powerful guardian of human rights and personal freedoms.

When it was founded in 1949, many Europeans hoped that it would pioneer a new form of integration on the Continent, embracing the aims of political union, social progress and the protection of human rights. Although these early aspirations quickly proved too ambitious, the Council of Europe has none the less developed a substantial system of cooperation among its members which covers areas as diverse as culture, education, scientific and technological research, harmonization of legal standards and documents, communication and information, social questions and environmental protection. Many of these initiatives and activities have been overshadowed by the work of the European Community, with its programmes such as EUREKA and ESPRIT, and its new bodies such as the European Environmental Agency. Nevertheless, the Council's central and indispensable role in the field of human rights, European parliamentarism and the codification and standardization of European law is likely to remain unchallenged for many years to come (Nowotny 1990: 60). Indeed, the CSCE Copenhagen Conference in June 1990 recognized the 'important expertise' of the Council of Europe in the field of human rights and agreed to consider further ways and means to enable the Council to make a contribution to the Human Dimension of the CSCE.

The Council of Europe has certainly played a significant role to date in facilitating and encouraging the transition to democracy in Eastern Europe. It has been able to draw on its experience in helping with the construction of legal systems and pluralist democracies in Spain and Portugal during their transitions from dictatorship to democracy. It has also demonstrated that it provides a means of putting international pressure on those countries that renege on democracy, such as Greece during the Colonels (1967–74) and, more recently, Turkey since the 1980 coup.

In the wake of the democratic upheavals of 1989, the Council of Europe decided to provide assistance to the countries of Eastern Europe embarking on political democratization at three different levels: firstly, consciousness-raising, information and dialogue (on the major principles of democracy and human rights); secondly, assistance and cooperation (in order to strengthen the democratic changes under way and to train new leaders); and thirdly, integration (in other words, bringing the East Europeans into the programmes and activities of the Council of Europe, and opening the way to their possible accession to the organization as full members) (*The Council of Europe and Human Rights* 1990: 27). More specifically, at its Special Ministerial Meeting held in Lisbon from 22–4 March 1990, in which all East European states except Romania participated, the Council approved the 'Demosthenes' programme. This programme was designed with two broad aims in mind: firstly, 'to strengthen the reform movement towards genuine democracy', and second, 'to facilitate their smooth and progressive integration in the circles and institutions of European cooperation'.[22] The content of the programme draws heavily from three areas which have traditionally been regarded as the three pillars of the Council of Europe: pluralist democracy, human rights and the rule of law. One important point to note concerns implementation of the programme. Most activities under the Demosthenes programme take the form of short meetings such as seminars and workshops, which are relatively cheap to organize. All initiatives under the rubric of the programme must come from the democratizing state and not from the Council. This is both to avoid charges that the Council of Europe is forcing its concept of democracy on the post-communist states, and to minimize the risks of duplication.

One interesting area of work under the Demosthenes scheme is the Demo-Droit programme, which is concerned with legislation and the transformation of the legal systems of states participating in Council of Europe activities. Help is provided in the drafting of new constitutions and in the framing of other important laws which influence the character of the political system. To facilitate the Demo-Droit programme, a special commission was organized in 1990 specifically to assist countries draft new constitutions. This body is the European Commission for Democracy through Law, also known as the Venice Commission. It is composed of experts on constitutional law, administrative law and international law, and help has already been given to, amongst others,

Romania, Bulgaria, Albania, Estonia, Latvia and Russia. The Commission also assisted Hungary in drafting its law on minorities. It should be noted, however, that some doubts have been raised about the effectiveness of the Venice Commission in certain cases. It has been suggested, for example, that the Romanians approached the Commission with their constitution already drafted in order to provide it with a form of international legitimation. On the other hand, it does seem as if the Bulgarians and the Baltic states were willing to engage in a more effective dialogue with the Commission.

In order for democratizing post-communist states to participate in Council of Europe schemes, they had to first be accorded 'special guest status' in the organization's Parliamentary Assembly. This was a new category created by the Council in response to the changes in the former Soviet bloc brought about by the Gorbachev reform programme in the late 1980s. Hungary, Poland, Yugoslavia and the Soviet Union were given special guest status on 8 June 1989; Czechoslovakia on 7 May 1990; Bulgaria on 2 July 1990; and Romania on 1 February 1991. Full membership was only granted once fully free elections had been held. This meant that Hungary became a member in November 1990, Czechoslovakia in February 1991, Poland in November 1991 and Bulgaria in May 1992.

The Council of Europe is widely regarded in Eastern Europe (particularly in the Visegrad states of East-Central Europe) as an important international organization which can play a key role in strengthening the process of political democratization in the post-communist world. As Gabor Kardos, a specialist in international law at Budapest University, has argued, 'The Council of Europe which has served to reinforce parliamentary democracy internationally for decades, could definitely contribute to the protection of the new [democratic] institutions, especially through its legal regime to protect human rights in Europe' (Kardos 1991). He has also stressed the important role the Council can play in the 'transmission of political culture':

> the well-developed legal culture and the more sophisticated legal regulations of the West should find their way to Central and Eastern Europe. The best method to pave the way for this process is to join the Council of Europe. This international organisation can provide a kind of 'maturity test' for these newly democratized states, before admitting them [to the EC], which is of crucial importance.
>
> (Kardos 1991: 152)

Membership of the Council of Europe is therefore widely seen as signifying the acceptance of a country as a democratic member of the

European comity of nations. It may consequently provide a valuable safeguard against subsequent backsliding on matters concerned with human rights and democratic practices. It also has a powerful symbolic value which should not be underestimated.[23] Membership of the Council offers to the new democracies a badge of political maturity, tolerance and respect for human rights. For this reason, as Kardos has made clear, countries such as Hungary, Poland and Czechoslovakia hope that their membership of the Council of Europe will prove their credentials as stable democracies when they apply to join the European Community – which is the real prize to which they all aspire.

CONCLUSIONS

In this chapter, I have attempted to assess the impact of the external environment on the democratization process in Eastern Europe. The evidence I have considered suggests that – at the very least – involvement in multilateral organizations, along with Western economic aid and political support, provides a favourable external environment for the democratization process in the former communist bloc. This contrasts sharply with the international climate in the interwar years, which was largely inimical to the stabilization of parliamentary government in the region. By contributing to the continued stability and security of the European continent, Western organizations (including the EC, NATO and the WEU) are thus helping to provide some of the necessary external prerequisites for the transition to democracy in Central and Eastern Europe.

However, Western policy has also been more directly focused on supporting the process of institutional reform in post-communist countries. The central aims of Western policy are evident from the remarks of the US Deputy Secretary of State, Lawrence S. Eagleburger, in a speech in May 1991 at the annual conference of the US Export–Import Bank (EXIM Bank). He argued that,

> One thing we in the West should not do is sit in judgement on our East European friends, or attempt to dictate choices which are theirs to make. We should, after all, remember from our own historicial experiences that democracy is perhaps the most challenging form of government under the best of circumstances.
>
> However, there are certain things which the West, particularly we in the United States, can do to help ensure that the difficult economic transition underway does not destabilize either the fragile new democratic institutions or the peace of the region as a whole.

. . . we must continue to provide advice and technical assistance in
the field of democratic institution-building. Our friends in the region
tell us that such help to date has been absolutely critical to the success
achieved thus far – the elections held, constitutions written and the
like. Henceforth, we must concentrate on strengthening democracy
at the grass-roots level, namely, the institutions of local government
plus those bodies which safeguard and mediate a healthy pluralist
society – such as unions, press organs, and the judiciary. Our aim
must be to help create a system from top to bottom in which debate
and opposition are channeled constructively and democratically, a
system which can absorb the inevitable shocks to come.

(Eagleburger 1991)

Such Western policies can play an important role in reinforcing
progress in democratization. However, I believe that the West needs to
play an even more active and committed role in facilitating the difficult
process of economic and political reform in the region. In this task, the
main responsibility will fall on the shoulders of the West Europeans
rather than the Americans (in contrast to the late 1940s). Above all, it
is the European Community which will be called upon to develop a
much closer and more supportive relationship with the new democracies to its east. The EC – in collaboration with the Council of Europe
and the CSCE – must therefore face up to the new demands and
responsibilities placed on it by history, and recognize that it cannot
isolate itself from developments in Central and Eastern Europe. Sadly,
most West European governments have not yet recognized the need to
play a more constructive role in supporting reform in Eastern Europe.
This can be seen from the EC's half-hearted trade concessions, and the
dearth of initiatives and lack of imagination shown towards the
problems arising from minority rights and demands for national self-
determination in the region. Following the traumatic process of ratify-
ing the Maastricht Treaty, and faced with the seemingly insurmountable
problems of ethno-national conflict in Eastern Europe, the EC has
become increasingly inward-looking and self-absorbed. As doubts
about the integration process have grown, the prospects for more open
markets and further institution-building with the East Europeans have
become bleaker and bleaker. This does not bode well for the consolidation of democratic institutions in the post-communist countries of
the former Soviet bloc.

The strategic aim of Western policies towards Eastern Europe should
be to enmesh these countries in an ever-deepening network of political,
economic and social interdependencies. In the short-term, Western

governments and multilateral organizations such as the EC and the Council of Europe can provide positive economic and financial incentives for democratic reform in the East. By raising the costs of political recidivism, a significant disincentive can be created which might help deter East European elites from reverting to pre-war patterns of authoritarian populism. More importantly, expanding the existing networks of multilateral cooperation and supranational integration through the gradual inclusion of the East European states will help with the diffusion of common normative values and the socialization of the new post-communist elites (on the role of multilateral bodies in fostering socialization and common norms, see Archer 1983: 156–63). By providing positive incentives for democratic reform and developing an even more extensive institutionalized framework for multilateral cooperation, it will be possible to give practical encouragement to liberal and reforming coalitions in the East, and to impede the emergence of autarkic, repressive and nationalist policies in these fragile polities (Snyder 1990).

These political goals, however, can only be achieved by a more active and engaged Western policy towards Central and Eastern Europe. All too often, the countries of Western Europe seem too preoccupied with their own national concerns and narrow sectional interests to commit themselves fully to a policy of building a more united and integrated Europe. Only by a substantial long-term programme of strategic interaction with the countries of Eastern Europe can the West effectively reinforce the process of political democratization in the region.

There are, none the less, limits to the influence that Western governments and multilateral agencies can have on the democratization process in Eastern Europe. As Lawrence Eagleburger pointed out, democracy cannot be imposed on the peoples of Eastern Europe, any more than could Soviet-style socialism. External agents can provide a favourable international environment which is conducive to democratic reform, and can also try and support the efforts of the East Europeans themselves to build democratic polities and flourishing civil societies. The political will to construct democratic societies is much in evidence in the post-communist East, especially in East-Central Europe. But the structural obstacles to political and economic reform are considerable, and Western policy must be designed to help the East Europeans overcome these imposing obstacles. None the less, at the end of the day the main burdens of democratic transition will inevitably be born by the East Europeans themselves. The benefits will, however, be experienced by Europeans in both East and West, in the form of a more stable, secure and democratic continent. It is for this reason that the West has a strong incentive for stimulating, encouraging, and supporting the democratization process in Eastern Europe. As the former Director of the International Institute of Strategic Studies, Francois Heisbourg, has succinctly noted,

> If reform fails because of a lack of financial support, or through a lack of openness to Central European exports to Western Europe, or because of excessive reticence toward membership in the European Community system, then we all pay in security terms.
>
> (*International Herald Tribune*, 30 May 1991)

NOTES

1 'The word has become fashionable in Latin America, and now in East-Central Europe too. This is to be welcomed. In order to do more than just write constitutions, and to build institutions, what is needed above all is the creative chaos of civil society. Indeed, civil society is the common denominator of a functioning democracy and an effective market economy. It is only if and when a civil society has been created that political and economic reform can be said to have credence' (Dahrendorf 1990: 15).

2 David Roche, the managing director of Morgan Stanley International, has suggested that, for example, 'the Czechs did not profoundly disagree with an egalitarian economic system. The revolution of 1989 . . . was about political oppression, rather than living standards . . . that means that the Czechs and Slovaks are more likely to keep seeking to retain the positive aspects of the old regime than most other central European states' (*Financial Times*, 15 August 1990). Similarly Gavril Popov, the radical mayor of Moscow, wrote in August 1990 of the 'contradictions' in the new democracies of the former communist world developing between the market-oriented economic policies of the new regimes on the one hand, and the people whose revolts ushered in the governments now instituting these policies (which will inevitably lead to greater social and economic inequalities). Warning of the possible emergence of a 'left populism' based on the old trade unions, Popov has argued that 'The masses long for fairness and economic equality. And the further the process of transformation goes, the more acute and the more glaring will be the gap between those aspirations and the economic realities . . . the interest (in economic transformation) is based not an understanding of the new but on a hatred of the old – a destructive motive' (*Financial Times*, 27 December 1990).

3 'Democratization and Institution-Building in Eastern Europe', Institute for East–West Security Studies (henceforth IEWSS) Meeting Report, 1–3 March 1990: 1.

4 Morgan Stanley, the International Investment Bank, predicted a fall in national income of 3 per cent in 1990 and 10 per cent in 1991 in Czechoslovakia; 5.5 per cent in 1990 and 5 per cent in 1991 in Hungary; 20 per cent in 1990 but a rise of 4 per cent in Poland; and a fall of 7 per cent in 1990 and 10 per cent in 1991 in the Soviet Union. The fall in national income will be accompanied by an equally serious fall in industrial outputs

and investments, with adverse consequences for employment levels. Indeed, unemployment may reach a peak in 1994 of 12m in Eastern Europe and 47m in the Soviet Union (see Lloyd 1990).

5 In a speech in New York at a meeting of CSCE foreign ministers, the British foreign minister Douglas Hurd stressed that one of the tasks of the proposed new security system in Europe was to consolidate democracy in Eastern Europe; 'As countries escape from the deep frost of communism they may discover that some of their problems, as well as all of their freedoms, have been put on ice. They may be prone to new forms of intolerance which find their expression in extremes of nationalism or hostility to minorities' (quoted in the *Financial Times*, 3 October 1990: 3).

6 German state-funded political foundations have already been actively involved in aiding the democratization process in Eastern Europe, particularly in helping to foster political parties. The Konrad Adenauer Foundation, attached to the CDU, for example, now has offices in Warsaw, Budapest, Prague and Moscow. Similarly, the Friedrich Ebert Foundation, linked to the SPD, has offices in Moscow, Warsaw, Budapest and Prague. Somewhat belatedly, the British government has also been considering establishing a state-funded foundation which would offer help to political parties in fledgling democracies. Plans under consideration since the summer of 1990 are currently being finalized at the Foreign and Commonwealth Office. They envisage a board of trustees comprising academics and civil servants. UK political parties, or other organizations would be able to apply on behalf of political parties in other countries. A budget has not yet been agreed with the Treasury, but aid is likely to be small scale, focusing on advice or perhaps paying for equipment. Additional sponsorship is likely to be sought from private sector charities or business. Such a fund would extend British aid for emerging democracies under 'know-how' financing, and its aim would be to promote pluralist systems without favouring any political creed. (See the *Financial Times*, 28 February 1991: 22.)

7 It is envisaged that the newly established European Bank for Reconstruction and Development (EBRD) will play a crucial role in this regard, because it is specifically designed to provide investment and financial support for the emerging private sector in Eastern Europe.

8 For the view that Western economic diplomacy in Eastern Europe is a malign attempt to impose capitalism on the region and prevent the development of an indigenous 'Third Way', see Gowan 1990: 63–84.

9 The USA has established what it calls its SEED programme, i.e., 'Support for Eastern European Democracy'.

10 A limited trade agreement was signed between the EC and Romania in 1980, and in 1987 negotiations began to enlarge its provisions to include agriculture and cooperation. However, these were suspended, together with diplomatic relations, on 24 April 1989, because of both the deteriorating human rights situation and Romania's failure to meet its obligations under the 1980 agreement. On 20 December 1989, the day of the Timisoara uprising, the Commission finally decided to freeze the 1980 agreement.

11 'Twenty-four governments, countless non-governmental institutions, up to seven multilateral agencies, combined with some 30 policy categories and up to eight target countries (including the Balkans and the USSR), all suggests a major problem of ensuring coherence and effectiveness for the West' (Rollo *et al.* 1990: 128).

12 Indeed, *The Economist*, in its leader of 25 November 1989, portrayed this in typically colourful terms as the East Europeans 'gatecrashing' a sedate West European 'dinner party' for the Twelve.

13 In the summer of 1990 the government bussed miners into Bucharest to beat up and disperse anti-government protests (led primarily by students and intellectuals).

14 In 1990, the Community provided ECU 500m (£350m) to Eastern Europe under the PHARE scheme; in 1991, the figure was ECU 850m.

15 The Agreement with the Czechoslovak Federation lapsed on 1 January 1993 when the Federation broke up. Subsequently new Association Agreements were negotiated with the two republics, and these were eventually initialled on 23 June 1993.

16 A major reduction in quotas for agricultural products was opposed by the French government (with the tacit support of Ireland and Belgium), which was sensitive to the domestic political pressures of French farmers. This French move generated considerable controversy at the talks, and led to a temporary withdrawal of the Poles from the negotiations on 19 September, 1991. A major reduction in quotas for textiles was opposed by the less-developed members of the Community such as Portugal, whilst the Spanish, along with the French, Italians and Portuguese, opposed significant reductions in quotas on steel.

17 The Six Institutes Report (see Bonvicini *et al.* 1991: 82–3) proposed a doubling of the Community's budgetary allocation for Eastern Europe. Financial assistance to the East Europeans should, it suggested, be increased to the level of the structural funds formula, which would amount to 0.2 per cent of the EC's GNP.

18 Quoted in 'The New Western Ostpolitik: Challenges, Current State and Issues' by Michael Andersen and Mette Skak, a paper presented to the workshop on Responses of Western European Institutions to Changes in the Former Soviet Union and Central and Eastern Europe at the ECPR Joint Sessions, Leiden, 2–8 April 1993.

19 'The section of the Concluding Document on "Co-operation in Humanitarian and other Fields" is replete with cross-references to international human rights law. The obligations of the participating states are expressed in terms of "They will" rather than "They shall" or "They agree to". Moreover, there is an increasing tendency to draw on the specific language of the International Convenant on Civil and Political Rights' (McGoldrick 1990: 924).

20 The four-stage monitoring procedure essentially involves (1) the exchanging of information and responding to requests and representations; (2) holding bilateral meetings concerning 'situations' and 'cases' with a view to resolving them; (3) drawing the attention of other participating states to those situations and cases; (4) and finally bringing the matter to one of the three main human rights conferences (Paris, May–June 1989; Copenhagen, June 1990; and Moscow, 1991) and the main CSCE Follow-Up Meeting in Helsinki in 1992. In the period between the Vienna Conference and April 1990, the mechanism was used about 100 times. At the Copenhagen Conference in June 1990, a number of measures were agreed to enhance the effectiveness of this new mechanism: a four-week time limit for a written response to requests for information and to representations made to

them in writing by other participating states under Paragraph One of the Mechanism; a three-week limit on the holding of the bilateral meeting held under Paragraph Two of the Mechanism; and an agreement to refrain, in the course of a bilateral meeting held under Paragraph Two, from raising situations and cases not connected with the subject of the meeting unless both sides agree to do so (McGoldrick 1990: 925, 939).

21 In 1988, Hungary became the first East European country to accede to the Optional Protocol.
22 Council of Europe Cooperation and Assistance Programmes for Countries of Central and Eastern Europe, Council of Europe, SG/INF (91) 2,3.
23 See for example the speech by the organization's Secretary-General, Catherine Lalumiere, 'The Council of Europe in the construction of a wider Europe', given at the Royal Institute of International Affairs, London, on 28 February 1990.

BIBLIOGRAPHY

Andersen, M., and Skak, M. (1993) 'The new Western Ostpolitik: challenges, current state and issues', Paper presented at the ECPR Joint Sessions, Leiden, 2–8 April.
Andriessen, F. (1990) 'Change in Central and Eastern Europe: the role of the Community', *NATO Review* 38 (February): 1–6.
Archer, C. (1983) *International Organisations*, London: Unwin Hyman.
Ash, T. G. (1989) 'Refolution: the springtime of two nations', *New York Review of Books* 36: 3–10.
—— (1990) 'Eastern Europe: the year of truth', *New York Review of Books* 37: 17–22.
Bonvicini, G., *et al.* (1991) *The Community and the Emerging European Democracies: A Joint Policy Report*, London: Chatham House.
Brada, J. C. (1991) 'The European Community and Czechoslovakia, Hungary and Poland', *Report on Eastern Europe* 3, No. 49: 27–32.
Buzan, B., Kelstrup, M., Lemaitre, P., Tromer, E., and Waever, O. (1990) *The European Security Order Recast: Scenarios for the Post-Cold War Era*, London: Pinter.
The Council of Europe and Human Rights CIM-DH (90)4 (1990), Strasbourg: Council of Europe.
Council of Europe Cooperation and Assistance Programmes for Countries of Central and Eastern Europe SG/INF (91) 2, 3 (1991), Council of Europe.
Dahrendorf, R. (1990) 'Roads to freedom: democratization and its problems in East Central Europe', in P. Volten (ed.) *Uncertain Futures: Eastern Europe and Democracy*, New York: Institute for East–West Security Studies.
Deak, I. (1990) 'Uncovering Eastern Europe's dark history', *Orbis*, Winter.
Dunn, F. S. (1937) *Peaceful Change: A Study of International Procedures*, New York: Council on Foreign Relations.
EC–Eastern European Relations 1990, ICC Background Brief, Brussels: Commission of the European Communities, 7 November.
The Economist (1989).
Eagleburger, L. S. (1991) 'Central and Eastern Europe: a year later', Speech at the annual conference of the EXIM Bank (16 May 1991), *Official Text*, United States Information Service, London, May 21.

Featherstone, K., and Hiden, J. (1991) *East meets West: Policies for a Common European Home*, Fabian Discussion Paper No. 3, London.

Financial Times (1990–1).

Ghebali, V.-Y. (1992) 'The July CSCE Helsinki Decisions: a step in the right direction', *NATO Review* 40, 4.

Gowan, P. (1990) 'Western economic diplomacy and the new Eastern Europe', *New Left Review*, No. 182 (July–August): 63–84.

Huntington, S. (1968) *Political Order in Changing Societies*, New Haven: Yale University Press.

Hyde-Price, A. (1991) *European Security Beyond the Cold War: Four Scenarios for the Year 2010*, London: Sage Publications.

Institute for East–West Security Studies (IEWSS) Meeting Report (1990), 1–2 March, New York: IEWSS.

International Herald Tribune (1991–2).

Janos, A. (1970) 'The one-party state and social mobilization in Eastern Europe between the wars', in S. Huntington and C. Moore (eds) *Authoritarian Politics in Modern Society*, New York and London: Basic Books.

—— (1982) *The Politics of Backwardness in Hungary 1825–1945*, Princeton, N.J.: Princeton University Press.

Kardos, G. (1991) 'A Hungarian view on the all-European protection of human rights', *All-European Human Rights Yearbook* 1: 151–5.

Keane, J. (1988a) 'Democracy and civil society', in J. Keane (ed.) *Civil Society and the State*, London: Verso.

—— (ed.) (1988b) *Civil Society and the State*, London: Verso.

Kux, E. (1991) 'Revolution in Eastern Europe – revolution in the West?', *Problems of Communism* 40: 1–14.

Lloyd, J. (1990) 'The dilemmas of freedom', *Financial Times*, 27 December.

Long, D. (1993) 'The prospects for peaceful change in Europe: the contribution of the CSCE', Paper presented at the ECPR Joint Sessions in Leiden, April.

McGoldrick, D. (1990) 'Human rights developments in the Helsinki process', *International and Comparative Law Quarterly* 39, October.

Michnik, A. (1990) 'The two faces of Europe', *New York Review of Books*, 19 July.

Moisi, D. (1991) 'A reunited Europe?', in G. Bonvicini *et al.* (eds) *The Community and the Emerging European Democracies: A Joint Policy Report*, London: Chatham House.

Nowotny, E. (1990) 'The role of the CSCE and the Council of Europe in facilitating a stable transition toward new political structures in Europe', in P. Volten (ed.) *Uncertain Futures: Eastern Europe and Democracy*, New York: Institute for East–West Security Studies, Occasional paper no. 16.

Pinder, J. (1991) *The European Community and Eastern Europe*, London: Pinter for the RIIA.

Reich, A. (1990) 'The gasoline war: order of chaos?', *Report on Eastern Europe*, 9 November.

Rollo, J. M. C., with Butt, J., Granville, B., and Malcolm, N. (1990) *The New Eastern Europe: Western Responses*, London: Pinter for the RIIA.

Rothschild, J. (1974) *East Central Europe between the Two World Wars*, Seattle and London: University of Washington Press.

The Secretary General's Contribution to the Informal Ministerial Conference on Human Rights, CIM-DH (90)3 (1990), Rome: Council of Europe.

252   *The external dimension*

Snyder, J. (1990) 'Averting anarchy in the new Europe', *International Security* 14: 5–41.

Sobell, V. (1990) 'Eastern Europe and the European Community', *Report on Eastern Europe*, 23 February .

Strasbourg Conference in Parliamentary Democracy (1993) *Democracy Newsletter*, p. 4.

Vanhanen, T. (1990) *The Process of Democratization: A Comparative Study of 147 States, 1980–88*, New York: Taylor and Francis.

Part IV
Conclusion

9 Conclusion

Geoffrey Pridham and Tatu Vanhanen

The aim of this volume has been to describe and explain democratization in Eastern Europe from different perspectives and to relate this to democratic transitions in other parts of Europe. We wanted to explore to what extent it could be explained by common factors or particular factors, and what those factors might be.

In drawing together our results, it is best to start with basic explanatory factors of democratization. We can easily differentiate two simple main categories: (1) domestic and (2) external factors. Contrast between these two categories is of special interest in the case of Eastern Europe because of the hegemonic position of the Soviet Union among the former East European communist regimes. External factors have been dramatized by the circumstances surrounding the fall of these regimes and subsequently underlined by the alternation in the international system which has accompanied regime change. Domestic factors can then be classified by five sub-categories: (1) socio-economic structures, (2) historical factors, (3) political factors, (4) various conjunctural factors and (5) personalities. External factors can be classified by four main categories: (1) the influence of the Soviet Union, (2) the influence of Western countries, (3) the influence of multilateral organizations and (4) the diffusion of ideas.

From a different perspective, we could classify explanatory factors as: (1) ultimate or long term and (2) proximate factors. The first have preceded democratization by decades or at least by many years, whereas the second refers to those that were effective immediately before democratization or concurrently with the process of democratization. Finally theories and hypotheses about democratic transition can be classified as (1) universal and (2) particular, depending on whether they are limited to particular regions, periods, or countries.

Studies of democracy show that many different conditions may affect the chances of democracy in a given country. These may well be cross-nationally variable. But experts on democratic transition have found difficulty in measuring the relative impact of different factors or even agreeing on what are all the relevant factors. One fundamental disagreement in the study of democracy concerns the relative significance of social conditions vs political factors. Has democratization been due more to favourable social structures or rather to political choices and other purely political factors? The same controversy appears in the explanations given in this book. The chapters of this book therefore reflect the state of the art in studies of democratic transition, but it is nevertheless important to try and establish some common patterns. In the following summary, we first discuss the different sub-categories of domestic and external factors with comparative reference to the chapters in this book; and, then, we attempt to evaluate their relative importance as part of a collective interpretation of democratization in Eastern Europe.

FACTORS OF DEMOCRATIZATION

Socio-economic structures

Vanhanen and Kimber limit their attention and measurement to some operationally defined socio-economic variables that are assumed to indicate the distribution of economic and intellectual power resources. They are used as independent variables in their statistical analysis. Waller refers to economic development and economic plight among the factors influencing change, but he does not specify these variables. Pridham notes that economic factors may be extremely important, but they cannot be treated in a deterministic manner as usually suggested by functionalist theories. Cotta assumes that socio-economic structures and cleavages affect the formation of political parties and through them the nature of the democratic system. And Niklasson argues that some domestic structural factors made reforms acute in the Soviet Union, but he does not differentiate between them. Socio-economic variables are thus dominant explanatory factors in Vanhanen/Kimber's study, whereas they tend to play a secondary albeit important role for the other authors.

Historical factors

Waller analyses current changes in Eastern Europe in terms of three sets of factors. The first set is historical (the others are systemic and conjunctural). He says that 'in each country of the region the past exercises a significant influence on the present. Any analysis of recent change must deal with layers of history, to some extent shared, and to some extent individually experienced.' Pridham also pays attention to historical factors, such as authoritarian and pre-authoritarian legacies, although they are not absolute determinants of democratic transition. Historical factors are clearly very important in Cotta's hypotheses on party formation.

Political factors

Several authors stress the significance of political factors, as in Waller's analysis where they have the dominant role. He relates the formation of political groups to various political factors more than social conditions. For instance, the period of communist rule provides his second and distinct set of factors shaping the process of change in Eastern Europe. Pridham also pays more attention to political factors than to social conditions, and stresses the crucial influence of political choice and strategy during the transition process. In Cotta's study historical factors refer principally to political variables.

Conjunctural factors

Various random and unique factors always play an important role in political change. Consequently, some researchers tend to emphasize the significance of conjunctural factors, i.e., the role of unique and random determinants of democratization. According to Waller, these include the shift in the Soviet Union's policy towards Eastern Europe and the attraction of the European community for countries in that region. Conjunctural factors are generally discussed by Pridham, and they play an important role in the analysis by Lewis, Lomax and Wightman of the emergence of multi-party systems.

Personalities

One controversy in the comparative study of democratization concerns the actual significance of political leaders. It is easier to agree that personalities matter in politics than to measure their relative significance. Waller pays only marginal attention to individual political leaders like Gorbachev, Zhivkov and Ceausescu. Pridham refers to several leaders in illustrating political choice and strategy by actors during the transition process. Individual political leaders have a prominent role in the analysis of Lewis, Lomax and Wightman, and in

Niklasson's article one particular leader (Gorbachev) has a central role. There appears, therefore, to be some disagreement about their overall importance as a determinant of regime transition.

The influence of the Soviet Union

Because the communist systems in Eastern Europe depended on the support of the Soviet Union and the CPSU, it is reasonable to assume that the policy of the Soviet Union toward Eastern Europe was a highly relevant factor. Democratization was hardly possible as long as the Soviet Union was committed to the Brezhnev doctrine that the Soviet Union had the right to defend communist systems in the countries of Eastern Europe even by military force. Niklasson's study concentrates on the influence of the Soviet Union and the significance of Gorbachev. He concludes that domestic changes in the Soviet Union, changes in Soviet foreign policy, and policies of Gorbachev helped to start the process of democratization in Eastern Europe. However, the explosion would have come even without Gorbachev, because the internal dynamics in the Eastern and Central European states was already ripe for radical change. The significance of Soviet influence is stressed in several other chapters (Waller, Vanhanen/Kimber, Pridham, Lewis *et al.* and Hyde-Price). Waller refers to 'the fatal weakening of the party's monopoly caused by the withdrawal of Soviet support'. Vanhanen and Kimber argue that communist systems in Eastern Europe survived for four decades with the support of external power resources. When 'the threat of external intervention disappeared, domestic governments were no longer able to suppress the demands of democracy and socialist systems collapsed'. Pridham notes that in Eastern Europe the international context has been more salient (than in Southern Europe) by virtue of the crucial role played by Gorbachev's Moscow.

The influence of Western countries

Hyde-Price stresses that Western Europe has presented an attractive political model for Eastern Europe and that Western influence on political developments there was enhanced by the revolution in information technology that occurred in the 1970s and 1980s. This attraction of Western Europe gradually undermined the support of the communist systems. Waller refers to the attraction of the west of Europe as a conjunctural factor that furthered democratization in Eastern Europe, just as Pridham also refers to 'Western influences'.

The influence of multilateral organizations

Hyde-Price includes some multilateral organizations, particularly the European Community, the CSCE, and the Council of Europe, among the external factors that encouraged democratization in Eastern Europe, although he stresses more their possibilities for offering political support and advice to new democracies. In particular he pays attention to the fact that the Community 'made explicit from early on that the granting of associate status to East European countries would be conditional not only on market-oriented economic reform but also on progress towards political democratization'.

The diffusion of ideas

Pridham refers to the diffusion of democratic ideas. He says that the 'rapidity of the successive collapses of communist regimes in Eastern Europe in the autumn of 1989 underlined more dramatically than in Southern Europe how contagious liberal democracy can be, reinforced as this was by the opening up of Eastern Europe to Western influences and especially by the role of the mass media'.

EXPLANATIONS COMPARED

We can start from the observation that some of the explanatory factors are assumed or claimed to be universal, some others are assumed to be regionally relevant, and some are assumed to be only locally important (applying to particular countries), conjunctural, or unique. Vanhanen's socio-economic explanatory factors are assumed to be universal. External factors discussed by Niklasson and Hyde-Price are clearly regional by nature. Historical factors are regional and local. Waller, Pridham, and Lewis *et al.* refer mainly to conjunctural and local, but also to some regional factors. These three types of explanatory factors do not need to contradict each other. It is conceivably possible that democratization is a simultaneous consequence of universal, regional, local and conjunctural or random factors. On the other hand, explanations of democratization obviously contradict each other if the same case is explained by dominant universal factors in one study, and in another study by dominant regional factors, and in some other studies by locally unique and conjunctural factors. Besides, there are also different universal, regional, and local factors. How to solve this problem?

It is true that all types of explanatory factors have been used in chapters of this book, but the authors admit that their explanations are only partial, leaving room for other determinants of regime change. For example, the results of Vanhanen and Kimber's study indicate that their universal explanatory factors accounted for approximately 70 per cent of the variation in the level of democratization in the 1980s, but this percentage is the average of no less than 147 states. The explained part of variation seems to have been considerably less than 50 per cent in the case of Eastern Europe. Pridham is probably right in his claim that conjunctural factors have been more significant than universal structural determinants in this region, but it is difficult to test his hypothesis exactly because his conjunctural and volitional variables as well as political determinants of regime change are not operationally defined and measurable variables. The conclusions of Niklasson and Hyde-Price on the significance of external factors do not as such contradict the hypotheses of Vanhanen/Kimber and Pridham because they do not claim that external factors have been dominant explanatory factors. Therefore, it seems that the explanations given in this book are rather more complementary than contradictory.

We have to bear in mind that, taken as a whole, the various explanations given for democratization in Eastern Europe in this volume do not completely overlap. Some chapters focus on political systems in general (such as Vanhanen/Kimber, Pridham, Niklasson and Hyde-Price); others are concerned with only certain aspects of political systems. Furthermore, there is some difference of geographical scope between certain chapters and also, in a few cases, differences of time period analysed.

However, universal, regional, and local explanations do not necessarily contradict each other, because universal factors and hypotheses may explain one area of the variation in democratization, regional factors and hypotheses another, and various local and historical factors and hypotheses a different part of variation. The basic problem is that we cannot be sure precisely how much of the variation in democratization has been explained by certain hypotheses and factors because most variables used in this book are qualitative. This means that we are restricted in measuring the relative significance of different explanatory variables and the explanatory power of different hypotheses. Only rough estimations are possible. Besides, a part of variation in democratization ultimately remains unexplained for the simple reason that random factors always play a role in politics.

TOWARDS A COMBINED EXPLANATION

Let us start from the general question: was democratization in Eastern Europe caused by some known and definable factors, or was it a more or less accidental event? On the basis of our analyses, it is reasonable to conclude that the breakthrough of democracy in Eastern Europe was not completely determined nor was it completely accidental. This means that there were objective causes for the collapse of the communist systems. However, on the other hand, conjunctural and partly accidental factors affected the timing of the breakthrough and the process of regime change.

The most fundamental objective causes of democratization in Eastern Europe can probably be traced to technological inventions that changed social conditions and structures, i.e., the domestic and international environment of the communist systems. The regimes were ultimately unable to control the consequences of technological change. The scientific-technological revolution created new forms of wealth and furthered the spread of education and knowledge. Economic and intellectual resources became more widely distributed within societies, and it became increasingly difficult for governments to control people's activities and ideas effectively. These changes in environmental conditions were, for example, conducive to group formation (cf. Waller and Lewis *et al.*). It is noteworthy that intellectuals were the first to establish autonomous groups, illustrating the importance of intellectual resources. We have quantitative data on environmental changes, particularly on the phenomenal rise in the level of education. The strengthening of social pluralism helps to undermine authoritarian political systems. Structural changes in the Soviet Union and in the other East European socialist countries hence created a different social environment, in which it became possible for a reformist figure like Gorbachev to gain power in the Soviet Union and for the Catholic Church to challenge the communist regime in Poland. However, objectively measurable structural changes were not enough to lead automatically to democratic revolutions. Many types of conjunctural and accidental factors played a role in the inception of changes and in the process of democratization, but these conjunctural factors should be seen in the context of changed environmental conditions.

In this connection, it is also useful to differentiate ultimate and proximate factors and explanations of democratization. Structural changes caused by the scientific-technological revolution represent ultimate factors, which preceded democratization and occurred independently from political decision-makers. Various conjunctural factors, particularly political ones (both domestic and international), represent proximate factors of democratization. They affected political systems immediately before the transition process started and during the process of democratization. They include the formation of autonomous political groups, the role of individual political leaders and their choices, the diffusion of democratic ideas, and the influence of external forces, especially the liberalization process in the Soviet Union and the attraction of the Western political and economic model. This key difference in the nature of explanatory factors affects the nature of possible explanations. At least some of the ultimate long-term factors are quantifiable, which means that their effects can be measured and compared across countries, whereas proximate factors are usually not measurable, as they are qualitative variables and probably limited to particular cases.

Thus we come to the general conclusion that democratization in Eastern Europe was partly due to measurable structural changes, but that a significant part of it, particularly the timing of transition process, was due to non-measurable proximate factors and unpredictable choices made by political leaders. It is not possible for us to determine exactly the relative significance of theoretical explanations based on universal quantitative variables and of explanations based on particular and conjunctural factors. It seems to be clear, however, that democratization in Eastern Europe was not completely accidental and unpredictable. Material and measurable environmental circumstances had become ripe for system change, although the time of change was not predetermined and sure. Niklasson has expressed this interaction between changes in objective circumstances and unpredictable conjunctural factors well: 'regardless of the actions of the Soviet Union or Mikhail Gorbachev, there was an internal dynamic in all of the six Eastern and Central European states which led to a situation ripe for radical change. In a way, the changes in the Soviet Union made the explosion come earlier, but an explosion would have come even without Gorbachev.' He continues: 'Without the pressure within the East European states themselves due to a lack of legitimacy for the existing authoritarian regimes, basing their power on support from Moscow, changes would not have followed automatically from changes in the Soviet Union, and, vice versa, that pressure itself would eventually have toppled the old regimes'.

We want to emphasize that politics is not fully deterministic and predictable. There are predictable regularities in politics, but random factors also have a significant part in politics. Therefore, complete explanations of political phenomena are theoretically impossible. We can achieve only partial explanations. So it is in the case of democratization in Eastern Europe. Hence, our collective explanation that structural changes in the Soviet Union and in the other East European societies created the necessary social conditions for democratization, but that various conjunctural factors, both domestic and external, determined the timing of transition process and affected the form of emerging democratic institutions.

What lessons have we reached from studying democratization in Eastern Europe that could be applied to the study of democratization in other regions of the world? Democratization is not an accidental phenomenon in the sense that it could as easily take place in any social conditions. Structural changes that increase resource distribution within societies improve necessary social conditions for democratization. The diffusion of democratic ideas across borders may speed up the starting of transition and support it, but the diffusion of democratic ideas without other favourable conditions is not sufficient for instigating it. External factors can hamper democratization in a particular country or a region (the dependence of East European countries on the Soviet Union until the middle of the 1980s) or further democratization (the liberalization in the Soviet Union in the latter half of the 1980s and the attraction of the Western model and the European Community). Historical legacies and cultural factors may hamper or further democratization by affecting a country's ability to adopt democratic institutions and behaviour patterns, but this ability is not independent from other conditions. Several conjunctural factors may become crucial in the transition process. Finally, the success or failure of the transition to democracy seems to depend more on domestic conditions and on leadership than on external pressures, except in the cases of complete or vital dependence on a foreign power. Democratization in the six East European countries, which were previously dependent on the Soviet Union, highlights the significance of external factors, whereas the starting of democratization in the Soviet Union itself highlights the crucial significance of domestic conditions.

Index

Petkov Agrarian Union 113;
Social Democratic Party 113;
Soviet influence on
democratization 213; Union of
Democratic Forces 54, 57–8, 113,
152
Bunce, V. 204

Calfa, M. 157
Canada 238
Catholic Church; *see* Church
Central Europe 15, 197, 198 (*see
also* Eastern Europe; East-Central
Europe; Southern Europe;
Western Europe)
Ceausescu, N. 51, 53, 159, 216, 231,
257
Chile 77
China 212–13, 228
christian democratic parties 111,
120–1
Church 52, 56, 60, 102, 121–2;
Catholic 27, 52, 54, 121–2, 182,
261; evangelical churches 50–2;
German Lutheran church 121
civil/military relations 23, 27–8, 30,
32, 35, 212
CMEA; *see* COMECON
COCOM 228
Cold War 30
Collins, G. 228
combined explanation of
democratization 260–3 (*see also*
conclusion); choices made by
political leaders 262; conjunctural
and accidental factors 261–2;
influence of external forces
262–3; importance of intellectual
resources 261; structural changes
262; technological change 261;
ultimate and proximate factors,
294–5
COMECON (Council for Mutual
Economic Assistance) 198, 228,
232, 235
Commonwealth of Independent
States 209
communist party 7, 35, 41–2, 46,
50–1, 54–7, 69, 115–16, 120,
153–4, 213–15; in Albania 146–7;
communist power monopoly 43–5

(*see also* nomenklatura); in
Czechoslovakia 156, 165–8, 171;
in Hungary 136, 155, 158–9; in
Poland 130–1, 176–7; in Soviet
Union 129–30, 198; in Spain 117
communist systems (regimes) 8–9,
33–5, 39–41, 43–7, 59, 112,
116–19, 121, 129, 151–7, 160,
165, 175, 184, 197, 206, 227, 236;
atomized society 39–40; collapse
of communist rule 3, 33, 38, 45–6,
53–8, 100, 111, 128, 147, 151,
154, 165, 176, 220, 261; group
process of politics in 44; mass
organizations 44, 49–50; reform
communism and communists 34,
48, 158–9, 210–13, 216; trade
unions 44–5, 49, 54, 58
comparative approaches 15, 17, 35,
100
conclusion (Pridham and Vanhanen)
255–63 (*see also* factors of
democratization); the aim of this
study 255; conjunctural factors
257; the diffusion of ideas 259;
explanations compared 259–60;
explanatory factors of
democratization 255; domestic vs
external factors 255; historical
factors 256–7; the influence of
multilateral organizations 259; the
influence of the Soviet Union 258;
the influence of Western countries
258; personalities 257–8; political
factors 257; social conditions vs
political factors 256; socio-
economic structures 256; towards
a combined explanation 260–3
(*see also* combined explanation of
democratization); universal and
particular hypotheses 255
Conference of Security and
Cooperation in Europe (CSCE)
10, 221, 226, 227–8, 236–41, 245,
259; Helsinki Final Act 236–7;
Paris Charter in 1990 237–8; and
the process of democratization in
Eastern Europe 238–40
constitutional reforms 22, 242–3;
abolition of the privileged role of
the communist party 54–5; in

274 *Index*